THE CHINESE IN THE CARIBBEAN

THE
Chinese
IN THE
Caribbean

EDITED AND WITH AN INTRODUCTION BY
Andrew R. Wilson

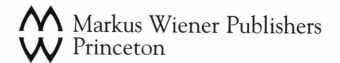

Markus Wiener Publishers
Princeton

For information write to:
Markus Wiener Publishers
231 Nassau Street, Princeton, NJ 08542
www.markuswiener.com

Library of Congress Cataloging-in-Publication Data

The Chinese in the Caribbean / edited and with an introduction by
Andrew R. Wilson.
    p. cm.
    Includes bibliographical references.
    ISBN 1-55876-314-7 (hardcover : alk. paper)
        1. Chinese—Caribbean Area. 2. Chinese—West Indies, British.
    3. Chinese—Cuba. 4. Immigrants—Caribbean Area. 5. Immigrants—
West Indies, British. 6. Immigrants—Cuba. 7. Caribbean Area—Emigration
and immigration—History. 8. West Indies, British—Emigration and
immigration—History. 9. Cuba—Emigration and immigration—History.
10. China—Emigration and immigration—History. I. Wilson, Andrew R., 1967-
    F2191.C46C45 2004
    304.8'729051—dc22

Paperback ISBN 1-55876-315-5

Printed in the United States of America on acid-free paper

CONTENTS

v

PART II. CUBA

PART III. RE-MIGRATION
AND RE-IMAGINING IDENTITY

Introduction
New Perspectives on the Caribbean Chinese
ANDREW R. WILSON

The massive outflow of émigrés from the Chinese mainland that began in the 1830s has had a profound effect on global history. Since then, millions of migrants have left China to sojourn or settle overseas. This movement was driven by domestic chaos in China and by global demand for labor—demand that was driven by the hunger for the commodities and raw materials that fueled the industrial revolution. In large measure the Chinese facilitated the emergence of the modern global economy. Moreover, the export of Chinese was just one human wave among many (African, South Asian, etc.) that supplied labor to and transformed the world economy. The macro-historical significance of Chinese emigration is undeniable.

That the Chinese were so important to global history goes beyond simply the vast number of Chinese who emigrated or the economic forces pulling Chinese into the global market. Virtually whatever the developed or developing world needed in terms of manpower, China could provide. Merchants, craftsmen, and laborers of every stripe existed by the millions in China, and since China also possessed an immense and complex economy, where trade in skills was equally important as trade in goods, there was a preexisting system of internal labor migration. If a European colony, even one as far off as Spanish Cuba, could "plug in" to this massive economy, they could almost immediately fill their labor needs—that is, if they could provide sufficient incentives.

Chinese émigrés were not passive subjects of mechanical "push" or "pull" forces; they played a major role in the process. The sending communities of Southeast China (called *qiaoxiang* or "native-places") were key nodes in elaborate migration networks that bound sending and receiving communities in a dialectical relationship. For example, a *qiaoxiang* might begin to specialize in exporting a particular type of labor, and migrants might work to create demand in the receiving society's economy for those specific skills. The fact that the various flows of Chinese emigration were not one single surge, but rather coincided with specific labor needs—such as with the decline of slavery or the building of the Panama Canal—and that once in the Caribbean, the Chinese worked to exploit or open market niches that required subsequent inputs of Chinese talent, demonstrates the dialectical connection between China as a source of labor exports and the Caribbean basin as a labor market.

Not all Chinese émigrés, however, enjoyed such a high degree of agency: there were tens of thousands of victims in this process. The coolie trade, by which many Chinese were imported to the Caribbean, was characterized by the use of recruiters, or "crimps," that either tricked Chinese laborers into unfair contracts or simply kidnapped them. The inhuman conditions under which coolies were transported and subsequently employed were so deplorable as to become an international scandal requiring multilateral treaties to end. It is the cruel forced migration of the coolie that has largely become the symbol of the Chinese migration experience. Many of the Chinese who made the arduous journey to the Caribbean fell under the category of coolies and were destined to fill the labor shortages created by the decline of slavery and the industrialization of sugar processing. Other Chinese went to work on the Isthmian railroad and later on the Panama Canal. For these émigrés, life in the Americas was often one of hardship and disease—a far cry from the Chinese merchant elites who grew rich in the emporia of the east. For other Chinese in the Caribbean, migration was voluntary and strategic. Many of these émigrés prospered and encouraged friends and kin to follow them.

Beyond the tragedy of the coolie trade, millions of Chinese traveled abroad willingly, and while their migration was a significant event, it was not necessarily the violent uprooting and alienation suffered by the coolie. Many Chinese migrations were little more than pragmatic efforts to enhance the economic well-being of an individual or a family. The majority of Chinese migrations consisted of unremarkable border crossings that, when viewed at the regional and global levels, are remarkably important. The intentions of the average Chinese traveling overseas were mundane, yet the consequences of his migration and those of his peers were tremendous.[1]

We should thus remain cognizant of the nearly infinite range of migration experiences that make up the larger history of Chinese emigration. Even while we view this spectacular human wave as a single historical phenomenon, the great range of personal and family experiences, types of migration, and degrees of interconnection between sending and receiving societies should alert us to the dangers of historical reductionism. The contemporaneous migration systems that directed Chinese migrants out from China into the global labor market were not identical parts of the same "Chinese diaspora." Rather, the unique structures and specializations of the migration systems of China's southeastern provinces were dictated by distinct local systems, regional economic developments, and the labor market of the receiving society. As such these systems only converged as part of the same larger historical process at the global level.

Not even China's moribund Qing dynasty could ignore the significance of these massive labor flows. To bind expatriate Chinese more closely to their homeland, the dynasty introduced the term *huaqiao*, or "Chinese sojourner," into its official vocabulary. This new term emphasized the migrants' membership in a larger cultural-ethnic Chinese community (*hua*) and directed their loyalty toward the homeland as "sojourners" (*qiao*) rather than toward their places of residence as immigrants. A later Nationality law of 1909 declared, by the principle of consanguinity, that all Chinese, everywhere, were subjects of the emperor. Beijing also tried to co-opt the money and talent of the Chinese overseas for its "self-strengthening" program. Chinese merchants and students were encouraged to return to China to either invest or serve in the bureaucracy. At the same time the Qing established embassies and consulates overseas which, not surprisingly, corresponded to the major concentrations of Chinese émigrés. An intense interest in Chinese migrants was shared by Western governments, who saw the import of industrious Chinese as an expedient way to fill labor shortfalls, exploit colonial possessions, and meet the rising global demand for commodities. Both the British and the Spanish enacted policies to attract Chinese to the sugar islands of the

Caribbean for exactly this purpose. As Anne-Marie Lee-Loy's "Kissing the Cross" shows, the authorities in the British West Indies consciously sought to portray Chinese labor as the most desirable way to develop the economy and craft a more harmonious structure for colonial society.

When the multiple migration systems emerging from China were drawn to the Caribbean basin by these policies, the possible trajectories of individual, family, and community narratives increased exponentially. The history of the Caribbean is a history of migrations. The non-native peoples of the region came as conquerors and planters, slaves and indentured laborers from all parts of the globe. Each group contributed to the social fabric, culture, and commerce of the region by weaving the traditions of their native-places into the warp and weft of the New World. The Chinese exist both as distinct ethnic groups within Caribbean societies and as shapers of unique Caribbean cultures. Given the malleability of Caribbean cultures and societies at the end of the nineteenth century, a time of upheaval and experimentation, the integration of the Chinese into the numerous cultural tapestries of the region was remarkably rapid. Economic growth and the emergence of new market niches in Jamaica, for example, allowed Chinese, once their indenture contracts had expired, to move quickly into small-scale retail. By the early twentieth century, "Chinaman" had become virtually synonymous with shopkeeper.

Caribbean Chinese communities are certainly a more recent phenomenon than those of the major Southeast Asian entrepôt ports, such as Manila and Batavia, where Chinese have lived and traded since at least the sixteenth century. Still, the great influx of hundreds of thousands of Chinese laborers, merchants, and craftsmen in the late nineteenth century quite literally changed the course of Caribbean history and fundamentally transformed the societies in which the Chinese settled. The unique social, economic, and cultural landscape of each locality exercised a powerful influence on shaping the Chinese experience there. As a result, to be a "Chinaman" in Kingston or Demerara differed in many subtle (and a few not-so-subtle) ways from what it was to be a *chino* in Havana.

We have chosen the Caribbean as a discrete unit of analysis because

of the intra-regional diversity, but also because larger historical trends
—trade, migration, sugar, and colonialism—bind the region together
and therefore allow for some degree of generalization. The present volume offers a broad sociohistorical definition of the Caribbean basin
that embraces islands in the Caribbean Sea and bordering coastal
areas such as those in Panama, and this definition can even be extended to the Caribbean diaspora. Such a definition permits the contributors to work across traditional boundaries, such as those between the
Spanish- and English-speaking Caribbean. The Caribbean region
forms a microcosm for examining the diversity of issues facing Chinese
in the Americas (and in the diaspora), as they came into contact with
different cultures and polities.

After the initial spectacular surge of migration, there followed periods in which multiple paths of community evolution can be traced.
Some Chinese fully assimilated into local society; others intermarried
to form a Creole group that created a new stratum in colonial society;
yet other émigrés self-consciously advertised their "Chineseness,"
founded Chinese schools and Chinese Chambers of Commerce, and
tried to develop more robust linkages with the Chinese state. These
processes were the product of personal choice, local conditions, economic opportunity, and global historical developments. The result
was, in the words of G. William Skinner, "a wondrous array of adaptive, acculturative, and assimilative phenomena."[2]

In the twentieth century, seismic historical forces were at work and
the attentions of the Chinese state were continuously drawn to the
Chinese overseas. Chinese consulates, like the one founded in Havana
after a Chinese investigative mission in the 1870s, were followed by
Chinese Chambers of Commerce, which began to crop up in the early
1900s, further enhancing the linkage between Beijing and *huaqiao*.
Such developments would seem then to encourage Chinese in the
Caribbean to more readily identify themselves with the Chinese state
and as Chinese. Beijing, however, was not the only political entity
that took an interest in the émigrés; nascent Chinese political parties
like those founded by Kang Youwei and Sun Yat-sen thrived among
the *huaqiao*. In many ways, Chinese communities overseas were the
birthplace of Chinese republicanism and were the place where many

ethnic Chinese first began to identify with the Chinese nation. The strength of these ties between the Chinese state and Chinese overseas ebbed and flowed throughout the tumult of China's long revolution in the twentieth century. Simultaneously the Chinese in the Caribbean were also under pressure to identify more closely with their host societies. These conflicting demands of loyalty required a subtle hand to manage.

With the fall of the Qing dynasty in 1911 and the subsequent failure of China's first republican government, followed as it was by two decades of political chaos known as the Warlord Period, formal ties to the Chinese state were of marginal value. Only with the emergence of a relatively unified Kuomintang government under Chiang Kai-shek in the late 1920s did formal ties to the Chinese state regain their value. During this interregnum, the Chinese in the Caribbean, like Chinese elsewhere, directed their attention and energies toward local rather than national projects. Despite the chaos in China, links to native-places often remained strong and provided a small but steady stream of new émigrés to staff the shops, truck gardens, and restaurants in the Caribbean, as well as a means to send remittances back to China.

At the same time that the Chinese were responding to developments in China, other historical forces were converging on the Caribbean basin. Booms and busts driven by market demand, rebellion in Cuba, the Spanish-American War, the completion of the Panama Canal, World War I, and the emergence of the United States as the dominant regional power (to name just a few challenges of the modern era) forced the Chinese to re-craft existing social and economic strategies or to invent wholly new responses. While native-place ties remained critical, some ethnic Chinese attempted to gain a degree of control over their surroundings by tentatively engaging in local politics. They leveraged their economic clout and used venues of collective action, like Chambers of Commerce, to enhance their prosperity and establish themselves as players in emerging Caribbean polities. And yet there was no single or typically "Chinese" formula for success. The essentially comparative nature of the essays in this volume allows us to evaluate the individual, family, and community responses to these events across a wide spectrum. It helps to illuminate certain patterns within the history of the Chinese overseas and provides fresh perspectives on the history of the Caribbean. The most skillful and successful Caribbean Chinese deployed an array of strategies and identities. What immediately strikes the reader about these essays is the remarkable variation in experiences and sense of identity among the Caribbean Chinese.

The Japanese invasion of China, which began in earnest in 1931 and accelerated in 1937, in many ways sharpened the national identity of the Chinese overseas. The Chinese in Jamaica, for example, raised more than £200,000 for China's war effort. Yet the global character of World War II meant that the Caribbean Chinese participated in the conflict both as Chinese expatriates and as local residents. Support for China's defense had to be balanced by contributions to the war efforts of the United States and Great Britain and with participation in the wartime economies of the region.

Following the Communist victory in China's civil war, Chinese overseas faced even starker choices. Because of Mao Zedong's victory, linkages to native-places were often severed. Correspondence once readily shared became impossible. Only recently, as Kathleen Lopez shows us in "One Brings Another," have the connections been reforged between Chinese in Cuba and their *qiaoxiang* of Southeast China. Throughout much of the Caribbean, the range of identity, social, and economic choices were significantly narrowed. This went beyond local Chinese having to choose between Beijing and Taipei, but also included having to deal with changes occurring in the Caribbean. Decolonization, emerging Caribbean nationalisms, and the pressures of the Cold War all compounded the dilemmas that many of Chinese descent faced. The Chinese in Castro's Cuba were in a particularly awkward position, given the tensions between Moscow (Havana's benefactor) and Beijing and the fact that petty entrepreneurship, which was the foundation of Havana's Chinese community, was anathema to the Communist regime. One response to changes in the Caribbean was re-migration, both within Latin America as well as to the United States and Canada. This opened new types and varieties of linkages and fostered new systems of identity. The native-place ties that once connected Caribbean Chinese to the sending communities of coastal China are now supplemented and even replaced, for example, by ties between the large and active Jamaican-Chinese community in Toronto and their families and "hometowns" in Jamaica.

The subsequent essays will explore not merely the arrival and experience of Chinese in the Caribbean but also the ways in which Chinese have adapted to and altered the region. Included are the histories of Chinese people in Cuba, Panama, and the British West Indies, their arrival as indentured laborers, the discrimination they suffered and overcame, their slow rise to economic independence and success, their contributions to cuisine and literature, their roles in the region's national revolutions, their place in post-colonial polities, and the subsequent re-migrations of individuals, families, and entire communities. The authors highlight the uniqueness of numerous Caribbean Chinese histories to assess the impact of geographic, economic, religious, and policy factors on the history of Sino-Caribbean interaction. The Caribbean is an ideal venue in which to study migrant communities not merely because there are so many migrants but also because of the dramatic social, economic, and political changes outlined above that have shaped the region over the last century and a half.

Of late, there has been a boom in Chinese emigration studies, and scholarly products run the gamut from the macro (Lynn Pan's *Sons of the Yellow Emperor*) to the comparative (Adam McKeown's *Migrant Networks and Cultural Change: Peru, Chicago, Hawaii, 1900–1936*) to discrete histories of individual migrant communities (such as my own *Ambition and Identity: Chinese Merchant Elites in Colonial Manila, 1880–1916*).[3]

Unlike the study of Chinese communities in Thailand, Singapore, Indonesia, and (in recent years) the United States, the field of Caribbean-Chinese studies has been relatively dormant. This is not to say that it has been entirely neglected. There are several historical, sociological, and anthropological studies of the Caribbean Chinese, many of which have been produced by Caribbean scholars and by ethnic Chinese themselves, that shed light on the complexity of community dynamics. We are fortunate to have as one of our contributors perhaps the leading figure in the field, Walton Look Lai of the University of the West Indies in Trinidad.[4]

Nonetheless, whereas Chinese migrations to Southeast Asia and North America receive significant attention, the experiences of Chinese migrants in the Caribbean remain a poorly understood and largely unchronicled chapter in the region's history. And yet the Chinese, as we will see, have played a significant role in the economies of Caribbean nations and have contributed immensely to Caribbean cultures. To date, no single book has attempted to systematically place these Chinese communities in the history of the broader Caribbean region or to place the Caribbean Chinese within the larger history of the Chinese diaspora. This is not necessarily a bad thing. It may be premature to attempt a comprehensive history of the Chinese in the Caribbean. The experiences are too varied over space and time, as many of the articles in this volume demonstrate, and we have yet to develop a sufficient corpus of quality scholarship comparable to that on the Chinese in Southeast Asia or the United States from which to craft a more general history. Rather, it may be better to first build a foundation of discrete studies of phases of migration, communities, families, and individuals.

Moreover, the range of academic disciplines—history, anthropology, sociology, biography, and cultural studies—that are applicable to this topic are as diverse and as complementary as the historical forces that converged in the Caribbean basin in the modern era. Therefore, as impossible as it is to confine the history of places as unique as, say, Havana or Kingston—liminal points, where numerous global, regional, market, national, and personal histories converged—within a national or even regional history, it is equally impossible, at present, to tell the story of the Caribbean Chinese as a single narrative. The assembled authors view this book as a unique opportunity to bring together numerous disciplines and community histories and perhaps inspire future research into this fascinating but little-understood field.

This volume opens with four chapters that lay out the historical background of Chinese emigration to the British West Indies and the evolution of these communities over the course of the twentieth century. Walton Look Lai, in his chapter on the Chinese indentured labor system, situates Chinese labor movements within the contexts of both Chinese and Caribbean history. The pressures of rebellion and over-population in China impelled many Chinese to move overseas, but their settlement in the British West Indies was far from inevitable. In fact, the first attempt to recruit Chinese labor to work Trinidad's plantations was a complete failure; rather, the eventual migration of almost 18,000 Chinese to Britain's Caribbean colonies in the late nineteenth century was the result of planter lobbying for new labor inputs and the presence of British officials on the China coast to facilitate out-migration. Nonetheless, the Chinese migration to the British West Indies was dwarfed by those of other ethnic groups, notably Africans, Portuguese, and more than 400,000 South Asians, primarily from British India. Quite different patterns obtained elsewhere in Latin America, such as Cuba and Peru, where Chinese immigration topped 100,000 in each locale. In British Singapore, there was more of a balance between Chinese and Indians, but even there the Chinese dominated despite the proximity to India. Disparate patterns such as these force us to seek explanations of why migration streams take certain trajectories. Obviously supply (abundant in China) and demand (significant in the British West Indies) equations are insufficient. The mechanisms of migration, such as recruitment systems, contracts, and transportation, as well as conditions in the receiving society are equally, if not more, important. Likewise, the ability of local officials and the migrants themselves to guarantee follow-on migrations deserve scholarly attention.

As to the conditions under which the Chinese migrated and worked, Look Lai has mined contracts, shipping manifests, and British official documents from both China and the West Indies for a wealth of detail on the contract system and local conditions encountered by the Chinese. Look Lai also locates the Chinese within the multicultural landscape of the British Caribbean. Chinese interacted with other groups in the islands in a range of ways: from outright ethnic hostility and fierce economic competition to mutual participations in each other's hobbies and holidays.

Having explored the early history of Chinese migrations to the West Indies through the experiences of the émigrés, Anne-Marie Lee-

Loy's "Kissing the Cross" allows us to look at the import of Indian and Chinese labor from the perspective of colonial officials and the planter elite. Drawing from her larger work on popular representations of ethnic Chinese in Jamaica, Trinidad, and Guyana, Lee-Loy shows that British officials and planters viewed the import of Chinese as not only a response to labor demand but also a way to craft a stable ethnic hierarchy in the midst of tumultuous times. To the British, the Chinese were more industrious, frugal, and sexually abstemious than the Africans or Indians—a set of assumptions not shared by officials elsewhere, such as in the American West. The British also believed the Chinese to be more inclined to assimilate European values and Christianity. They hoped that this cultural flexibility would allow Chinese immigrants to form a loyal cadre of subalterns to facilitate the colonial enterprise and create an ethnic "firewall" between the whites at the top of colonial society and the Indians and Africans filling out the lower strata. Whether or not the Chinese consented to this positioning is unclear, but this chapter does highlight the range of social and economic roles that different ethnic groups can play in their host environments. Migrants, especially those moving into societies undergoing significant changes, are not automatically destined to fill specific roles. In other words, first-generation Chinese immigrants are not fated to be launderers or stevedores. Rather, government policy, the skill sets and inclinations of the migrants themselves, as well as local conditions can all inform where they end up in the socioeconomic landscape.

Li Anshan turns his significant expertise, gained from the study of Chinese in Africa, to a brief history of the Chinese community in Jamaica. In addition to providing a narrative of early migrations to complement Look Lai's chapter and exploring the Chinese transition from agricultural laborers to petty entrepreneurs, Li uses community institutions to help frame his chapter. Beyond descriptions of Chinese newspapers, homes for the elderly, sports clubs, and political party branches, it is Li's description of the Chinese Benevolent Association (CBA) that serves as a parable for the community's evolution.[5] Initially founded in the 1890s as a venue for collective action and to protect fledgling commercial interests in an often hostile environment, the CBA rapidly became the dominant Chinese organization, and leadership of the Association was synonymous with prominence in the Chinese community. In the early 1900s the CBA's board was more concerned with intra-community functions and local projects—hospitals and old-age homes—and preserving Chinese culture and language through the establishment of a Chinese school. By the 1920s and 30s the CBA, thanks to the rising economic clout of the Chinese, was more active in extra-community affairs, such as lobbying the colonial government and raising funds for China's anti-Japanese resistance. As second- and third-generation Chinese moved toward assimilation on the eve of Jamaican independence, the need for institutions that defined the Chinese community as something apart from Jamaican society declined and the influence of the CBA waned. We are thus reminded of the integrative function of institutions in shaping community dynamics and informing identity choices among émigrés. The example of the ebb and flow of community cohesion and the varied patterns of assimilation evident in Li's story of the Jamaican Chinese also challenge reductionist tropes of characteristically "Chinese" insularity.

Gail Bouknight-Davis uses her chapter to show that class and occupation, as much as race, account for ethnic distinctions. She chronicles the Chinese rise to prominence in Jamaica's grocery sector in the early twentieth century: a rise facilitated by the immaturity of the Jamaican retail sector and the ability of the Chinese, many of them Hakka,[6] to leverage family connections for labor inputs and market information. The high profile of Chinese shops contributed to a general, albeit inaccurate, perception that the Chinese monopolized retail groceries and served to sharpen ethnic distinctions in Jamaica. Not only did the family network structure of Chinese businesses encourage insularity, but retail competition was directly equated with competition between Chinese and Afro-Jamaicans—a view that may have been perpetuated by the white elite. Ethnic tensions further encouraged the Chinese community to cohere for self-protection. Thus Bouknight-Davis argues persuasively that the formation of ethnic identity must be understood as a process of interaction driven by context. There were numerous commercial advantages to being "Chinese" in colonial Jamaica, and both government policy and the economy encouraged the Chinese to define themselves as a community apart. This self-identification was complemented by external "othering" and ethnic antagonism. Following independence, Jamaica's Chinese took one of three main paths. A small group stayed the course of insularity, another group—the second and third generations of Jamaican- and American-educated Chinese—integrated into the island's new Creole elite, while a third group fled to Toronto. Although they are not covered in this chapter, it is interesting to note that those who moved to Toronto identify themselves as Jamaican-Chinese while simultaneously locating themselves as members of the larger Chinese diaspora and more specifically as members of the global Hakka community.

Turning from the West Indies to Cuba, Kathleen Lopez describes the fluid environment through which Cuba's Chinese moved in the early twentieth century. More than just providing an excellent community history, Lopez demonstrates that her subjects were, in the words of Adam McKeown, both "here and there." In other words, the *chinos* in Cienfuegos and Havana were both firmly entrenched in their local environments and at the same time remained intimately linked with their native-places (*qiaoxiang*) in China. Being both "here and there" was how Cuban Chinese recruited talent, moved money, researched markets, sired heirs, and invested. Lopez judiciously applies the concept of transnationalism that has gained currency in international migration studies over the past decade.[7] The case study of the Chinese in Cuba demonstrates how one group of migrants developed a "transnational social field" linking places of origin and settlement.[8] Lopez's work provides a set of local and personal histories that underscores the utility and ubiquity of transnational migration networks in exploiting economic opportunities in Cuba and providing income and employment in the native-place.[9] But "transnational" is perhaps a misleading term without significant qualification and refinement. These transnational linkages were usually quite narrow, if not parochial, in terms of the connections between the "sending" community and the "host" community.

By following the intimate and dialectical relationship between Xinhui County in Guangdong Province and Cienfuegos, Lopez highlights the inherent local character of migration and shows that the ties that shaped migration, settlement, and employment patterns of Chinese overseas were primarily translocal and transurban. For a Chinese *tendero* (shopkeeper) or coolie it was the link between his immediate locale and his *qiaoxiang* that mattered most. The same was true for family members who remained behind in China and whose fortunes were inexorably tied to the Cuban countryside. The distance between China and Cuba and the intervention of historical forces, notably war, revolution, and the emergence of nationalism, could significantly disrupt migration networks, but *qiaoxiang* ties were remarkably resilient. Ironically, it was Castro's revolution that ultimately spelled the end to robust linkages between Southeast China and Cuba.

One of Lopez's main interlocutors during her research in Cuba was the archivist Mitzi Espinosa Luis. Ethnic policy in Castro's Cuba was largely successful in achieving social leveling and fostering the belief that all Cubans, regardless of race, are equally "Cuban." This achievement, however, often came at the expense of a more nuanced understanding of individual ethnicity. Luis is representative of a generation of young Cubans who have recently been encouraged by the state to explore their ethnic backgrounds. For Cubans of Chinese descent this process has primarily consisted of pilgrimages to Havana's once vibrant, but now faded, *barrio chino* as well as participation in academic colloquia and Chinese cultural festivals. At Chinese New Year in 2001 Luis met two elderly men who were from the same village and shared the same family name as her grandfather. Following this chance encounter, Luis adopted the two men as "relatives." While far more personal and certainly less scholarly than the other chapters in this volume, Luis' retelling of her "grandfather" Felipe's life story is worthy of inclusion here. Many of the colorful vignettes drawn from Felipe's experiences are valuable, especially the descriptions of *barrio chino* in its heyday, but it is Luis' delivery that is most illuminating. In many ways the author has become the subject and Felipe the prism through which she grapples with her own identity. That Luis portrays Felipe, who has spent more than seven decades in Cuba, as something of a quaint oddity says a lot about race, ethnicity, and identity in contemporary Cuba.

The third section of this book offers up two provocative chapters dealing with identity and belonging among contemporary Caribbeans of Chinese descent. Lok Siu uses four life stories of Chinese in Panama to introduce the concept of "serial migration." Serial migration is the cumulative process of an individual's or family's multiple border crossings that shape a life experience. Siu is thus seeking to move beyond classical migration studies, which focus on unidirectional migrations and sending/receiving society dichotomies, and show her subjects as participants in cyclical and multidirectional flows that shape "notions of identity, home, and belonging in diaspora." Nor is serial migration a new process, but it definitely takes on new significance in an era when the forces of globalization exist in tension with more classical concepts of the nation-state and ethnic identity. For some, discovering and exploring the multiplicity of identities and experiences within the Chinese diaspora enhances their sense of belonging in a global "Chinese" community, while for others this same process contributes to a sense of alienation. Two of her subjects, Marco and Pedro, are at opposite ends of this spectrum, yet both explain their sense of belonging or alienation as typically "Chinese." Siu therefore not only introduces a provocative and useful concept into migration studies, serial migration, but, like the other authors in this volume, challenges those who would seek homogeneity in the Chinese experience overseas.

Andrew Meyer's study of New York's Cuban-Chinese restaurant fad in the 1980s seems at first to illuminate a classic experience of the new immigrant transitioning from employment to entrepreneurship. Here we have refugees from Castro's Cuba finding employment as dishwashers and cooks before opening their own restaurants. The fading of the craze also seems to be explicable in straightforward terms as the children of Cuban-Chinese restaurateurs sought their American dream as lawyers and doctors in the suburbs. But Meyer finds that there is far more to this story. The fact that some Cuban-Chinese restaurants opened in the early 1960s challenges the classic employee-employer transition. Moreover, market demand must also be taken into account. The vogue of "fusion cuisine" in the 1980s (when the fad peaked) partly explains why a Cuban-Chinese restaurant would be viable, but New York's Cuban-Chinese were not only a remarkably cohesive group, resisting assimilation into the city's large Chinese population; they also had a ready-made clientele. These restaurants served up the flavors of pre-Castro Cuba for a Cuban expatriate clientele. Going out for Chinese food was as commonplace in Havana as it is here in the United States, but the dishes varied dramatically. Meyer shows that Cuban-Chinese are members of two different diasporas, the Cuban and the Chinese, which are often in tension with each other. The cultural gravity imparted to the Chinese community during its long sojourn in Cuba remains potent in exile, a potency enhanced by the nostalgia of the larger community of Cuban expatriates for the flavors of home. Like Siu, Meyer thus alerts us to the need to understand how the migration/re-migration of the Chinese to/through the Americas is a fundamental part of pan-American culture. That cuisine is commodifiable and exportable comes as no surprise, but the fact that "Chinese" cuisine is so elastic and has taken so many trajectories may serve as a metaphor for both culture and identity among the Chinese overseas.

The comparative and local approach that the authors of these essays employ is an important corrective to more essentialist and totalizing portrayals of Chinese migrations, Chinese communities, and Chinese identity. The migrant communities portrayed in this volume show remarkable variations: in agency, in political orientation, in sense of belonging in the host environment or to a Chinese community, and in the strength of linkages with the native-place. But we are not trying deconstruct the term "Chinese" to the point where it becomes meaningless. While no one can provide a definitive portrayal of either Chinese identity or the Chinese diaspora, China and native-place ties do exercise potent influences on many of these subjects. Moreover, labels like *chino*, "Chinaman," etc., whether self-identification or external "othering," are so pervasive that there is meaning to the marker "Chinese" and substance to a shared experience among the Chinese overseas. In sum, this book is a tentative coalescing of various subdisciplines from which we can craft a better and more historically accurate view of the Chinese experience in the Caribbean and beyond. We hope that this project invites further study, similar to what has occurred in the study of the Chinese in

Southeast Asia and the United States: discrete community histories, building to a more nuanced view of the multiple roles played and multiple directions taken by the Chinese in the Caribbean.

These chapters can further research in two disciplines: Caribbean studies and Chinese diaspora studies. For Caribbean studies, this book encourages comparisons of Chinese communities across the Caribbean, considerations about secondary migrations of Chinese within the Caribbean and from the Caribbean to North America, and comparisons between the historical and contemporary experiences of different ethnic groups in the region. More comparative work on the experiences of various migrants—European, African, Chinese, South Asian, Portuguese—is needed. Lok Siu's introduction of serial migration as a way of understanding contemporary Chinese in the Americas invites us to ask whether serial migration is a shared experience among other Caribbean peoples. Likewise, we would welcome more studies of how local attitudes and government policies across the Caribbean facilitate or impede assimilation or hybridization. With regard to the Chinese diaspora, the variations in the strength and structure of *qiaoxiang* ties might be used to explain the patterns of development and relative socioeconomic success of Chinese communities overseas. Are there uniquely Chinese migration strategies and network structures that transcend regional variations in the émigré experience? How are the dialectical relations between the sending and receiving societies managed across these transnational and translocal networks? Clearly this is far from a comprehensive list of potential avenues of inquiry; nonetheless, it is indicative of the wealth that further exploration of the Chinese experience in the Caribbean can uncover.

PART I
The British West Indies

He longed for vestiges of his family mirrored in the men who came, in their gesticulations and corroded faces, in the Morse code of their languages, which he didn't even understand anymore, but anything to remind him that he wasn't alone there on that wretched island.

—Patricia Powell, *The Pagoda*
(New York: Alfred A. Knopf, 1998), p. 33

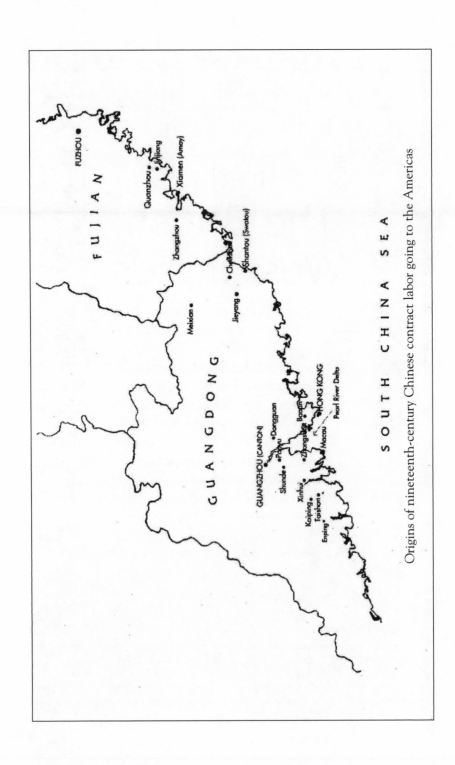

Origins of nineteenth-century Chinese contract labor going to the Americas

CHAPTER 1

The Chinese Indenture System in the British West Indies and Its Aftermath

WALTON LOOK LAI

The first Chinese migrations to the British West Indies took place at the same time as the worldwide Chinese migrations in the nineteenth century, and from the same cluster of emigrant districts around the Pearl River Delta in Guangdong province (see map at left for names of key districts involved).[1] With the post-1840 large-scale arrival of Europeans, led by the British, and the imposition of the treaty port system, which rapidly opened a series of coastal and riverine ports to both foreign imports and labor exporters, China's rural and urban poor were presented with new emigration horizons that had not existed before. Several of these new destinations turned out to be catastrophic for the average Chinese migrant, and a large number of people were actually coerced or tricked into migrating during the nineteenth century, but many destinations (among them the West Indies) proved in the long run to be beneficial, despite the local hardships encountered in the passage from sojourner to settler, from alien immigrant to citizen.

The circumstances of the early West Indian migrations are to be found in a combination of a number of factors: the conditions of life in Guangdong in the mid-nineteenth century, British migration and recruitment policy in China, and the condition of the West Indian sugar economy after slave emancipation in 1834. Guangdong in the mid-nineteenth century was afflicted, like much of rural China, with a population explosion that could not be properly accommodated on

3

available lands. Local and imperial authorities also exacerbated the plight of the average rural dweller with exorbitant taxes and cruel local administration, helping to create a social environment of anti-imperial rebellion, widespread social unrest, and personal insecurity. Social upheavals in the form of the massive Taiping Rebellion ravaged southeast China from 1850 to 1864 and almost toppled the Qing Dynasty (1644–1911). These disruptions were compounded by tribal and ethnic struggles for scarce land between "native" Cantonese or "Punti" and the more recently arrived Hakka (literally "guest families").[2] As such, there were massive forces pushing Chinese laborers out of rural Guangdong, toward China's treaty ports and even beyond. In the midst of this unsettled situation, eagerness to migrate overseas became one of the many responses to the domestic condition. It was a natural response, especially since Canton and its environs, with their centuries-old overseas trade connections, had long been, along with Fujian province, the major outlets for the pre-nineteenth-century Chinese overseas migrations to Southeast Asia.

In the course of the nineteenth century, more than 7.5 million Chinese émigrés left Guangdong and Fujian provinces to travel overseas. About 6.5 million went to familiar regional destinations in Southeast Asia. Another million ventured beyond the familiar to newly available destinations, sometimes with the help of Chinese middlemen (such as to the United States), and often under the auspices of various Western middlemen who had entered into the business of transporting Chinese overseas. About 100,000 went to Australia, and 600,000 to the Americas. Of the migrants to the Americas, about forty-five percent went to Latin America and the Caribbean, mainly as contract or indentured laborers. The main receiving countries were Cuba (125,000), Peru (100,000), and the British West Indies (ca. 18,000), with a remaining six percent siphoned off in smaller streams to Central America (Panama and Costa Rica), the Dutch and French West Indies, and Brazil.

British officials along the coast of China in the nineteenth century were not initially concerned with issues of Chinese labor migration, although a substantial spontaneous movement of labor had already begun toward the British-held possessions in Southeast Asia, notably

4

Penang in Malaya, and a few British shipping firms had already been involving themselves in the transportation of laborers overseas.[3] An official based in Malaya, who was familiar with this growing migration to British Southeast Asia, suggested in 1802 that a trial emigration to newly acquired and sparsely settled British Trinidad should be tried under official auspices. This resulted in the arrival in 1806 of the vessel *Fortitude* with 192 Chinese males (eight having died on the voyage). Interestingly, all the workers were recruited in Macao, Penang, and even Calcutta, rather than directly from the Chinese mainland. This Trinidad settlement became the first organized Chinese settlement in the Americas in the nineteenth century, coming as it did a full forty years before the first major arrivals in Cuba and California. Fated to be a solitary shipment, rather than the beginning of a regular migration, the Chinese were housed west of Port of Spain in North Trinidad, and were given a choice as to whether they would work on the sugar plantations or as independent small farmers. They were also given a chance to return home, passage paid, if at any time they were dissatisfied with their new environment. All except for about two dozen exercised the return option within three years, and about sixty Chinese returned aboard the *Fortitude* itself.[4]

It was not until the 1850s, after the forced establishment of the treaty port system in China, that the British began to formulate a coherent policy on Chinese labor migration, in an atmosphere of growing migration to new destinations like Cuba and Peru, the United States, the Sandwich Islands (later Hawaii), and Australia. A few hundred had already been shipped under private auspices to Demerara (British Guiana) in 1852–53. The main intermediaries in this early traffic were often English,[5] and some of the tensions arising out of the recruitment process exploded into violence at Xiamen (Amoy) in Fujian (Fukien) as early as 1852.[6] One of the clauses of the Treaty of Beijing (Peking), concluded in 1860 after the Second Opium War, explicitly endorsed the emigration of Chinese to British colonies. The emigration to the British West Indies was specifically designed to alleviate the labor shortage in the West Indian sugar industry, then going through the difficulties of the post-Emancipation experience.

In the aftermath of Emancipation in 1834–38, the West Indian planter elite was beset with a number of problems:

The Labor Problem. Having gained their freedom, ex-slaves exercised the full range of their expanded options. They increasingly left the plantations for lands elsewhere in their respective colonies (acquired either by purchase or by squatting). Those who remained on the plantations often agitated for higher wages and pressured owners by providing reduced or irregular work. According to many planters, collective work discipline also suffered under the new dispensation, with a resulting impact on productivity. On some islands where land availability was low, or where wages remained unsatisfactory, such as Barbados and the Leewards, and to a certain extent the Windwards, freed slaves migrated to the newer British colonies like Trinidad and British Guiana in search of higher wages, often initially in the sugar industry.

Capital and Credit Access. By the late nineteenth century the British capital that had once financed the West Indian sugar industry was increasingly siphoned away to the many alternative and lucrative outlets of an expanding British Empire. Many of the old merchant houses on which the West Indian planter elite relied also went through financial travails of their own during this period, with the resultant tightening of credit. Some planters were more fortunate than others, but many lost their plantations to metropolitan creditors. Other plantations were carved up and sold in smaller plots to newly mobile middle-class elements, and even to ex-slaves who could buy them either outright or with the assistance of church groups.

Markets and Prices. Global competition required that West Indian planters produce more efficiently and cheaply than the new sugar-producing countries of the nineteenth century,[7] and those who did not modernize and/or resolve their labor problem were vulnerable to being undersold by the competition.

It was within this context that the West Indian sugar planters lobbied for, and eventually won, the right to bring in laborers from other countries under arrangements that would tie workers to the plantations for a fixed minimum number of years, since they could no longer tie them there forever. The indenture experiment was the result. This

6

followed a larger trend in the world sugar industry, which in the nineteenth century came to rely heavily on indentured labor.[8] In the British West Indies, labor migrations can be broken down into two discrete phases. During the first phase, 1850s to 1870, the laborers were multi-racial, as the planters experimented with various sources of migrant labor. This was the period that saw the arrival of Europeans, Portuguese, Chinese, Indians, and "liberated" Africans under various short-term indenture contracts. From the early 1870s the labor supply became overwhelmingly Indian, down to the end of the indenture experiment in 1917. All in all, a total of 536,310 migrants entered the West Indies between the 1830s and 1917. They were made up as follows:

Table 1.1
Migrants to the West Indies, 1830s–1917.[9]

Period	Nationality	Number of immigrants
1838–1917	Indians	429,623
1835–1881	Portuguese	40,971
1834–1867	freed Africans	39,332
1853–1884	Chinese	17,904
1834–1845	Europeans	4,582
1835–1867	others (mainly Black Americans)	3,898

Thus 83.5 percent of these immigrants came from Asia: 80 percent from India and 3.5 percent from China. British Guiana alone absorbed 56 percent (300,967) of the total migration, 55.6 percent (238,909) of the Indians, and 76 percent (13,533) of the Chinese. Trinidad absorbed 29.4 percent (157,668) of the total migration, 33.3 percent (143,939) of the Indians, and 15 percent (2,645) of the Chinese. Jamaica received 10 percent (53,940) of the total migration, 8.5 percent (36,412) of the Indians, and 6.4 percent (1,152) of the Chinese total.

From these figures it can be seen that the Chinese contribution to the survival of the West Indian sugar industry was marginal. This stood in marked contrast to its counterpart in Cuba—where about

7

125,000 Chinese were brought into the sugar industry between 1849 and 1874—or Peru, which received about 100,000 during the same period.[10] In total, there were fifty-one voyages from China to the British West Indies between 1853 and 1884, the year the last ship arrived in Jamaica: thirty-nine to British Guiana (13,539), eight to Trinidad (2,645), two to Jamaica (1,152), one to British Honduras (474), and one to Antigua (100). (If one includes the 1806 experiment, this would bring the number of shipments to fifty-two, and the Trinidadian total to nine). The more extensive traffic to Cuba and Peru between 1847 and 1874 saw 347 vessels bringing Chinese to Cuba, and about 276 vessels to Peru.

Similar, more sporadic, efforts at Chinese labor importation were made during this period by the Dutch government in Surinam, and by the French West Indian colonial authorities. In 1853 the Dutch authorities in Surinam began with one vessel bringing a small group of fourteen Chinese from Java, and the British Guiana legislature also briefly considered importing Chinese from Holland's Southeast Asian colonies. Two further shipments of five hundred were attempted in 1858, under state auspices, this time from Macao. With the end of slavery in 1863, the issue was again raised, and between 1865 and 1869, a private company, the Surinam Immigration Corporation, brought seven more shipments of Chinese from Hong Kong. In 1869, however, the Hong Kong government banned further shipments of contract laborers to non-British territories, and the Surinam government turned once more to Java, bringing in another 115 laborers between 1872 and 1874. All in all, about 2,645 Chinese arrived in Surinam between 1853 and 1874. [11] The French West Indies also imported Chinese labor from Canton, as well as a few from Shanghai. Only a handful of vessels carrying Chinese workers, however, made the voyage to this part of the Caribbean. In 1862 there were 800 Chinese in Martinique, and 112 in Guadeloupe, along with 8,000 and 98,389 Indians, respectively. [12]

The indenture arrangements under which the Chinese came to Trinidad, British Guiana, and Jamaica were closer to those under which the Indians came than to those under which Chinese immigrated to Cuba or Peru. The key factor here was British policy on

8

indenture, which was shaped under the stern gaze of metropolitan abolitionists and human rights activists preoccupied with the possibility of the re-imposition of slavery under a new name. One consequence was the active involvement of the state and its agencies in all aspects of the migration process, from recruitment and transportation in the East, to arrival and distribution in the West Indies. All recruitment—mainly in Hong Kong and Canton—was done under the supervision of an Emigration Agent responsible to the British government; officially permitted vessels under the Chinese Passengers Act did all transportation; and all allocation of jobs was coordinated by the Immigration Agents based in the different territories. This helped to avoid the worst abuses associated with the privately operated indenture recruitment conducted out of Portuguese Macao by vessels recruiting for Cuba and Peru, as well as those abuses resulting from the private sale and distribution of the immigrants on arrival in Cuba or Peru, often indistinguishable from the slave trade.

The British emigration agent in the East deliberately tried to distinguish the British efforts from Latin American recruitment, which used Chinese recruiters or "crimps" who were paid a fee for each migrant "recruited." Naturally, this per capita system led to myriad abuses. The unscrupulous tactics (kidnapping, deception, and physical coercion) of these crimps had become something of a scandal in coastal China and colored much of the labor export business. At the end of the 1860 season, the British Emigration Agent J. Gardiner Austin reported as follows:

> Mr. Parkes, the British Commissioner of Canton, Mr. Lobscheid, a German missionary, and myself, were all agreed that as our acts and intentions were as different to those of the Chinese crimps as day to night, so should every step taken be dissimilar. Instead of collecting people by force or fraud, I therefore employed the press to sow the good seed over the length and breadth of Quantung, and to make known to those who were in poverty that the British Government offered them a new home where comparative affluence was the reward of honest labor.

Instead of the Swatow dens of filth and iniquity where the sustenance barely sufficed to support life, and where husbands and children torn from their families were caged till their purchasers called for compulsory removal to the ships, I offered the best and amplest food at houses to and from which there was FREE ingress and egress, where every information was available from maps, pamphlets and notices, and from whence the laborers were at perfect liberty to return to their old homes, or to seek the new one offered to them.

Instead of forcing the emigrants to indent themselves to worse even than slavery by renunciation of the advantages of free British citizens, [I offered] the current wages of the colonies, house and garden rent free, correspondence free of cost with relatives left behind, and the punctual payment at Hong Kong or Canton monthly from the day of embarkation, of such portion of the wages to be earned as the emigrants desired to appropriate in China.

Lastly, instead of placing my ships where oppression could be practised with impunity, I selected Hong Kong and Canton for their anchorage, and facilitated their inspection, by the Chinese authorities and people as much as possible. You may judge of the influence of this over the feelings of the emigrants when I tell you that the first Canton ship, the *Red Riding Hood*, left with 10,000 crackers blazing at each yard-arm, amidst cheers which told far and wide that there was no compulsion, and you may judge of the character of the emigration by the contrast afforded in the behaviour of our people in the *Dora*, and those of the *Flora Temple* for Cuba when sailing down the China seas, the latter—800 in number—rising in the bitter agony of despair, only to meet grape shot, imprisonment, cruel abandonment on the reef, and a watery grave, whilst the former, to use the words of the surgeon, passed Anjer after the quickest passage ever made, singing hymns and joining regularly in the morning and evening services.....[13]

The public notices posted by the British in Canton emphasized these differences:

- There is no slavery wherever the British Flag flies.
- The Law is the same to rich and poor. All Religions are tolerated and protected, and the Queen of England has appointed Special Magistrates in her West Indian Colonies, to look after and protect the strangers, who go there to seek their fortunes.
- All Chinese may therefore go without fear to the British West Indies.
- The climate is very much like that of Southern China.
- The cultivation is chiefly that of the Sugar Cane.
- The wages offered during five years service under contract, are in accordance with the current price of labor in the West Indies, and vary from 2 shillings to 4 shillings[14] per day, according to the industry and ability of the emigrant. House, garden ground, and medical attendance, are supplied free of charge.
- Any laborer entering into a contract for five years, and desiring to cancel it at the end of the first year, and work where he pleases, can do so on repayment of four fifths of the passage money from China to the West Indies, estimated at $75. At the end of the second year, he can cancel it on repayment of three fifths, and so on, one fifth being deducted for every year's service.
- Special means of remitting money, and of corresponding with relatives gratuitously, will be afforded.
- A free passage is offered, and clothing for the voyage.
- A special Law has been passed by the Parliament of England, for the feeding and protection of the emigrants during the voyage.
- An advance of wages to the extent of twenty dollars for the married men, and ten dollars for the single men, will be made, either by monthly payments in China to the families of male emigrants, or to themselves. If an emigrant

desires to draw the whole advance himself he can do so, but if leaving a monthly allotment of one or two dollars to his family, the first six monthly payments will be deducted. The cash payment to the emigrant will be deducted from the wages to be earned by him, at the rate of one dollar per month, and the payments to his family in equal amounts monthly.

• To such emigrants as may be desirous of taking their families, a gift of twenty dollars will be made to the wife, a similar sum to each adult daughter, and five dollars to each child.

• Provision will be made in the West Indies, for the education of children.

• Women will be unfettered by any engagement whatever, being free to work or to attend to their household duties, solely as their wants and inclinations determine.

• Lastly a Depot has been established by me at   for the reception of emigrants, where those enrolling themselves can be housed and fed until a vessel is ready for sea, and where those who desire further information, can obtain it from the Officer in charge.

J. GARDINER AUSTIN.[15]

Because of the unsettled environment in coastal China in the 1850s and 1860s, and the instability of British personnel at the China end of the recruitment system (there were three emigration agents between 1859 and 1866), during its short life-span (1852–66) the labor export process was neither as smooth nor as well-regulated as the British authorities would have liked. The contracts offered to potential recruits were never standardized, and there were several versions of indenture contracts offered to the Chinese. The most important difference had to do with the redemption or cancellation clause. Some contracts allowed redemption by the immigrant after one year, subject to repayment, by the immigrant, of the balance of the passage monies, calculated at one-fifth for each year of the five-year contract. Some contracts allowed no redemption during the five-year period. In addition, the contracts made in 1859 were actually altered on arrival in British Guiana by the Agent-General for Immigrants, changing the start of the redemption period from one year to three years. The redemption sums were also made specific: $50 for two years, $25 for any single year.

There were other differences as well. Some contracts specified the amount of wages to be paid monthly, while others did not, offering only an amount corresponding to that earned by free laborers at the time. Some arrangements even gave the migrants a choice between timework at specified wages, and task work at unspecified wages, measured against corresponding wages earned by free laborers. Even when the wages were specified, the amounts were not always the same. Many specified $4 plus free rations, some specified $5 plus rations, and one even offered $2 plus rations.[16] Contracts made after 1860 did not mention free rations at all.

In addition to all these discrepancies, the Chinese contracts differed from the standard Indian contracts in substantial ways.

- There was no provision for a pre-paid return passage to China at the end of the five-year term, or any period of service. [17]
- The contractual workday for the Chinese was generally stated as seven and a half hours, while for the Indians it was nine hours for Trinidad and seven for the British Guiana immigrants.
- The Chinese were given repayable loan advances as well as bounty payments for accompanying family members ranging from $10 to $20, whereas their Indian counterparts were not.
- Indians were expected to pay for their own food rations, delivered for only a short period ranging from 3 months to a year.
- Many Chinese contracts also mentioned free garden grounds, although it is not clear how many actually received such grants.
- Most important, Chinese women were not allowed to enter into contracts of indenture, but instead into what were called contracts of residence, which bound them to their designated plantations for the full term but did not oblige them to work at all.[18]

In addition to the instability regarding the contracts, British recruiting efforts were not free from some of the very questionable methods they tried to avoid. The 1859 efforts to bring Chinese to

British Guiana were deeply flawed. It was claimed that emigrants had been recruited at Hong Kong, when in fact most had been obtained in Macao, home to the "crimps" and crooked foreign agents responsible for the infamous shipments of Chinese to Latin America. The same was true for the 1866 shipments, which were done via a private mercantile firm utilizing suspect recruiting procedures at Amoy, while the Emigration Agent himself remained based at Canton. The matter was cause for some official correspondence, and the Emigration Agent was sanctioned.[19]

The Chinese migration to the West Indies, episodic and marginal, was eventually terminated because of a dispute over a treaty concluded in 1866 between China, Britain, and France known as the Kung Convention. Articles VIII and IX of the Convention granted every emigrant the right to a return passage for himself and his family at the end of his five-year term of service, or a cash grant in lieu of passage. Article IX further specified that in the event that a migrant should reindenture himself for a second five-year term, he should receive a bounty equivalent to half the amount of his return passage, while still retaining his right to a free passage at the end of the second term. These agreements had a significant impact on the future of Chinese immigration to the British West Indies. The West Indian planter elite and the Colonial Office objected to this Foreign Office–negotiated concession, on grounds of cost, and looked to alternative sources of labor. By the time the Chinese government made concessions in 1872, reducing the obligation to a single cash grant of $50 in lieu of return passage after five years, Indian indenture had already taken root as the more financially viable and better organized alternative. A few vessels came in the 1870s and 1880s, but the vibrancy of the Chinese emigration effort had long since subsided.

Settlement Patterns

The Chinese were employed on sugar plantations along with other free and indentured immigrants who had arrived in the 1860s: Portuguese Madeirans, Indians, and Black immigrants from the other West Indian islands and West Africa. The Chinese were widely dispersed in British Guiana and Trinidad, ending up on 116 out of 153 estates in the former, and 70–76 out of 153–58 estates in the latter. What we know of the social conditions on the British Guiana plantations comes from an 1869–70 investigation by an official commission of enquiry. The resulting report was published as a parliamentary paper in 1871.[20] In addition to the official report, there was a dissenting independent view, which the commission found too harsh in its judgments to be accepted as part of the final report, authored by Ex–Chief Justice Beaumont. Beaumont subsequently published his version under the title *The New Slavery: An Account of the Indian and Chinese Immigrants in British Guiana*. Although the conditions described were nowhere as damning as the 1874 Chinese government commission report on conditions among Chinese laborers in Cuba, the two Guiana reports demonstrated that life was far from satisfactory for many of the Chinese (and Indians) who had migrated to the British colonies.[21]

Some of the main irregularities pointed out by the Guiana critiques involved

- Misrepresentation by recruiters in China of the actual level of wages a prospective immigrant could hope to earn in the new environment;
- Arbitrary wage delays or deductions for minor violations, a penalty not sanctioned by the laws but widely applied;
- Violations of minimum wage stipulations, especially in periods of economic downturn;
- Abuse and intimidation by plantation officials like drivers and overseers, as well as managers, ranging from physical brutality to bribery and extortion for favors rendered;
- Frequent resort to prosecutions for minor offenses, as a way of disciplining the rebellious, with the result that the jails were often full of immigrants imprisoned for minor and major offenses against the labor laws, living side by side with hardened criminals;
- Court partiality toward planters in the dispensation of justice;
- Defective health care and housing conditions, as individual planters evaded the formal provisions of the law.

How did the Chinese themselves respond to conditions of life in their new environment and in the new societies in general? As was to be expected, these responses were quite varied.[22] The social and regional backgrounds of these migrants were diverse, and this reflected itself in their adjustment patterns. Those from stable, hardworking peasant backgrounds were the most praised by the planters for their diligence and enthusiasm. Even migrant women occasionally joined voluntarily in this collective adjustment to plantation life. On some voyages, however, the émigrés included a large number of social miscreants, "recruited" from China's coastal ports. Their habits of opium smoking and chronic absenteeism were cause for frequent complaints from the planters and their representatives. Some Chinese even brought with them a propensity to brigandage and social parasitism that characterized the unstable, war-torn environment of South China. Non-Chinese villagers often had to guard their property and produce from thieving and plundering raids by Chinese, whether acting individually or as part of an organized gang.

Frustrated with their lot, many Chinese ran away from plantation life, to pursue independent lives as fruit and vegetable growers or as small proprietors in the villages beyond the reach of the planters, occasionally engaging in illicit rum smuggling and distillation, and even the keeping of gambling houses and brothels. In Belize (British Honduras), a number of Chinese migrants even fled into the interior to make common cause with the indigenous peoples of the colony. In Guiana, there was an independent settlement of free Chinese upstream along the Demerara river where runaways could seek refuge. One observer recorded that "it would be a bold policeman who would attempt to execute a warrant in their midst."[23] Violent confrontations between laborers and plantation personnel were not unknown. On the island of Antigua in 1883, two migrants were tried and executed for the murder of a plantation manager.[24] Beaumont's 1871 account of the fate of the Chinese and Indians in British Guiana, *The New Slavery*, as well as the pages of the (Demerara) *Royal Gazette*, chronicled the many graphic incidents of violence by and against Chinese workers in the colony, including the retaliatory murder of a cruel white overseer by a Chinese plantation hand who subsequently received ten years' imprisonment for manslaughter for that offense. In Trinidad in 1866, at the height of the Chinese labor influx, as many as 902 Chinese spent some time in prison for various offenses. While the majority were jailed on matters of work discipline for which all indentured laborers, both Indians and Chinese, were often incarcerated for short periods, there were also offenses ranging from resisting a police constable, to larceny, to trespass and assault, to using violent and obscene language against officials.

Chinese interactions with their fellow Asian laborers and with Black villagers were never systematically chronicled, and we do not have insider accounts like the Afro-Cuban Esteban Montejo's *Autobiography of a Runaway Slave* to enlighten us. Given the colonial obsession with law, order, and good government, the documentary record covers mostly ethnic interactions that required a legal response. There are official reports of early clashes between Chinese and Black villagers in Guiana, triggered by language difficulties and motivation misunderstandings. There was also the constant friction between some Chinese and both Africans and Indians over Chinese praedial larceny. There are likewise accounts of rebellious Chinese laborers killing Black drivers or foremen in plantation-related disputes, as well as accounts of harsh treatment by the latter group toward immigrant laborers. There are also accounts of clashes between Chinese and Indian workers, as well as Chinese siding with one side or the other in Indian-Black clashes. [25]

At the same time there are indications of less contentious ethnic interactions, such as laborers of all colors sharing one another's recreational pastimes. A frequent complaint by planters was the tendency of some Indians to indulge in the Chinese pastime of opium smoking, and also of Africans learning and popularizing among themselves Chinese games of chance. One account spoke of the Chinese actively participating in the Indian Muslim festival of Muharram ("Hosay"), which in the West Indies seems to have become an all-inclusive festival with the active participation of Hindus and Africans.

> This year the [Indian] Coolies called in the aid of the
> Chinese to build their gaudy temples, and these ingenious
> fellows gave the Coolies better temples than they have ever

had before. As on former occasions the black people followed the procession in thousands, and seemed to look on the [Tadja] festival as one designated as much for their spiritual benefit as for that of the Coolies. [26]

The post-indenture fortunes of the Chinese were also quite varied. In Trinidad, the Chinese moved quickly off the plantations as early as the 1870s. Beginning often as small peasant food cultivators and truck gardeners, former indentured laborers quickly gravitated toward the rural and urban petty commerce in which a small number of Chinese had been active since the 1860s. We get brief glimpses of these shopkeepers in the writings of missionaries and others who lived or traveled in Trinidad and British Guiana in the 1880s and 1890s: the Abbé Massé, the Reverend Cothonay, the Reverend Kingsley, Edward Jenkins, Henry Kirke, the Reverend Bronkhurst.[27] In British Guiana, where reindenture was actually a common practice up until the mid-1870s, many Chinese remained on the plantations for as many as ten years or more.

Nonetheless, even the Chinese in Guiana explored a wide variety of post-indenture options in the late 1870s and beyond. A few hundred actually returned to China at their own expense, having amassed small savings during their stay in the colony. Many chose to relocate within the Caribbean region itself. About three thousand had left British Guiana by the mid-1880s for Trinidad, for Surinam and Cayenne, for Jamaica and Panama. Contemporary reports spoke of a restlessness among the Guiana Chinese between the 1860s and 1880s that was due to the inability of many to get past the hurdles of Portuguese domination of the small-scale retail merchant sector. The immigration reports spoke of them heading in large numbers for Trinidad, where the Chinese had in fact gained a foothold in the retail trade sector and were being described as "the Portuguese of Trinidad." The reports also described the Chinese as attracted to the Surinam and Cayenne goldmines, and spoke of some who received bounty to reindenture themselves in the Nickerie district of Surinam. A small number found their way to St. Lucia in the Eastern Caribbean in the 1870s, under a dubious labor exchange arrangement which was terminated when discovered by the Guianan authorities. Census reports for the Leeward Islands in the Eastern Caribbean islands in 1881 recorded minuscule numbers of Chinese in St. Christopher (13), Dominica (4), and Anguilla (1). This was one year before the small group of 100 landed in Antigua.[28] For those who relocated as well as those who stayed on in their original destinations, the census reports recorded the occupational transition they had made out of the sugar plantation environment by the 1880s and 1890s.[29]

After the period of indenture, a small but steady trickle of voluntary free migration from China continued into the region in the 1880s and 90s. Some of this was family- and village-related—managed through migration networks based on the native-place (*qiaoxiang*), or more narrowly the kin of a first generation émigré—while other migrations were part of a larger deflection of migration flows toward Latin America and the Caribbean in the period after the ban on Chinese immigration to the United States in 1882. These flows were subsequently augmented as a result of the social turmoil arising from the fall of the Qing Dynasty in 1911 and the Warlord Era that followed. By the mid-1920s, there were over twenty-four thousand Chinese in Mexico, a destination which had assumed significance only in the 1880s. There was also a new influx of about seventeen thousand in Cuba, many of whom came under a special agricultural worker program between 1917 and 1921. Several hundred Chinese had also migrated to Panama. At the same time a small number— probably between six and seven thousand—found their way into the three main West Indian territories and Surinam. Unlike the earlier migrants of the mid-nineteenth century, most of these new migrants gravitated toward the small-scale retail trades, rather than toward agriculture. Most of them also went to Jamaica and Trinidad, while far fewer went to British Guiana, in significant contrast to earlier indentured migrations. The growth of the Jamaican-Chinese community in fact dates from this period at the turn of the century. While the number of Chinese in Jamaica rose from 99 in 1881 to 2,111 in 1911, and to 6,879 in 1943, those in Surinam rose from 784 in 1920 to 2,293 in 1941. The foreign-born Chinese of Trinidad alone increased in number from 832 in 1901 to 2,366 in 1946. Meanwhile the Chinese community in British Guiana showed a steady but not nearly as dramatic increase, from 2,622 in 1911 to 3,567 in 1946.[30]

Originating in the nineteenth-century global labor dispersals, the turn-of-the-twentieth-century migration flows to the British West Indies built on the connections established by the first generation, but the new influx was motivated more by domestic factors pushing émigrés out of China rather than by economic opportunity or other forces within the Diaspora pulling them in. The networks were also dominated by small traders looking for cheap and trustworthy clerks and/or by families seeking to reunite overseas or to pool manpower to exploit the modest commercial opportunities available in the colonial West Indies. By the 1940s, the descendants of the original indentured laborers in the British West Indies were significantly replenished by these new inputs, but thereafter, especially following the Communist victory in the Chinese Civil War, migration flows declined. The history of the Chinese in the West Indies between the 1950s and the 1990s has therefore been one of adjustment and assimilation to the multi-racial post-colonial polities of the region rather than one of continuing migration.

Although migration from Asia has not played a large role in the life of this community since the 1950s, there has nevertheless been a small influx since the 1980s. These new elements do not necessarily originate from the same older emigration districts. The arrival of this new group has instead been the result of different island government policies (in Guyana, through invitation by the late Forbes Burnham; in Jamaica, as part of the development of export processing zones). Many are also transients intending to relocate to the United States as soon as circumstances allow, and they have been spontaneously trickling into several islands in the Eastern Caribbean as well as Trinidad.[31] Ironically, for the mainstream Chinese community in the West Indies, outward migration toward North America (Canada and the United States) has played a more significant role in shaping the community since the 1970s than immigration from China into the West Indies. These new patterns of migration have opened a new chapter in the history of these communities, which are an appropriate and rich topic for future scholarly inquiry.

Table 1.2
List of Vessels traveling to the British, French, and Dutch West Indies from China between 1853 and 1884

Name of Ship	Whence	Destination	Arrived	Total Embarked	Total Landed	Females Landed	Infants Landed
Glentanner	Amoy	B. Guiana	12.1.53	305	262	0	0
Lord Elgin	Amoy	B. Guiana	17.1.53	154	85	0	0
Samuel Boddington	Amoy	B. Guiana	4.3.53	352	300	0	0
Australia	Swatow	Trinidad	4.3.53	445	432	0	0
Clarendon	Canton	Trinidad	23.4.53	254	251	0	0
Lady Flora Hastings	Swatow	Trinidad	28.6.53	314	305	0	0
Merwede	Batavia	Surinam	20.10.53	18	14	0	0
Epsom	H. Kong	Jamaica	30.7.54	310	267	0	0
Vampire	Panama	Jamaica	1.11.54	195	195	0	0
Theresa Jane	Panama	Jamaica	18.11.54	10	10	0	0
Minister Pahud	Macau	Surinam	18.4.58	257	257	0	0
De Twee Gezusters	Macau	Surinam	21.4.58	243	243	0	0
Galilee	Canton	Martinique	.59	426	(?)426	0	0
Admiral Baudin	Shanghai	Martinique	.59	355	331	0	0
[?]	Shanghai	Guadeloupe	.59	—	208	0	0
Royal George	H. Kong	B. Guiana	29.3.59	300	249	0	0
General Wyndham	H. Kong	B. Guiana	13.5.59	461	450	0	0
Whirlwind	H. Kong	B. Guiana	11.3.60	372	372	60	1
Dora	H. Kong	B. Guiana	3.4.60	385	383	133	12
Red Riding Hood	Canton	B. Guiana	8.4.60	314	311	10	0
Minerva	H. Kong	B. Guiana	23.5.60	310	307	67	2
Thomas Mitchell	Canton	B. Guiana	9.6.60	252	252	0	0
Norwood	H. Kong	B. Guiana	23.7.60	331	317	52	3
Sebastopol	Canton	B. Guiana	28.3.61	333	329	43	0
Red Riding Hood	Canton	B. Guiana	13.4.61	314	310	47	4
Claramont	H. Kong	B. Guiana	13.4.61	282	282	87	1

Continued on p.22

21

Table 1.2, continued

Name of Ship	Whence	Destination	Arrived	Total Embarked	Total Landed	Females Landed	Infants Landed
Saldanha	H. Kong	B. Guiana	4.5.61	500	492	67	1
Chapman	Canton	B. Guiana	9.6.61	303	290	53	1
Mystery	H. Kong	B. Guiana	9.6.61	360	337	40	1
Montmorency	H. Kong	B. Guiana	27.6.61	290	283	17	1
Sea Park	Canton	B. Guiana	7.7.61	293	263	40	0
Whirlwind	H. Kong	B. Guiana	31.7.61	365	352	51	2
Lancashire Witch	H. Kong	B. Guiana	5.8.61	461	433	26	3
Agra	Canton	B. Guiana	15.2.62	287	287	35	1
Earl of Windsor	H. Kong	B. Guiana	17.3.62	325	303	126	3
Red Riding Hood	Canton	B. Guiana	11.4.62	326	324	46	1
Maggie Miller/ Wanata	H. Kong	Trinidad	3.7.62	547	467	125	2
Persia	H. Kong	B. Guiana	10.7.62	531	525	112	0
Lady Elma Bruce	Amoy-Swatow	B. Guiana	15.8.62	385	384	32	0
Sir George Seymour	H. Kong, Canton & Swatow	B. Guiana	20.8.62	324	289	29	0
Genghis Khan	H. Kong, Canton & Swatow	B. Guiana	20.8.62	512	480	88	3
Ganges	Canton	B. Guiana	29.6.63	413	396	96	2
Zouave	Canton	B. Guiana	28.2.64	517	509	152	7
Brechin Castle	Canton	B. Guiana	26.1.65	270	269	76	2
Montrose	Canton	Trinidad	18.2.65	320	313	101	2
Queen of the East	Canton	B. Guiana	18.4.65	490	481	109	1
Paria	Canton	Trinidad	25.5.65	289	280	76	0
Light of the Age	Amoy	B. Honduras	12.6.65	480	474	16	3
Sevilla	Canton	B. Guiana	22.6.65	312	305	91	2
Arima	Canton	B. Guiana	18.7.65	343	311	50	0
Tricolor	H. Kong	Surinam	29.7.65	475	286	120	17
Bucton Castle	Canton	B. Guiana	28.8.65	353	325	60	4
Dudbrook	Amoy	Trinidad	12.2.66	286	272	1	0

Name of Ship	Whence	Destination	Arrived	Total Embarked	Total Landed	Females Landed	Infants Landed
Red Riding Hood	Amoy	Trinidad	24.2.66	327	325	6	0
Light Brigade	Amoy	B. Guiana	14.4.66	493	487	5	0
Whirlwind	H. Kong	Surinam	30.3.66	409	404	—	—
Whirlwind & Golden Horn combined						} 203	} 28
Golden Horn	H. Kong	Surinam	9.7.66	416	403	—	—
Pride of the Ganges	Canton	B. Guiana	31.7.66	305	302	30	0
Veritas	H. Kong	Surinam	28.1.67	291	—	9	0
Veritas & Marie Therese combined					} 516		
Marie Therese	H. Kong	Surinam	20.8.68	252	—	3	0
Veritas	H. Kong	Surinam	13.5.69	202	—	—	0
Veritas & Ferdinand Brumm combined					} 405	} 11	
Ferdinand Brumm	H. Kong	Surinam	23.8.69	298	—	—	0
Wilde Man	Batavia	Surinam	3.11.72	11	11	0	0
Krommenie	Batavia	Surinam	23.11.72	10	10	0	0
Kosmopoliet	Batavia	Surinam	6.3.73	13	13	0	0
Julius	Batavia	Surinam	21.5.73	5	5	0	0
Adriana Johanna	Batavia	Surinam	19.6.73	16	16	0	0
Willem Jacobus	Batavia	Surinam	27.8.73	7	7	0	0
Kosmopoliet	Batavia	Surinam	12.9.73	17	17	0	0
Lida	Batavia	Surinam	5.11.73	18	18	0	0
Adriana Johanna	Batavia	Surinam	18.12.73	5	5	0	0
Hendrik Daniel	Batavia	Surinam	12.2.74	13	13	0	0
Corona	Canton	B. Guiana	23.2.74	388	388	45	4
Dartmouth	H. Kong	B. Guiana	17.3.79	516	515	52	9
Clara	H. Kong	Antigua	1.2.82	128	100	0	0
Diamond/Prince Alexander	Macao, H. Kong	Jamaica	12.7.84	681	680	122	3

Sources: (1) Annual Reports of the Colonial Land and Emigration Commission, 1859–73. (2) Great Britain, Colonial Office Correspondence, C.O.111 Series (British Guiana) and C.O.295 Series (Trinidad). (3) Cecil Clementi, The Chinese in British Guiana, Demerara 1915.

Table 1.3
Natives of China in the British Caribbean, 1861–1946

	1861	1871	1881	1891	1911	1921	1931	1946
B. Guiana	2,629	6,295	4,393	2,475	634	376	423	548
B. Honduras	1	133	68	52	27	12	n/a	42
Antigua	—	—	—	111	13	4	n/a	—
Trinidad	461	1,400	1,266	1,006	1,113	1,334	2,027	2,366
Jamaica	—	—	140	347	1,646	2,413	n/a	2,818
All Others	—	—	—	—	—	—	—	—
TOTAL	3,091	7,828	5,867	3,991	3,433	4,139	n/a	5,774

n/a = not available
Source: West Indian Census Report 1946 (with corrections of 1946 figures)

CHAPTER 2

Kissing the Cross:
Nineteenth-Century Representations
of Chinese and Indian Immigrants in
British Guiana and Trinidad

ANNE-MARIE LEE-LOY

In March, 1870, a small article appeared in British Guiana's *Royal Gazette* newspaper that described the final hours of life for two immigrants who were executed in the colony. The article details how, the night before their deaths, an Indian migrant spent his final hours dancing in his cell, while a Chinese prisoner was engaged in prayer.[1] The differences between the two men were made explicitly clear on the scaffold. The Indian resolutely refused to be attended by any clergyman. In contrast, "the Chinaman was very attentive to the prayers of the Roman Catholic Priest who accompanied him on the scaffold and kissed the cross that the Priest presented to him just before the drop fell" (RG 22 March 1870).

Why would West Indian colonists be interested in such an article? Why did the author pay so much attention to the differing behavior of the two prisoners? In particular, why was it so important to record and report that moment when the Chinese prisoner chose to kiss the cross of the priest? Contemporary readers' sympathies might lie with the Indian migrant, who seemed to demonstrate a powerful resistance to the domination of the European colonists even in the face of death; but this is not how a West Indian colonist would have read this story, and it was most certainly not the intention of the article's author to celebrate the behavior of the Indian. Instead, the article makes the most sense when it is understood to be part of a nineteenth-century discursive comparison between immigrants from India and China to the West Indies that sought to represent the Chinese as key elements in the maintenance of the colonial status quo. More specifically, colonial discourse imagined the Chinese migrants as a middle-stratum addition to a population that was deemed to exist hierarchically, with Europeans at the apex and slaves and ex-slaves at the bottom. Representations of the Chinese assimilating to European standards and norms or maintaining colonial order were an important element of this vision. A contrast between the behaviors of the members of the Chinese and East Indian communities—between their reactions to or impact upon the colonial economy and culture—was a discursive strategy that served to both underpin the position accorded to the Chinese in the colonial hierarchy and to support the hierarchy itself.

Nineteenth-Century Chinese and Indian Immigration

Nineteenth-century immigration of Chinese and Indians to British Guiana and Trinidad was connected to the fortunes of the sugar industry. In both regions, as with the British possessions in the West Indies in general, sugar production was well established as the backbone of the economy by the end of the eighteenth century. In the 1800s, however, a series of legislative decisions in London threw the West Indian sugar enterprises into crisis. The first was the decision to abolish the slave trade in 1807, an act that directly interfered with the ability to acquire labor for the sugar estates. The labor shortage was intensified by a second important decision made in the British Parliament: the emancipation of the slaves in 1834.[2] The abolition of slavery not only meant a potential reduction in the work force, it also meant new labor relations between estate owners and workers. Finally, the Sugar Duties Act of 1846 removed the protective tariffs on British West Indian produced sugar, placing it in direct competition with foreign sources, most notably Cuba (where slavery was still legal and sugar production was therefore thought to be cheaper). This combination of free trade and radically different labor relations hit the sugar industry hard. Indeed, from 1838 onward, many areas of the British West Indies saw a severe decline in sugar production. The situation was perceived to be so extreme that one observer claimed that three quarters of West Indian planters were on the verge of absolute ruin in 1851 (Stanley 35).

Despite the fact that a number of elements had converged to produce the decline in the sugar industry's fortunes, the sugar crisis was commonly blamed on a perceived lack of discipline and controlled labor and increased costs, caused by the new demand for wages, since slavery had been abolished.[3] It was argued that indentured labor was the only way in which the sugar industry, and by extension the economy of the British West Indies as a whole, would be revitalized; or as one letter to an editor of a colonial newspaper put it more poetically:

> Immigration to the province may be likened to supplying with water a reservoir employed to afford power to extensive mechanical appliances; when the supply is abundant the machinery will work up to its full power; but, when it proves to be deficient, when the source is obstructed by any circumstances, the water in the reservoir will sink below its working level and the machinery will stop. (RG 12 February 1850)

Both China and India were viewed as areas that could supply such labor.[4]

There were, of course, other sources of labor explored by British West Indian planters in the period following slave emancipation. By the mid-nineteenth century, African-Americans, "liberated" Africans, and Europeans had all been brought to the West Indies to work. None of these groups, however, was able to provide the stable and plentiful labor force required by the planters. In the face of such reality, the British possessions in the East began to appear to be an ideal source of labor.

The earliest Indian immigrants to the British West Indies arrived in British Guiana in 1838, the same year that mandatory apprenticeships ended. Known as the "Gladstone Coolies,"[5] after the name of the

27

planter who had received permission to import them, this early experience in labor importation from the East was a failure, in part because of public outcry arising from accusations of abuse suffered by the new laborers. Nevertheless, the pressing needs of the planters meant that the potentially abundant labor source in India could not long be overlooked. Indeed, once immigration resumed, India would become the major source of indentured labor for the West Indies. Lasting until 1917, the indentured labor scheme would bring hundreds of thousands of Indians to Trinidad and British Guiana before it ended.

Chinese indentured immigration to the British West Indies actually began earlier than the Indians with the arrival of just under two hundred men in Trinidad in 1806. This initiative, however, did not become the true basis for the Chinese communities of the West Indies, as most of the migrants quickly left.[6] Chinese immigration did not resume until 1853, when British Guiana and Trinidad each received three shiploads of migrant workers. The bulk of nineteenth-century Chinese migrations took place between 1853 and 1866, when the Kung Convention, which effectively ended the indentured Chinese coolie trade, was signed, at which point it became much more financially feasible to import Indian laborers than Chinese.

As indentured laborers, the Chinese and Indian migrants were to be part of the "water in the reservoir" that would keep the colonial machinery running, and on these grounds alone it would seem that the colonial imagination would be predisposed to depicting the migrants favorably upon their arrival in the colonies. In the case of the Chinese, such an inclination was furthered by the fact that the Chinese were expected to provide something more than labor. From the very beginning of their migration, the Chinese were afforded another role within the colonies. It was imagined that they would provide a neutralizing buffer zone between the European and slave (and later ex-slave) populations. Prior to the arrival of the first Chinese, the Colonial Office made this agenda explicit when it wrote:

> The events which have recently happened at Saint
> Domingo necessarily awaken all those apprehensions
> which the Establishment of a Negro Government in that

Island gave rise to some years ago and render it indispensable that every practicable measures [*sic*] of precaution should be adopted to guard the British possessions in the West Indies as well against any further indisposition of power so constituted as against the danger of a Spirit of insurrection being excited amongst the Negroes in our colony.

It is conceived that no measure would so effectually tend to provide a security against this danger as that of introducing a free race of cultivators into our islands who from habits and feelings would be kept distinct from the Negroes and from interests would be inseparably attached to the European proprietors.

The Chinese people are represented to unite the quality which constitute this double recommendation . . . (CO 295/14)

Nineteenth-century Chinese migrants to Trinidad and British Guiana were entering a space that was in a state of explicit social and economic transition. British colonists in the West Indies wanted the Chinese newcomers to help re-establish both the economic and the cultural superiority of the Europeans within the colonies as well as stabilize the sugar industry. It is in this context that colonial comparisons between the Chinese and Indian migrants of the nineteenth century must be read.

The Importance of Industry

One of the most popular nineteenth-century images of the Chinese in the West Indies was that of a people who were characterized by an innate and indefatigable industry. Indeed, when it was originally proposed that Chinese laborers might serve the needs of West Indian sugar production, the proposal was partially based on the claim that the Chinese were much more efficient and hard-working than slaves. Specifically, it was claimed that an estate worked with Chinese labor could be done so at an annual savings of just under £3,000 compared to an estate worked by slaves (*Chinese in the West Indies*, 26). Nearly fifty years later, when Chinese immigration was revived by the Colonial Office, it was justified on the same grounds; it was the purported "indomitable industry and perseverance" of the Chinese that made them appear to be such attractive immigrants (PP vol. LXVIII).

The image of the "industrious Chinese" was often played out in contrast to that of the "Lazy Negro"—a depiction of the ex-slave lying around and eating pumpkins and yam made particularly popular in the nineteenth century by the work of men like Thomas Carlyle and Anthony Trollope. Similar comparisons, however, were also being made between the indentured laborers from China and India. Since the value of these immigrants was seen to lie mainly in their labor, that is, their ability to help maintain the economy, positive representations of the Chinese were directly related to how much more it was perceived that they would serve the economy than their contemporaries from India. In British Guiana, for example, the Chinese migrants were praised for being "more muscular and athletic than the Cooly"; while in Trinidad, newspapers suggested that the Chinese were more valuable immigrants because they appeared to be "healthier and stronger than the Coolie" (RG 16 July 1853). West Indian planters were even more explicit in establishing the grounds for the comparison between the two groups when they reported that the Chinese were preferable to the Indians because of the simple fact that ". . . they consider [the Chinese's] physical strength greater" (RG 16 February 1854). The Colonial Office went so far as to call the Chinese a "middle class" for the West Indies largely because they were said to be "more energetic than the East Indian" (PP vol. LXVIII).

The importance that the perceived economic impact of the Chinese in the colonies had on their representation in colonial texts is also evident in a subtle yet significant difference in colonial attitudes toward Chinese and Indian women. Overall, there is a striking lack of attention paid to Chinese women throughout nineteenth-century texts. Very few depictions or comments about Chinese women actually exist. This is undoubtedly linked to the simple fact that very few Chinese women participated in the nineteenth-century migration to the West Indies. Indeed, the Colonial Office had been advised on a number of occasions of the impossibility of female immigration from China. Nevertheless, since its goal was to establish a permanent work-force in the colonies, the Colonial Office actively pursued family migration from China during the mid-part of the nineteenth century. As part of this initiative, the Colonial Office offered incentives for female immigration, including additional bounty money for wives and the provision that Chinese women would not be bound to labor, although their residency on specific estates would be mandatory. In comparison, Indian women were recruited as indentured laborers, and a significantly larger number of Indian women migrated to the British West Indies during this period.

Despite the fact that Indian women labored on the estates and therefore contributed to the overall well-being of the colonial econo-my in a way that their Chinese counterparts did not, the Indian migrants were not automatically deemed to be a more attractive addi-tion to West Indian society. In fact, due to the disproportionate num-bers of men and women emigrating from India, the presence of the Indian women was often seen as a cause of violence and disruption within the colonies. When Commissioners reported on the treatment of indentured immigrants in British Guiana in 1871, for example, they made reference to the number of violent attacks against Indian women that had been perpetrated by their husbands or lovers when they were suspected of, or found to be carrying on illicit affairs. Colonial newspapers of the period also commented regularly on such events. These affairs and the violence they spawned often disrupted labor on the sugar estates. Indeed, so concerned were the Com-missioners by these disturbances that they recommended that penal provisions be created to punish those who seduced individuals away from their respective spouses.

It is within this context of a concern for the smooth running of estate labor that an 1869 article in the *Royal Gazette* claiming that "Chinese women are more chaste than the Coolies" (RG 16 September 1869) must be placed. What was at issue is not so much the sexual behavior of the Chinese women but the *effect* that their behav-ior had on the estates. For example, this article was written to report on an apparent anomaly in Chinese sexual behavior, namely that a

31

Chinese man was said to be hiring out his wife to other men on pay day. The article makes no real comment about the moral implications of the situation; nor are questions raised as to whether or not the woman is a willing participant. Instead, the article's main concern is how this activity might affect the behavior of the Chinese laborers on the estate.

A similar attitude is demonstrated toward Chee-Shee, one of the rare times that a Chinese woman actually appears in a nineteenth-century colonial text. Chee-Shee's story is reported in Edward Jenkins' *The Coolie: His Rights and Wrongs*, written after Jenkins had participated in the Royal Commission's investigation into the treatment of indentured laborers in British Guiana mentioned earlier. According to Jenkins, Chee-Shee is seduced away from her husband and moves in with another man. Despite threats that her husband will commit suicide if she does not return to him, Chee-Shee is adamant that she is not leaving her lover. Jenkins reports that the estate's management would probably intervene and transfer her lover to another estate, thus forcing a reunion between Chee-Shee and her husband. Again, estate managers are not concerned with Chee-Shee's personal feelings or freedom of choice. Rather, their focus is the desire to keep matters on the estate under control so that sugar production can proceed without interruption. Chee-Shee's behavior draws the negative attention of colonial society, as do the affairs of the Indian women to some extent, largely because of the fact that it has the potential to disrupt this production. That such occurrences were rare among the Chinese helps account for the slightly more positive attitude toward Chinese women than Indian women that runs throughout colonial texts.

For the Love of Money

Comparisons between immigrants from India and China were also made on the grounds of what were believed to be their attitudes towards money. In such comparisons, the Chinese are again depicted more favorably than the Indians; and, once again, the basis for their more positive representation lies in the fact that their behavior is interpreted as being in line with the capitalist ambitions of the colonists. Throughout the nineteenth century, both the Chinese and the Indians were described as having an inordinate, even unnatural, love of money. It was even argued that the Colonial Office would easily recruit Chinese indentured laborers because it was believed that the Chinese were so "eager for gain, and [willing to] do anything for money" that they would certainly migrate to the West Indies and undertake the difficult and demanding task of sugar production if they were simply offered enough money. Similarly, the pursuit of gold was deemed to be "characteristic of the Hindostan" (RG 28 January 1854). But whereas the Chinese migrants participated in the colonial economy by spending their money on goods, colonists complained that the migrants from India did not use their earnings in a way that was understood to benefit the colonial economy. Herein lay the basis of the more positive representations of the Chinese as seen in the examples set out below:

> There is another broad distinction between the East Indian and the Chinese. The former is essentially parsimonious and content with a low standard of food, and with little and cheap clothing. The latter has large and more varied wants, is indulgent of his appetites and tastes and liberal in his expenditure. His standard of food is high—his holiday dress is of rich and varied materials. He earns money not to hoard but to spend it. (RG 25 August 1860)
>
> [The Chinese] are a sober, diligent, industrious, intelligent, and money-loving people, without being a miserly one . . . They like to make money, but they have not the faculty of hoarding it that distinguishes the penurious Hindoo, for they live more comfortably, and, when they can, more luxuriously than other Asiatic people . . . (PP vol. XXXV)

So integral was the relationship between positive images of the Chinese and the impact that they were perceived to have upon West Indian economies that in the 1870s the sugar planters of British Guiana petitioned the Combined Court to provide money to introduce more Chinese laborers to the colony, even though it was considerably more expensive to import Chinese labor than Indian labor. Clearly, the attraction of the Chinese lay not only in their labor, but in their potential status as consumers. As the planters themselves put it in their petition:

> [The Indian migrant] does no direct good, or almost none as his earnings, after supplying himself with the little food and very little clothing he indulges in, are either buried, put into the Savings Bank, or spent on uncirculating coins and jewellery, lost for all purposes of trade.
>
> The Chinese on the contrary circulate their earnings freely in trade channels . . . (RG 10 June 1875)

Signifying Superiority

The contribution of the Chinese to the maintenance of the colonial status quo was not simply economic. The newcomers provided British West Indian colonists with an opportunity to reinforce ideas of the cultural and moral superiority of their civilization in West Indian societies. Although the European elements of the British West Indian populations held significant sway over the political, economic, and social spheres in the colonies, their control was never absolute. In particular, fragments of African cultural heritage continued to make their presence felt in the language, food, music, and forms of religious worship among a significant proportion of the numerically dominant slaves and ex-slaves. Colonial discourse was, therefore, forced to continually reassert European superiority. One of the means by which this superiority was asserted during the nineteenth century was to portray the Chinese migrants as accepting and assimilating to the European norms and values within the colony rather than to the more African-derived elements of West Indian culture. Not only did such images justify the concept of European superiority, that is, that the Chinese recognized European culture as superior to both African and Chinese cultures, it also positioned the Chinese as an "in-between" people on the colonial hierarchy—somewhat lower than the Europeans, but certainly positioned higher than the ex-slaves. In a similar fashion, comparisons between the Chinese and the Indians that focused on the ways in which the members of the Indian communities remained unassimilated reinforced this positioning of the Chinese.

A surprising amount of attention is given in colonial texts to reporting how the Chinese dressed upon their arrival in the British West Indies. In his memoir of a tour in Trinidad, for example, Charles Kingsley notes the Chinese women attired in expensive European-styled finery at a church service, while in British Guiana, Governor Barkly took the time to include in his official reports to the Colonial Office comments indicating that the Chinese members of the population were purchasing articles of European clothing. This change in fashion was used as a powerful visible symbol of the Chinese communities' assimilation of European standards in colonial texts. More important to the discourse of European superiority, however, were the reports that the Chinese had, by and large, converted to Christianity.

That there were large numbers of Chinese Christians in British Guiana and Trinidad during the nineteenth century is indisputable. In British Guiana, for example, by 1863, the Chinese had their own Chinese Christian religious leader, a settlement of Christian Chinese and, in 1874, had laid the foundation of a Chinese church, an event which one newspaper suggested marked the first Chinese Christian church in the West (RG 15 August 1874). The number of Chinese conversions in the colony is less impressive, however, when one realizes that many of the Chinese who were coming to the West Indies during the mid-nineteenth century had already been converted in China or had been exposed to Christianity by missionaries there. Unlike in India, missionaries to China, like Reverend Lobschied, had been used extensively in the recruitment of Chinese laborers for Trinidad and British Guiana. Nevertheless, the seemingly receptive attitude of the Chinese towards Christianity was important to their positive representation in the colonies. In British Guiana, for example, Governor Barkly enthusiastically reported that the first Chinese migrants to arrive in the colony were "participating in the services at a missionary chapel," a fact that seems to lead directly to his conclusion that "the Chinese possess the energy and the intelligence attributed to them" (PP vol. LXVIII). In contrast, the Indian migrants were proving less amenable to conversion, as the article on the Indian and Chinese prisoners mentioned above suggests. As a result, in the nineteenth century, it was not uncommon to read arguments that China was a better source for immigrants to the colony than India because the Chinese appeared to accept Christianity more readily. As one newspaper article put it, the colonists were willing to welcome the Chinese in a special way, indeed to extend the "hand of fellowship," because they were coming into the colony "as fellow Christians" (RG 15 August 1874). It is doubtful whether such a welcome was extended to the "pagan" Indian migrant.

Although this portrayal of Chinese cultural acquiescence to the Europeans was an important element of West Indian colonial discourse, it was also extremely important to re-affirm the idea that the Chinese were equally acquiescent to the physical control that the colonists exerted over them in the colony. Early reports to the Colonial Office during consideration of the Chinese indentured immigration scheme often created images of the Chinese as inherently tractable and orderly. Descriptions of the Chinese demonstrating "docility and obedience" and "regular order, obedience and industry, together with a perfect degree of reconciliation, confidence and happiness" were common (RG 16 July 1853; PRO CO 295/14). Represented as a people content with their lot as laborers, the Chinese were cast as a stabilizing element in West Indian society.

Upon their arrival, in spite of very real evidence that the Chinese were not as tractable and controllable as they had been represented, colonial texts insist on portraying the Chinese as accepting the place constructed for them in colonial society and of supporting the colonial order itself. Colonial texts often take particular care to report on the behavior of the Chinese during incidents of labor unrest on the plantations, focusing on their non-participation or on their willingness to be used to diffuse such situations. For example, the 1871 Commissioners in British Guiana noted with some satisfaction that "The Chinese, as far as we are aware, have never combined with the Indians in disturbances on the estates" (PP vol. XX). A newspaper article from this period made a similar contrast between the behavior of the

Indians and the Chinese when it reported that while "the Coolies are found to be organizing themselves on plantations with fire arms and hackia sticks," anxiously anticipating the results of the Commission, the Chinese were "too sensible to be led away into riots" (RG 10 November 1870).

Colonial texts also focus much attention on events that could be interpreted to suggest that the Chinese were actually active supporters of the colonial order. Both the report of the Commissioners and news-papers of the period take care to note instances in which Chinese laborers rallied to the side of estate management when their East Indian counterparts became violent. After one such incident, a news-paper article confidently stated that "in the event of a disturbance the Chinese and Creoles would oppose the Coolies, who, with opposition from that quarter, from the Police, the troops and the special consta-bles, would be speedily defeated and crushed" (ibid.).

What is important in these comparisons is the image of the Indians' violence being contained by the Chinese. It is a depiction that places the Chinese in the role of a representative of colonial control and order. Indeed, when placed in the context of similar reports of the Chinese being used to quell uprisings by Black laborers, this recurring image of the Chinese being aligned with the estate owners and man-agement suggests that not only were the Chinese active participants in maintaining colonial order, they had no real allegiance to anything other than the colonial order itself. In this way, the comparison between Indians and Chinese served to reinforce the image of the Chinese that had been asserted from the time of their earliest immi-gration—that is, that they would be a people "inseparably attached to European proprietors" (PRO CO 295/14).

Conclusion

Despite the preceding discussion, it would be false to conclude that nineteenth century images of the Chinese in the British West Indies were unproblematically positive. Indeed, at this time, other represen-tations of the Chinese were much more negative—depicting them as innately violent, stubbornly pagan, and altogether undesirable additions to West Indian colonies. For example, Jenkins' novel *Lutchmee and Dilloo: A Study of West Indian Life* provides a very rare—if not the only—fictional representation of a Chinese character to appear in a nineteenth-century novel about the British West Indies. The character, called Chin-a-foo, is portrayed as being morally and physically repulsive—a very blight on the community within which he lives.

Neither are the boundaries between the immigrants from India and the Chinese migrants always absolute. Newspapers reported, for example, that the Chinese in British Guiana participated in celebrating *Tadja* with the Indian migrants; and the 1870 investigation into the treatment of the indentured laborers in British Guiana often lumped the complaints of both the Chinese and Indians together as mere evidence of "Asiatic craft and ingenuity" (*The Coolie*, 149). There also

Wood engraving made by a Chinese indentured laborer representing the experience of indentured laborers in British Guiana. The group under the house are migrants from India, while the group to the right of the house are migrants from China. Notice the attempt to flee by the Chinese indentured laborer in the bottom right-hand corner of the engraving.

(Source: Edward Jenkins, *The Coolie: His Rights and Wrongs*, p. 10)

appears to be some idea of a community among the indentured laborers themselves—an idea expressed in the woodcut by a Chinese migrant, depicting the abuse and suffering the laborers endured under the indentured system, that appears in Jenkins' *The Coolie: His Rights and Wrongs*. The artist takes pains to include *both* the immigrants from China and India in his portrait of misery, rather than to focus only on the Chinese.

Nevertheless, colonial discourses reverted again and again to a comparison between Indian and Chinese migrants that insisted that the Chinese were superior to the Indians. Why was it that the Chinese came across as being so much more desirable as immigrants than their Indian counterparts? The key to this difference can be seen in the negative description of the character Chin-a-foo mentioned earlier. What prevents Jenkins from providing a more positive portrayal of this Chinese character is that Chin-a-foo refuses to accept the authority of the estate management and the colonial order it represents. Instead, he runs a gambling den that not only is detrimental to other laborers, but provides him with a livelihood outside of the literal and discursive space on the estates provided for him in the colony. Indeed, Chin-a-foo's gambling den is positioned on the very borders of the bush, the symbol of primeval savagery, so that he becomes an emblem of barbarity and depravity, as well as a threat to colonial order and civilisation.

Chin-a-foo's decidedly negative representation, so much in contrast to the positive images of the Chinese that appear frequently in other nineteenth-century West Indian texts, reveals the very basis of the comparison between the Chinese and the Indians that so often represented the Indians as negative counterparts to the Chinese. The Chinese were depicted as positive additions to society when their presence reaffirmed, justified, or reinforced the continued dominance of the European colonists in the British West Indies. It was not that the Indians were somehow "bad" and the Chinese "good"; rather, the Chinese were deemed to be "preferred to all others" when their behavior could be read as supporting the interests of the colonial power—when they could be portrayed, in other words, as "kissing the cross" (PRO CO 295/18).

CHAPTER 3

Survival, Adaptation and Integration: Origins and Evolution of the Chinese Community in Jamaica (1854–1962)

LI ANSHAN

From the day of their first arrival in Jamaica to Jamaican independence in 1962, the Chinese struggled, first for survival, and then for development. Throughout that century the Chinese played important roles in Jamaican society and in the Jamaican economy. Yet while there have been influential works on the Chinese in the West Indies, especially on Chinese indentured labor,[1] and several articles about different aspects of the Jamaican Chinese experience, there has been a long-standing neglect of the Jamaican-Chinese community as a whole.[2] This study seeks to correct that historiographical snub of the Chinese community[3] in Jamaica, and uses materials in Chinese, especially Chinese newspapers published in Jamaica, which have yet to be fully explored. Compared with other data, the most valuable aspect of these Chinese language materials is that they reflect daily life and common concerns within the Chinese community. Sources produced outside the community allow us to look at this enclave from Jamaican and colonial perspectives, but the Chinese sources force us to look at the origins, adaptation, and integration of the Chinese in Jamaica from the émigré's point of view.

Community Origins and the Struggle for Survival

The abolition of slavery in the British West Indies created acute labor shortages, especially in the industrializing sugar industry. Following unsuccessful experiments with the recruitment of European contract laborers and East Indian coolies, Chinese indentured labor became an appealing source of new labor imports.[4] According to Christine Ho, "Chinese migration to the Caribbean was part of a larger population movement from China to *all* of the Americas."[5] This statement is only partly true. Ho is correct in the sense that Chinese migration to the Caribbean was closely linked to Chinese migration to the Americas, but she neglects the fact that more than three million Chinese were recruited as indentured labor to other parts of the world in the period between 1800 and 1925.[6] Since Chinese labor was both the product and producer of globalization, it would be better to put Chinese migration to the Caribbean in a wider global context.

According to previous studies, the first Chinese came to Jamaica in 1854, followed by about 200 Chinese laborers mainly from British Guyana and Trinidad between the 1850s and 1870s. It was only a third group that emigrated directly from China. This raises the question of how many Chinese arrived in Jamaica in 1854 and where were they from? There are three common figures: 195 (Olive Senior), 200 (Tomes) and 472 (Chen; Lind), and the usual story is that the first Chinese immigrants in Jamaica had re-migrated from Panama.[7] The Panama Railroad Company, which was building the isthmian rail-link, desperately needed laborers, and 709 Chinese were recruited. They arrived in Panama on March 30, 1854. On the difficult voyage to Panama, 16 died on board ship, and another 16 perished shortly after their arrival. This was followed by 80 more deaths after less than a week at their line camp at Matachin, Colon.[8] Several months later, some of them were transferred to Jamaica as laborers.

The high death rate seems to have been caused by the harsh climate, deadly fevers, a shortage of fresh vegetables, deplorable work conditions, managerial cruelties, and a lack of proper medical treatment. The conditions were so harsh in Panama that many Chinese committed suicide. In a short period of time, 125 Chinese coolies were said to have hanged themselves from trees and over 300 others were found dead.[9] Lucy Cohen has put this suicide phenomenon in a psycho-cultural framework and concludes that the Chinese had been subjected to such physical and psychological stress associated with the mode of recruitment, the ocean voyage itself, and the harsh environment and labor conditions in Panama, that suicide became "a culturally patterned mode of protest or of turning aggression inward."[10]

According to the *Daily Panama Star and Herald*, a Chinese gentleman arrived from Jamaica six months later to effect an exchange "with the Railroad Company and furnish them with an equal number of Jamaican laborers for such of his countrymen as are able bodied and in good health."[11] A ship carrying 195 Chinese indentured laborers arrived in Kingston in November 1854 from Panama. It seems that the exchange was not as satisfactory as the Jamaicans thought. Because of their poor health and desperate economic straits, Chinese were seen in the streets very soon after their arrival "'worn out and emaciated, heartbroken and miserable,' and they eventually found homes in the hospitals and alms houses of Kingston and St. Catherine where the majority died as paupers."[12] Most of them died shortly after their arrival. Thus the conventional wisdom has it that the first Chinese in Jamaica were from Panama, and this conclusion has been widely accepted by both Caribbean and Chinese scholars.[13]

Contrary to this, British documents show that the first Chinese in Jamaica actually arrived directly from China. They took the ship *Epsom*, contracted by James White, a British Guyana emigration agent. The vessel left Hong Kong for Jamaica in April 1854 with 310 passengers, 267 of whom survived the voyage. This shipment was regarded as the "first attempt to encourage a direct voluntary engagement of contract emigrants by the British." These immigrants, not those from Panama, became the first Chinese settlers in Jamaica. After their arrival, they were allocated to estates in Clarendon and the Caymanas estates near Kingston and were soon joined by a fresh contingent of 205 arriving aboard two ships (*Vampire* and *Theresa Jane*) by way of Panama.[14] It is clear that among the 472 arrivals, 267 were contract laborers from Hong Kong and 205 were indentured laborers from Panama. Among the first arrivals, only a few survived, such as Chen

Ba Gong (Robert Jackson),[15] Chang Shengbo, He Shou, Lin San, and Huang Xiu. They all later started up businesses in retail grocery, and laid the foundation for the Chinese community. For example, Chen Ba Gong employed Huang Chang (Wong Sam) as an assistant in his shop when Huang first arrived in Jamaica from British Guyana.

During the period from 1864 to 1870, about two hundred additional Chinese indentured laborers came to Jamaica through other Caribbean islands. As indentured laborers employed by plantations in Trinidad and British Guyana, they had already finished their three-year contracts when the plantations went bankrupt owing to natural disasters. At the same time, American agricultural companies were starting businesses in Jamaica and were therefore recruiting new laborers. Chinese laborers had already won a reputation for being intelligent, industrious, persevering, and reliable. In a period of local labor shortages, American companies went to Trinidad and British Guyana specifically to recruit Chinese indentured laborers. Some Chinese answered the call, and others came to Jamaica voluntarily from Trinidad, British Guyana, Panama, or Hawaii, totaling altogether about two hundred.[16] After their labor contracts had expired, some continued to work for the big companies, while others began their own businesses in the retail trade.

The third, and last, significant nineteenth-century influx of Chinese laborers came directly from China in 1884. The "last ship to reach the British West Indies from China with indentured laborers" left Hong Kong and arrived in Kingston after more than two months. The adults were all contract laborers recruited by Hong Kong agents. This shipment included 501 men, 105 women, 54 boys, 17 girls, and 3 babies, totaling 680.[17] The voyage was relatively safe, with only one fatality; the three children were born on board. Except for about 20 persons from Si Yi (Sze Yup, meaning the four administrative units of the Pearl River Delta),[18] the rest were all of Hakka origin from Dongguan, Huiyang, and Bao-an Counties in Guangdong Province. The interpreter on board was named Chen Yawei and the doctor Chen Pingzhang. It was this group that formed the nucleus of the Chinese immigrants in Jamaica. Subsequent émigrés came mostly from these Hakka sending-communities and emigrated with the help of clan members who had arrived in 1884.

How did they arrive in Jamaica? According to Ching Chieh Chang, "The first group of Chinese arrived in Jamaica directly from China in 1884 by way of Vancouver and Halifax. From that time on, the Hong Kong–Vancouver–Halifax–Kingston route was used by most of the emigrants to Jamaica until the early 1930s. Only a small number of them came by way of the Panama Canal."[19] I find this statement doubtful. One of the 1884 arrivals recorded his personal experience of the voyage in the late 1950s. Only nine years old at the time, Wencai came to Jamaica with his family. Their ship *Diamond* left Hong Kong on May 8, 1884. They encountered a storm and the ship's mast was broken, so they had to change to the *Prince Alexander* in Canada, which arrived in Jamaica on July 12, 1884. Their voyage was by way of a Hong Kong–Macao–Singapore–Suez Canal–Europe–Bermuda–Halifax–Cuba–Kingston route.[20] This story is more reliable for two reasons. First, it is a firsthand reminiscence. Second, prior to the opening of the Panama Canal in 1914, the time and expense of an overland journey from Vancouver to Halifax seems prohibitive for a poor immigrant family.

As regards family origins, it should be noted that most of the Chinese in Jamaica were not from the dominant sending-communities of the Pearl River Delta (the villages of Sam Yup and Sze Yup), but from a border region comprised of the three *xians* (counties) of Dongguan, Bao-an, and Huiyang. As such they were mainly Hakka, rather than Punti Cantonese. We have two sources to support this: the record of the Chinese Cemetery and the "who's who" section of Lee Tom Yin's *The Chinese in Jamaica*. According to the persons listed in this book, the overwhelming majority was from three counties, i.e. Dongguan (169), Bao-an (65), and Huiyang (57). Moreover, more than 70 persons were from Guanlan, a small township in Dongguan County (see table 3.1).[21]

Another source corroborates this demographic spread. The native-places (*qiaoxiang*) of Chinese immigrants in Jamaica were concentrated in a few localities and this pattern is represented in the Chinese Cemetery (Gah San) in Kingston. The cemetery was established in the early 1900s by the Chinese Benevolent Society (later Chinese Benevolent Association) for those Chinese who had died in Jamaica and could not be returned to their native-places. The burial record, dated September 9, 1957, shows that out of 1,436 Chinese buried in the cemetery, 303, or 21% of the total, bore the surname Chen. The top 8 clans (Chen, Li, Zhang, Zeng, Zheng, Huang, Liu, and He) together totaled 1,005, or 70% of the persons buried in the cemetery (see table 3.2).[22]

The majority of the Chens in Jamaica were originally from Guan-lan in Dongguan County, whereas most of the Zengs and the Zhengs were from Tangli in Dongguan. The Lis were mainly from Shawan in Bao-an and Longgang in Huiyang, while the Hes were mostly from Henggang in Huiyang.[23]

Table 3.1

Distribution of the Family Origin of Chinese in Jamaica

Family origin	Number	Family origin	Number
Dongguan	169	Hong Kong	10
Bao-an	65	Taishan	6
Huiyang	57	Enpin	4
No record	59	Xinhui	1
Born in Jamaica	33	Heshan	1

Table 3.2

Major Family Names Recorded in the Chinese Cemetery in Jamaica (to 1957)

Surname	Number	Surname	Number	Surname	Number
Chen	303	Liu	72	Dai	32
Li	182	He	69	Luo	30
Zhang	135	Qiu	48	Deng	25
Zeng	84	Ling	40	Liao	22
Zheng	84	Yang	32	Wu	21
Huang	76	Shen	32	Jiang	20

Organization and Adaptation

Eastern Lee, a prominent Jamaican Chinese writer, once said of the Chinese community in Jamaica, "the more the pressures came from the outside, the more they clung together."[24] This is true for all Chinese immigrants settling in strange lands. "Clinging together," that is, relying on the bonds of kinship or native-place to ease the transition to a strange land and to increase the likelihood of economic success, and "getting organized" into surname, trade, and charitable organizations, are the primary survival strategies for Chinese overseas. Generally speaking, in Jamaica there were three kinds of organizations: a general association to service all Chinese immigrants, specific ones for surname and native-place groups, and various kinds of trade guilds.

The Zhong Hua Hui Guan (Chinese Benevolent Association)[25] is the only organization serving all the Chinese in Jamaica. According to oral tradition, there were originally two Chinese Benevolent Associations. The one headed by Chen Yawei was not popular and dissolved after a short while. The other, the Chinese Benevolent Society, was set up in 1891, led by Chen Ba Gong (Robert Jackson), Zhang Sheng, Huang Chang (Wong Sam), and others. The society had about 500 members, who paid a primary membership fee of one pound. Maintenance of the common property was supported by periodic donations and by special income such as fees levied on gambling. From that point on, the society, later renamed the Chinese Benevolent Association (CBA), played a wide array of roles both within the community and as the interlocutor between the Chinese community and local authorities. Among its primary functions were the organization of collective action to protect community interests; the dissemination of information on regulations and rules, and of news from China; mutual aid; care for the elderly elders; and the coordination of different interest groups. Most important, the CBA sought to address the shared concerns of the community, whether immigration issues, business opportunities, or the settlement of internal conflicts.[26]

Beginning in 1928, the CBA became increasingly involved in protesting Japanese aggression in China. These activities consumed much of the Association's energies until the end of World War II. Through informational campaigns, the CBA called on the Chinese community for donations to help wounded soldiers and to buy airplanes for the Chinese air force. Altogether the Jamaican Chinese donated £200,554 during the Anti-Japanese War. These activities were praised by Chiang Kai-shek's government.[27] After the war, the shift to a new generation of Jamaican-born Chinese, and dramatic changes in the international situation (especially the subsequent Chinese Civil War and the decades-long conflict between Taiwan and the PRC), led to a gradual change in Chinese attitudes toward China and Jamaica. This shift increasingly informed their decisions to stay in Jamaica or return to China—decisions that, in turn, played a critical role in shaping their identity.

With the passage of time, the Chinese gradually adapted themselves to Jamaican society.[28] As the younger generation came to see themselves more as Jamaican than as Chinese, the CBA was gradually reduced to a center where the older generation could socialize with their peers or learn the latest about their hometowns back in China. Understandably, participation in the CBA was waning. By the end of the 1950s and the early 1960s, the CBA's annual electoral meeting and general membership meeting frequently had to be either called off or postponed for lack of a quorum.[29]

At its height, however, the CBA had five sub-organizations: a school, a hospital, an almshouse, a cemetery, and a newspaper. The predecessor of Huaqiao Gongli Xuexiao (Chinese Public School) was set up in 1920 by the Chinese Freemasons (Zhi Gong Tang) but it suspended operations two years later. In March 1924, the Chinese school was restarted on the site of the Chinese Benevolent Association, financially supported by the drama club (Xinmin Club), thus it was named "Xinmin School" (New Peoples School). After 1927, a Chinese club, the Ru Yi Tang (The As-You-Wish Club),[30] began to subsidize the school at £35 monthly. The school directors all volunteered, and tuition was £6 annually, although poor students could apply for a tuition exemption. In 1928, the Xinmin School was taken over by the CBA, renamed the "Chinese Public School," and relocated to a larger site, purchased by the association for the sum of £2,300.

In 1944, the school promulgated its new constitution, which stated that the school belonged "to the Chinese Benevolent Association" (article 1), and would "follow the institution of the Ministry of Education of the motherland" (article 3), etc.[31]

At the end of World War II there was a boom of Chinese schools in Jamaica.[32] With the establishment of a Jamaican Branch of Kuomintang (Chiang Kai-shek's Chinese Nationalist Party), the community was increasingly enthusiastic about developing formal linkages with the Chinese state, and with learning about China's language, culture and history.[33] By 1944, the pupils attending the Chinese Public School had increased to more than 300 and in 1945 the Chinese community decided to renovate and expand the school. In order to encourage donations, the Chinese Consulate went so far as to issue a bulletin calling for pledges.[34] The school was finally rebuilt with a donation of about £10,000 by the Chinese community. The Chinese Public School usually published its annual financial report in the *Huaqiao Gongbao* (Chinese Public Newspaper, Kingston).[35] After this first blush of China-orientation there were heated discussions in the 1950s and 1960s about how the school should be run. Some realized the limited utility of Chinese language courses and suggested that teaching should be more localized and English-oriented, while others thought that Chinese language and culture were the only proper symbols of the community, and to abandon Chinese language instruction meant a fundamental change in community identity.[36]

However, as previously noted, the new generation of Jamaican-Chinese regarded themselves as more Jamaican than Chinese.[37] Even if they learned Chinese, there few opportunities to use it except at home. By 1955, only two out of nine teachers at the school knew Chinese; and of the ten students boarding at the school, only one could speak Chinese.[38] Since the school was the common property of the Chinese community and funding came from the community, any significant change in policy or curriculum depended upon the opinion of the majority. The school constitution (1944) made it clear that in teaching "Chinese is absolutely the primary [language of instruction] while foreign languages are secondary" (article 3) and "the headmaster must be Chinese" (article 4). Both of these rules were broken in

49

1952 when the courses were made up according to the local educational bureau, with English as primary and Chinese as secondary, and "a westerner" with an M.A. was appointed as headmaster. Subsequently the Chinese Public School experienced cycles of prosperity and decline.[39]

Another major community institution run by the Chinese Benevolent Association was the Huaqiao Liu Yi Suo (Chinese Hospital or Inpatient Department). The Chinese Hospital was founded in May 1923 after a call from community leaders Chen Qiongguang, Li Tianpei, Dai Dinggui, etc. The community ultimately donated £4,000. The hospital was open 24 hours a day to provide local Chinese with more convenient medical care. Rooms were free, but with no resident physicians, patients had to pay for their own doctors.[40] Owing to the shortage of donations, the hospital was initially forced to operate on an irregular schedule. In 1944, however, the CBA held a meeting to discuss the issue of financing and decided that all Chinese wholesalers, retail businesses, and individuals should donate a set amount of money to support the hospital.[41] In 1952, Peng Zhaozhang was appointed the director and came up with the ingenious (and successful) idea of selling advertising space on the walls of the hospital. With the regular income provided by the advertisers, the hospital was eventually running so well that it was highly praised by the government and by the public.[42]

Also operating under the CBA was the Huaqiao Yi Lao Yuan or Lao Ren Fang, or Yi Qiao Yuan (Chinese Almshouse for the Elderly), which was specifically for impoverished and aged Chinese. As early as 1877, the community bought two neighboring houses in Kingston to house homeless elderly Chinese. Later, with two more houses purchased and an additional house donated by the Ru Yi Tang, the almshouse managed five houses to serve the elderly. Among the almshouse's regulations was the stipulation that any Chinese aged more than 60 years, unable to work and without family, could apply for a life subsidy and live in the almshouse.[43] In 1957, there were about 60 elderly residents in the various houses. Their upkeep was subsidized by donations from bakeries, stores, and individuals. At times, however, the CBA was forced to dragoon donations from the Chinese community.[44] In the early 1960s, the CBA decided to rebuild the Almshouse, and in the autumn of 1961, with a £1,000 donation from Luo Weisong, a Chinese architect, the project was started.[45]

The CBA's cemetery dates back to the first decade of the twentieth century. In April, 1904, Chinese community leaders Chen Liangao and Zhang Sheng bought twelve acres at Heart's East Ashley Road (now Waltham Park Road) in Kingston as a burial place for local Chinese. This was the origin of Zhonghua Yishan (Chinese Cemetery or Gah San). In the terrible earthquake of 1907, Chinese businesses and households suffered significant damage. After protracted negotiations, the British colonial government agreed to pay the Chinese community £500 as compensation for their losses. The community used this sum to build a formal cemetery at the Heart's East location. In 1927, six Chinese leaders, Chen Yaoguang, Xie Zhenhua, He Xuerong, Wu Yiguang, Chen Dasheng and Huang Huaxun, called on the community to donate funds to renovate the site. This job took about two years and £980 to finish.[46] The second renovation came thirty years later and the Chinese Benevolent Association took out a full page in the *Chung San News* (Chinese Weekly, Jamaica) to call for pledges.[47] The CBA collected donations of more than £4,820, £3,000 of which were spent on construction, and the opening ceremony was held on April 7, 1957. As of September 9, 1957, 1,436 Chinese were buried in the cemetery.

The first media outlet for Jamaica's Chinese community was the *Zhonghua Shang Bao*, the predecessor of the *Huaqiao Gongbao* (Chinese Public Newspaper), which was started by Zheng Yongkang on October 18, 1930, who then sold it to Lee Tom Yin and Zheng Weiyu in 1931. The newspaper was taken over in 1935 by the CBA, which changed the name to the *Huaqiao Gongbao*. From that point on the *Huaqiao Gongbao* became the principal voice of the CBA, and by extension for the entire Chinese community. As a means to disseminate information and provide a platform to discuss issues related to the Chinese, the newspaper played a very important function in community life. Publication was stopped in October 1956, but restarted in 1975.

During the period under study there were three other newspapers run by the Chinese. The *Minzhi Zhoukang*, an organ of the Chinese

Freemasons, was a handwritten weekly. Its first appearance is unknown but it also stopped publishing in 1956. The *Zhong Shan Bao* (The Chung San News) was formally started as the official newspaper of the Jamaican Branch of the Chinese Nationalist Party on December 1, 1953. Its political bent was occasionally so contentious as to cause conflicts within the Chinese community.[48] A third paper, *The Pagoda*, was the only English weekly run by Chinese. It was started on March 16, 1940, by Charles T. Chang (Zheng Dingcai), a talented young man who was also the founder of Cathay Club. Carrying reports on the Chinese community and news about various aspects of life in Jamaica, it was both a product of and a tool for Chinese adaptation into Jamaican society.[49]

Below this stratum of community-wide organizations subordinate to the CBA there were more specific membership institutions that generally fell into three categories: political, recreational, and religious. The difficulties that the Chinese had met in emigrating to Jamaica were enormous. As indentured laborers, they had to fight for fair treatment. In revolts against plantation owners, members of secret societies like the Hong Men Hui usually took the lead.[50] After the labor contracts for the 1884 arrivals had expired, Chinese laborers gradually gathered in Kingston. Yang Yaren, Wan Mai, and other Chinese decided to organize themselves as a branch of the Zhi Gong Tang, or the Chinese Freemasons. They thus became the first formal Chinese organization in Jamaica. The purpose of this organization is reflected in its three principles: wipe out internal traitors, be patriotic and loyal to the country, and be loyal to friends and preserve unity.[51] Although its origin was political and specific to former plantation workers, the Freemasons served the Chinese community in various ways, such as setting up a Chinese school, organizing donations for the elderly, and buying an administrative office for the Chinese Benevolent Association.[52]

Another political organization was the Jamaican Branch of the Chinese Nationalist Party. The Chinese Consulate was established in 1943 after a long process of petitioning by the Chinese community to the Chinese embassy in London and the Chinese home government.[53] The initial founding of the consulate was supported by donations col-

lected by the CBA. Since China was ruled by the KMT it was natural that the consulate was the first formal link between the Chinese
Nationalist Party and the Jamaican-Chinese. As World War II was
approaching its end, some Chinese in Jamaica were thinking of a
bright future for their motherland. Chinese Nationalist Party members
Zeng Gongyi, Lee Tom Yin, and others applied to establish a party
branch in Jamaica. The branch was set up on April 13, 1945.
Unfortunately, the war between the Communists and the Nationalists
broke out soon after, followed by decades of conflict between the com-
munist-held mainland and KMT-controlled Taiwan. However, as the
Jamaican Chinese community became less and less interested in political conflicts in China, the party branch gradually lost influence.
Nonetheless, the big playground with swimming pool and other facilities built by the local KMT became a popular place for community
leisure activities.

Unlike other parts of the world where overseas Chinese settled,
there were only a few native-place associations (*tongxianghui*) founded
in Jamaica, and those were not very active at all.[54] This can be
explained by the concentration of the émigrés' origins. Since the size
of the community was relatively small and primarily from a handful of
Hakka villages, it made little sense for the community to subdivide
along native-place lines, as occurred in locales where there was significant competition between larger groups of Chinese émigrés from different native-places. In addition to native-place associations, there
were also some recreational organizations, such as drama societies,
dance troupes, literary clubs, and basketball teams, which were formed
by Chinese born in Jamaica. The reasons for the establishment of
these organizations varied. First, there was the desire to get out from
under the control of the older generation—the "China-born," as
Christine Ho has called them. The older generations had been establishing and consolidating their authority since 1854. Recreational
associations provided an easy way to circumvent that deeply
entrenched authority. Second, the Chinese born in Jamaica were still
excluded from the social circles of the Jamaican middle and upper
class. As a response, they decided to set up their own organizations.
Third, during the Anti-Japanese War, different measures were adopt-

ed by the Chinese Benevolent Association to mobilize the Chinese community, and this stimulated interest in recreational activities.

The Xin Min She (New Peoples Club) was one of the earliest of these organizations. It was set up by Wu Yiguang in 1924 for the purpose of exchanging knowledge and developing Chinese education. The first Chinese school was started by this organization. The Zhonghua Tiyu Hui (Chinese Athletic Club) was another group that attracted a lot of young Chinese born in Jamaica. On September 15, 1937, 17-year-old Horace Chang founded the club for the promotion of leisure activities. The club had various facilities and organized different sports, such as baseball, football, table tennis, tennis, bridge, and *mahjongg*. The 1951 earthquake destroyed the club building, and only after the donation of land and money by the Chinese community did a new clubhouse reopen in 1954. The club sponsored various types of competitions between Chinese teams and "western" local teams, which in return accelerated the process of adaptation and integration by the Jamaican-Chinese.[55]

The late 1930s were significant for the Chinese community in Jamaica for two reasons. First, the Marco Polo Bridge Incident in 1937 marked the beginning of Japan's massive invasion of China. Japanese aggression in China aroused the nationalistic sentiments of and inspired vocal protests from Chinese all over the world. The same was true in Jamaica. In 1938, in the midst of this nationalistic fervor, there was also a major anti-Chinese riot in Jamaica, which greatly hurt Chinese businesses. In this context a sense of victimization and the desire for self-protection were common. After the riot, the Chinese formed trade guilds and merchant associations to protect their interests. For example, the Mianbao Lu Shanghui (Chinese Bakery Association) was created in October 1938. The association was formed for the purpose of stopping a vicious cycle of competition among Chinese bakeries. After its founding, the association immediately stipulated the average weight of bread loaves and fixed the sum of *yongjin* (commission) that bakers could collect. Thereafter, the Chinese baking business enjoyed a more stable and fruitful process of development.[56] One month later the Xian Tou Hang Shanghui (Chinese Grocery Association) was formed with the purpose of "protecting members' interests, promoting business progress" (article 1), and "exchanging information" (article 2).[57]

During World War II, other organizations were formed for the same purpose, such as the Huaqiao Lingu Shanghui (Chinese Retail Association, 1942) and the Xuegao Canguan Shanghui (Chinese Ice Cream and Restaurant Association, 1943). These organizations contributed a great deal to the development of Chinese business, especially during the difficult times of the 1940s and 50s. Among these various trade guilds, the Chinese Retail Association, founded by Ye Yunsheng, was the most popular. It worked hard to guard its members' interests and played an important intermediary role between Chinese merchants and the colonial authorities. For example, in 1945, some Chinese retailers were charged with selling goods above the wartime prices stipulated by the colonial government. The major reason for this was that the Chinese were unable to read English did not know about the wartime price limits. The association reported this to the government and the price list was republished in the local newspaper *The Gleaner*. The association itself issued a bulletin specifically announcing the prices, made copies of the price list for Chinese retailers, and advised them to respect the law.[58] The records of February 6, 1945, showed that of the twenty members who had sent petitions to the Retail Association, six had been settled and the rest were being dealt with.[59] In 1955, a law regarding the treatment of employees was issued, which affected all types of business. The Retail Association wrote a letter to the government explaining the difficult situation of the small retailers and got a favorable response from the minister in charge.[60] The association was so important to the community that it was called the "stronghold and lifeline of the Chinese in Jamaica."[61]

The Chinese community was also involved in religious activities. Most of the Chinese elite converted to either Roman Catholicism or Anglicanism. Two prominent Chinese clergymen were the Reverend Father Frances and the Reverend Father Vincent. Both priests were from Henan Province in China and had formerly preached in Taiwan and Southeast Asia. They came to Jamaica in 1957 and became the leaders of the Chinese Catholic community.[62] With more and more Chinese converting to Christianity, the former headmaster of the

Chinese Public School, He Rujun, launched a movement promoting Chinese Christianity in Jamaica in 1954, which attracted a lot of Chinese.[63] The large number of conversions in the 1950s demonstrates that the Chinese in Jamaica were increasingly trying to adapt themselves to local society.

For the Chinese community in Jamaica, the more pressures they were under from the outside, whether political, economic, social, or natural, the more they united; the more they were treated as strangers, the more they felt Chinese. In other words, it was because they were in a strange land that they truly felt their original identity as Chinese; only by uniting and clinging together could they survive and prosper.

Things had begun to change at end of the 1940s. New generations were reaching maturity, the re-orientation of thinking became obvious, and the dedication to Jamaica's cause and the island's social and economic life were increasing. Unity was certainly a key for both survival and development, but not necessarily exclusively within the Chinese community. *Spotlight*, a local journal, commented on the new generation, "this second generation are Chinese only because they look like Chinese. They think Jamaican, Jamaica is their home, and they never miss an opportunity to show their love for and patriotism for the country of their birth and upbringing. Psychologically, they are more Jamaican than the children born in Jamaica of European parents."[64]

Development and Integration

When the Chinese first started to establish their own businesses at the end of the nineteenth century, they usually began with a small investment of capital, usually no more than £20 or £30. Their shops were small and the goods they offered were few and often in small enough quantities so that cash-strapped locals could buy a few pounds of rice or sugar rather than buying in bulk. Among the pioneers in Chinese retail were several important figures, such as Chen Ba Gong (Robert Jackson), one of the first arrivals; Huang Chang (Wong Sam) from British Guyana; Lin Bing (James Solomon) from Costa Rica; and Qiu Yajia (Harris Carr) from the U.S.[65]

56

Facing adverse sentiments and unfriendly attitudes at the beginning, the Chinese nonetheless made significant progress, first in the retail business and then in other fields. They were initially concentrated in Kingston and St. Andrew, but quickly spread to the rural parishes around the country. According to the colonial census, in 1881, 84 out of 99 Chinese were in Kingston; in 1891, there were 482 Chinese, 295 lived of whom lived in Kingston. In the following decades, the Chinese gradually spread to other parts of the island (table 3.3).

Table 3.3
Chinese Population in Jamaica

	1881	1891	1911	1921	1943	1948	1953	1960	1995	1998
Kingston	84	295	754	1,180	4,154			3,196		
St Andrew	4	9	198	369	2,085			7,852		
Other places	11	178	1,159	2,347	6,155					
Total in Jamaica	99	482	2,111	3,896	12,394	12,401	18,655	21,812	20,000	22,500

Sources: Chen Kwong Min, The Chinese in the Americas, p. 700; Lee Tom Yin, The Chinese in Jamaica, pp. 44–50, 118; Orlando Patterson, "Contest and Choice in Ethnic Allegiance: A Theoretical Framework and Caribbean Case Study," in Nathan Glazer and Daniel P. Moynihan, ed., Ethnicity Theory and Practice (Cambridge: Harvard University Press, 1975), p. 324; S. Hurwitz and E. F. Hurwitz, Jamaica: A Historical Portrait (New York: Praeger Publishers, 1971), p. 162; Committee of Overseas Chinese Economy in Ten Years, Shi Nian Lai Huaqiao Jinji, 1972–1981 (Overseas Chinese Economy in Ten Years, 1972–1981) (Taipei: Qiao Wu Weiyuanhui Di San Chu, 1981), pp. 211–235; Huaqiao Huaren Jinji Nianjian 1995 (Overseas Chinese Economy Year Book, 1995) (Taipei: Qiao Wu Weiyuanhui, 1995), p. 558; Huaqiao Huaren Jinji Nianjian 1998 (Overseas Chinese Economy Year Book, 1998) (Taipei: Qiao Wu Weiyuanhui, 1998), p. 416; Phyllis Morrow, "Chinese Adaptation in Two Jamaican Cities," Honors thesis, Harvard University, 1972.

The majority of Chinese activity was in the retail business. Almost every scholar who has done research on the Chinese in Jamaica has noted that the Chinese controlled the lion's share of the retail sector.[66] In 1954, among 1,250 Chinese-owned businesses, 1,021 were retail stores.[67] Their skill in business was, however, not limited to retailing,

57

but obvious in wholesale grocery as well. Of the 14 leading wholesale merchants in Jamaica in 1946, 10 were Chinese. In 1954, 38 out of 46 wholesale grocers on the island were Chinese. Big wholesale grocery outlets provided goods to the retail stores and the small wholesale stores located in the countryside. The latter provided stock for the small retail stores throughout the rural parishes. [68] This network involved both capital and personnel, which helped a great deal in promoting Chinese business in Jamaica. Since the Chinese played such an important role in Jamaican retail and wholesale business, the spread of the Chinese in turn brought the spread of Chinese retail stores. This economic expansion facilitated the process of their social integration.

Why did the Chinese succeed in the retail business in Jamaica? Scholars have attributed their success to four factors: opportunity, character and service, social networks, and favorable policies. First, the Chinese started retail business when there was an economic niche waiting to be filled.[69] At the time of their arrival in Jamaica there was little competition in the retail sector. African slaves had just been emancipated and had not yet developed the requisite commercial skills, and other ethnic groups considered shopkeeping below their status. Second, the Chinese had a well-earned reputation for thriftiness and hard work, and they emphasized the practical education of children in the rudiments of commerce. What is more, they provided better service, and this helped them to establish and expand their business.[70] Third, the social networks they built had two important functions. They provided an abundant and efficient labor reservoir, mostly relatives from China, to work long hours and for low wages in rural shops. Moreover, the linkages between immigrants in wholesale and retail facilitated Chinese business expansion.[71] Finally, colonial policy played the key role in their success. If there was no favorable policy in the host environment, the Chinese could not have made as much progress. For a long time, there were no restrictions on Chinese immigration to Jamaica, provided the immigrants were coming to engage in commercial activities. This policy attracted experienced Chinese merchants from outside to try their hand at business in Jamaica.

Although the atmosphere in Jamaica was conducive to Chinese business, we should not conclude that the Chinese were working in a particularly friendly land, especially in the early twentieth century. In 1933 an Alien Restriction Law was enacted that was designed to restrict Chinese immigration. This law was "enacted by a Legislative Council on which the merchant class was well represented." What is more, there was a strong anti-Chinese feeling in Jamaican society, evidenced by the anti-Chinese riots of 1918 and 1938. In comparison, similar levels of hostility were not apparent in Trinidad or British Guyana.[72]

Sufficient attention should be paid to the unique character (peasants), condition (poor), and objectives (to return home with money) of the early Chinese immigrants. Most émigrés were poor and lacked either formal education or professional training. Early immigrants tended to be poor peasants who emigrated for a better life and tried to make their fortune overseas. Three years' hard labor under the indenture system, however, did not leave them much, only the little money they had managed to save, that is, if they could avoid the myriad tricks designed by the plantation owners to cheat them of their savings.[73] After the end of the contract, they could return to their home with what little they had, but this was not what they had had in mind when they left China. Rather, the common goal had been to *guangzhong yaozhu*, or "bring glory to their ancestors." Given the rudimentary state of the commercial economy in Jamaica, there was both opportunity and demand. A little money as capital was enough to open a retail store, which did not require a high level of professional skill, although many Chinese probably had some rudimentary trade knowledge, given the highly commercialized nature of the Chinese rural economy. Some did try their hand on the land by using their skills as farmers, but they were hard pressed to compete with the plantations, nor was farming as potentially lucrative as trade. Farming, moreover, required a long-term commitment which was unappealing to those whose desire was to quickly earn enough money and return to China.

Besides the retail and wholesale business, Chinese did quite well in other fields, such as food manufacturing and light industry (bakeries, bottling, ice cream, soap, etc.) as well as the import of foodstuffs. The baking industry was almost totally controlled by the Chinese, such as Chen Xuexian's Diamond Bakery and Liao Xiqing's Lyew Brothers Baking Company in Kingston. Cremo Ltd. was founded by Chen Luxiang in 1939. Updated and expanded in 1954, it became the biggest ice cream producer in Jamaica. In the early 1950s, supermarkets appeared in Kingston. Chinese soon realized the potential commercial advantages of supermarkets and sensed the growing pressure on their small shops from local competitors.[74] Within a few years there were numerous Chinese-owned supermarkets, including the biggest one in north Kingston, and Chin's Super Market owned by Masue Chin in Montego Bay. Hu Jingxian (Helen Chinsee) offers a good example of Chinese market sensitivity and commercial acumen.

In order to update her knowledge and "apply it to local raw materials adaptable for manufacture," Helen Chinsee decided in 1955 to take courses at Antioch College in Ohio, even though she had received a M.A. in Economics from the University of Chicago in 1939. After her application was turned down, she wrote a ten-page plea to the Antioch faculty. With the help of Dr. Arthur Morgan, president emeritus of the college, she was accepted. The Chinese newspaper *Zhong Shan Bao* issued a special editorial "To Encourage Ms. Hu Jingxian" to extol her spirit.[75] After she finished her studies, Helen Chinsee and her husband Chen Yinghao (Rupert Chinsee) took Dr. Morgan's advice and began a business manufacturing aluminum products, mostly cooking utensils. With help from the Jamaican government, they set up the Caribe Metal Works in Falmouth. "From a shoe string capital, they were now running a £40,000 industrial operation. From an initial production of crude stuff, they were now turning out a sophisticated line of over 70 quality products including palms, and coloured alumina ware." Two governors visited their factory and were greatly impressed by their achievements. No less than Premier Manley congratulated them on their efforts, and the media praised the Chinese couple that "had transformed the industrial and employment face of the old north coast town of Falmouth."[76]

Shifting Identities

With increased commercial success, the Chinese became inexorably linked with the emergence of modern Jamaica, but the process by which they came to see themselves as "Jamaican" was still in flux. Christine Ho has skillfully analyzed the processes of and differences between the *creolization* of the Chinese in Jamaica, Trinidad, and Guyana.[77] I prefer to use the term *integration* to describe the process in Jamaica, and will discuss two aspects of the process, social involvement and political participation of the Chinese in Jamaican life.

The older generation of Chinese immigrants in Jamaica established and consolidated the community on the basis of three elements: ethno-cultural superiority, economic specialization, and social isolation. However, this solidarity was challenged and eroded by new generations of Jamaican-born Chinese.

In the 1950s Andrew Lind described the emergence of a sizeable mixed Chinese population in rural parishes outside Kingston.[78] It seems the rural parishes lacked the center of gravity for Chinese identity that Kingston's "Chinatown" provided. But even in the cities like Kingston with larger Chinese populations, like Kingston, mixed marriages gradually increased and caused alarm among the older generation of Chinese. The problem that emerged was that Jamaican-born Chinese did not think highly of the "ethnocentrism of their parents." Young Chinese men even looked down on Chinese girls and preferred girls of other color as friends. Rather than being portrayed as a group apart, they preferred to be treated equally as Jamaicans.[79] As a result, the process of social involvement by the Chinese became more and more obvious, whether integration was pursued consciously or unconsciously. Realizing they were now part of Jamaican society, the Chinese, both the old and new generations, became more concerned about local issues, their role in Jamaican society, as well as their place in the colonial and post-colonial West Indies.

Some Chinese elites gradually merged into Jamaican society. Perusing the Who's Who Jamaica of 1951 shows that the majority of the Chinese listed in the book were deeply involved in Jamaican life. This integration took two main forms. First, most prominent Chinese had converted to either Roman Catholicism or Anglicanism, while others joined Protestant denominations. Among the 27 Chinese listed in the *Who's Who*, six were born in China and came to the island either at the end of the 1800s or in the early 1900s. Thirteen Chinese were Roman Catholic, eight Anglican, two Protestant, while four did not mention their religion. Another interesting phenomenon is that, in the section detailing the listees' recreational activities, every Chinese noted at least one favorite pastime. More traditional Chinese would have been unlikely to emphasize recreation, and the Chinese born in China usually mentioned popular activities that did not require much skill, such as swimming, walking, and listening to music. The Jamaica-born Chinese, on the contrary, mentioned more specific activities, such as tennis, dancing, biology, or even "all outdoor activities."[80]

This suggests that those Chinese eager to be accepted into Jamaican society tried to adapt themselves to or adopt the local values and mores of Jamaican society. As Jamaica approached statehood a new term appeared to describe Chinese in Jamaica as yet another part of the new island nation's multi-ethnic tableau—"Jamaicans of Chinese origin."[81]

Early in their history the Jamaican-Chinese evinced little interest in Jamaican society, in part because of the language barrier and a traditional disinterest in local politics. After World War II, and especially during the 1950s, this changed significantly. The Chinese in Jamaica became more and more concerned about the linkages between local society and themselves. Fair treatment and equality in both business and social life became a common cause. On April 8, 1954, Helen Chinsee wrote an open letter to the minister in charge of tax collection through the local newspaper *The Gleaner*. Complaining about her mistreatment by the official in a matter of business, Chinsee suggested that the tax department should have a clear direction regarding the registration and accounting of merchandise and the procedures to be followed. Her opinions, which went beyond the parochial concerns of Chinese businesspeople, were well received by the government.[82] Chinsee's ability to use an ostensibly "Jamaican" newspaper to advocate an issue of concern to all Jamaicans is indicative of the increasing Jamaica-orientation of the Chinese elite.

Prior to this point, it had been common for local newspapers to publish articles that contained either discriminatory descriptions of or slander against the Chinese community. Even in the early days, the Chinese were sensitive to the racist tenor of those articles, but they made no protest. This was either because no Chinese would take the trouble to criticize the authors or because their English was not good enough to issue a rejoinder. Moreover, the Chinese tended to adhere to the doctrine of *he wei gui*, meaning peace is the most precious virtue among people. This was all the more the case for a community settled in a foreign country. Nonetheless, things were changing.

An article in the Chinese newspaper *Huaqiao Gongbao* in August 1940 applauded a recent "victory" over anti-Chinese attitudes. In June of that year a local weekly had presented an ugly portrayal of the Chinese community, vividly describing the exotic and "alien" atmosphere of Kingston's Chinatown, characterized by gambling and opium smoking. As soon as the article appeared, a Jamaican-born Chinese wrote a letter to the editor, criticizing the fabrication and protesting against this anti-Chinese article. The editor of the Jamaican weekly took the protest seriously and published an apology on the front page of his July 27 issue. The editors of the Chinese-language *Huaqiao Gongbao* were thrilled with the result. "We believe that after this letter, the weekly would never be so provocative and wantonly vilify the Chinese community, and will be very careful about anti-Chinese language, not like this time." The letter-writer also blamed the older generation of Chinese for consistently submitting to such humiliations. No matter how bad the slight, older Chinese would prefer to swallow the insults and were never bold enough to protest. Even if they had recourse to legal action, the first-generation Chinese never dared take their cases to the courts and thus voluntarily gave up their rights. The article called on the Chinese community to stop yielding to anti-Chinese discrimination and instead fight back.[83]

Obviously, Jamaican-born Chinese were gradually immersing themselves in the social milieu of late-colonial Jamaica. They had a good command of the language, they understood Jamaican values and had developed ways to deal with social and political affairs. More importantly, they had the courage to fight for fair treatment. Their success is indicated by the change in tone of the local press. Newspapers that had formerly displayed a bias against the Chinese community gradually changed the tenor of their reporting. When several Chinese stores were robbed in 1954, a local newspaper published an article criticizing the tendency to attack Chinese shops, praised the Chinese community's contributions, and made it clear that Jamaican society should take an positive attitude toward the Chinese community. The Chinese responded with enthusiasm and had the article translated and published in the *Huaqiao Gongbao*.[84]

The process of integration was two-dimensional. In addition to Jamaicans changing their view of the Chinese community, organizations and institutions that had once been exclusively Chinese were changing their membership policies to be more inclusive. In December 1954, members of the Chinese Retail Association raised the issue of changing the association's name. The main idea was to delete the word "Chinese" in order to expand by enrolling "Xiren shops," meaning "westerners' shops." It was believed that the change would have three advantages: it would recruit more shopkeepers and thus raise the profile of the association; it was a more convenient way to interact with other ethnic groups; and it was a way to combine the two cultures of the east and the west. In an editorial entitled "The Chinese Retailers Association Changes Its Name," it was suggested that the name could be changed to "Jamaica Retailers' Association" which in turn raised three issues for consideration: "the ownership of association property, the revision of the constitution, and the working language for meetings."[85]

Sports, recreation, and education were yet other venues for integration. From the 1950s onward, the Chinese community began to organize its own Miss China contest, an event that was unthinkable for the older generation. The pageant was held annually and attracted great attention both within the Chinese community and among Jamaicans as a whole. There were more and more friendly contests between Chinese basketball teams and other local teams. In order to encourage higher education, Ye Junwan, a Chinese merchant, set up a scholarship in the Department of Pharmacy at the University of the

West Indies in 1957. As a five-year scholarship, it involved a gift of £1,500.[86] The 1960s began with a promising start for Jamaica with the referendum on the future of West Indies. After the Jamaican people voted for their own independence in 1961, the whole nation seemed caught up in the excitement. In this context the Chinese community sought to accelerate the process of integration.

Just prior independence, at the end of 1961, four separate events demonstrated the willingness of the Chinese to become an integral part of Jamaican society. In October 1961, British Honduras was devastated by Hurricane Hattie, a storm that caused a great damage to the Honduran capital and killed several hundred people. Upon hearing the news of the disaster, Huang Tusheng, chairman of the Chinese Benevolent Association, took the lead in calling for donations and other aid from the Chinese community. The Chinese actively participated in the donation drive and they sent four different installments of money in November.[87] Then in December the "Citizens Committee for a Better Jamaica" held a meeting to discuss plans for the celebration of Jamaica's independence. Together with more than 80 other organizations, the Chinese Benevolent Association took part in the meeting and agreed to sponsor a float in the celebratory parade.[88] As a strategic move, the CBA also called on the Chinese community for year-end donations to support the elderly poor, but not just for the Chinese elderly, but rather for all older Jamaicans in need. In order to carry out the donation drive, the association set up a committee to take charge. The purpose of these various moves was clear: "If we want to decrease the discriminatory crime against the Chinese, we must adopt a strategy of harmony, integrate with every nationality, be friendly with others, help the needy, treat others equally without discrimination, ..."[89] The Chinese Benevolent Association also opened the Chinese Public School to non-Chinese Jamaicans, and other formerly exclusive Chinese associations began admitting Creoles.[90]

Political Participation

As early as the 1940s, Chinese elites were involved in the process of political participation. During the colonial period, being named a justice of the peace was an honor "conservatively conferred to either native or Chinese and was highly cherished," and Chinese were occasionally appointed to the post. Tai Ten Quee was the first to be awarded this title in 1943 for the town of St. Andrew and he later became the first Chinese Member of Parliament. In the next year, Sidney Chang (Zheng Dingfa), the elder brother of Charles T. Chang (Zheng Dingcai), who founded the *Pagoda* magazine, became a justice of the peace for the same district. After his appointment, Mr. Chang served his community wholeheartedly and "made the office an active one, signing papers, giving advice, guidance, to humble Jamaicans most of them not of his racial origin."[91] In 1945, Chen Huafu was appointed as the Justice of Peace in Kingston, the first Chinese to hold the position in the capital. In the following decade (1946–55), nine Chinese were appointed justices of the peace in different districts.[92]

During the 1950s, the Chinese community was sensitive to the changing situations in both China and Jamaica. The continuing conflict between the PRC and Taiwan meant that the Chinese had to stay in Jamaica for some time, maybe forever. The optimal strategy was for the Chinese community to change its traditional low profile in local politics and take an active role in Jamaican politics. An editorial of April 15, 1954, suggested that the Chinese should not neglect their role in the election that year. But what was the significance of the Chinese, who counted for only one percent of the total population? "The result of the election is usually decided finally by the minority. If we take part in the election, any parties would approach us." The editorial also advised that the Chinese "should take an active action; but be cautious of our words towards outsiders. This is the best way to deal with the surroundings."[93]

We can sense the change of thinking among the Chinese in Jamaica by their rising prominence in the 1950s. It is common for Chinese immigrants to keep a low profile in their host country, especially soon after arrival. Chinese in Jamaica in the 1950s wanted a change, and wanted to make the best use of local politics to serve the interest of the Chinese community. This was the first step, a step forward, but not far enough, since political activism was still confined to a small circle of prominent Chinese. It took some years before the majority of the community began to look on Jamaica as their own country.

The Chinese tendency to keep a low profile in local politics stems not only from the political traditions of China, but also from local attitudes toward Chinese. In other words, when you expect not to be well received in local politics, you are usually reluctant to enter the fray. There had been a long-standing unwillingness to accept prominent Chinese into Jamaica's parliamentary life. This resistance was broken only in the late 1950s when Hubert Tai Ten Quee was nominated to the Legislative Council in 1959. His achievements in both professional and social life show clearly that he deserved both the honor and the responsibility. Born in Kingston and one of the Jamaica's first industrialists, Mr. Tai was Managing Director of Caribbean Products and a director of the Motor Owners Mutual Association, Tai Ten Quee, Pagoda, and the Caribbean Atlantic Instrument Company. As legal advisor to the old Chinese Consulate in Kingston, he had given "yeoman service" as a council member of the Chamber of Commerce, and as a member of the Princess Alice Appeal Fund Committee, the Coconut Industry Board, Jockey Club, and the Boys' Town Finance Committee. Mr. Tai was also one of the pioneers in organizing the Chinese Athletic Club. He was so popular within the Chinese community that he got the affectionate name "Sir Tai."[94]

With Jamaican independence approaching, those Chinese who had always taken China as their *zuguo* (motherland) began to realize that if they wanted to stay in Jamaica, they had to "learn to be Jamaican first." In 1961, when the Jamaicans were facing the vote on the future of Jamaica—to remain in the West Indies Federation, or become independent—the Chinese elites called the community to voice their choice: "To cast your sacred vote in order to fulfill your duty."[95] The Chinese were told to "take an active part in the vote," but "do not get together and join in any parade, do not tell others which choice you have made, do not vote for any side as others ask you to do. This is your free choice, do whatever you consider suitable to do. Make your own choice and cast your sacred vote. Those who have the right to vote should not give up the vote."[96]

When independence came in 1962, Rupert Chinsee became a sen-

67

ator in the new congress. In his career Chinsee had contributed a great deal to both the Chinese community and to Jamaica. As mentioned above, he and his wife, Helen Chinsee, built the Caribe Metal Works and changed the face of the small town of Falmouth. In the four years after its founding, the factory expanded from six machines and six workers to 25 machines and 30 men in 1960. "The old seaport town has been all the better for the unburied talents of the Chinsees."[97] Rupert Chinsee was a Jamaican-born Chinese, and earned an M.A. from Stanford University. He served the Chinese community for many years and became an industrialist with the help of his capable wife.

"Out of Many, One People" became the motto of independent Jamaica. After independence Sidney Chang was appointed by the governor-general, on the prime minister's recommendation, as Acting Inspector of Customs. Commenting on the event, *Spotlight* reported, "Although the position is an acting one, it underlines once again Government's and Jamaica's esteem for the Jamaican Chinese community." This was great news for the Chinese in Jamaica, or Jamaicans of Chinese origin, and a culmination of the evolution of a community in what had once been a "foreign land." It was a long and difficult journey: from the indentured labor to timid retailer, from a foreigner to a citizen of the nation, from Chinese to Jamaican.

In this chapter I have laid out the history of the Chinese in Jamaica: the origins of the community and the subsequent processes of adaptation and integration. "Integration" is used here to mean that the Chinese in Jamaica wanted and tried to be part of Jamaica, and they have succeeded. As one *Spotlight* reporter suggested in 1963, a year after independence: "Today the process of integration at first cautious, slow, rolls inexorably on, is close to a completion point where there will be no such thing as a Chinese community here, but Jamaicans all of Chinese origin. Already to second or third generation Chinese, Jamaica is home, their native land; the overwhelming majority think Jamaican, live Jamaican."[98]

CHAPTER 4

Chinese Economic Development and Ethnic Identity Formation in Jamaica

GAIL BOUKNIGHT-DAVIS

Introduction

The Chinese in Jamaica represent a small proportion of the population and yet maintain the greatest visibility in the grocery retail industry. Even though their numbers represent only a fraction of the total number of retail grocery establishments, their participation in the trade has been quite high and often misconstrued as a monopoly. The literature suggests that the character of Chinese-owned businesses in Jamaica has helped to foster economic success and consolidate Chinese ethnic identity (Silin 1962, Levy 1967, Morrow 1972, Patterson 1988). It has also been contended that the economic activity in the retail grocery trade has contributed to an antagonistic presence in Jamaica (Broom 1954, Morrow 1972, Silin 1962, Richardson 1983, Patterson 1988). This chapter addresses the myth of the Chinese monopoly and examines the social and economic factors influential in constructing a Jamaican-Chinese ethnic group and forming interethnic relations.

Chinese as an Ethnic Entity

The Chinese population in Jamaica grew out of several migrations. The initial contract labor migrants arrived under three waves of large-scale immigration in the nineteenth century under the contract system. The first ship arrived in August 1854 from China, the second in

November 1854 from Panama, and the third in 1884 from Hong Kong. These three immigration waves brought Chinese into Jamaica as indentured servants. However, the Chinese immigrants did not remain in agriculture for long, and by the turn of the twentieth century a number of Chinese had become shop owners.

The Chinese became successful shop owners, developing a particular style of retail grocery that brought economic prosperity. The creation of these economic establishments assisted the growth of the Chinese population by creating a network through which members could encourage Chinese relations and community assistance. By creating this kind of network, the Chinese had also created a social group distinct from the larger Jamaican community.

Chinese success in grocery retail facilitated their rise to the middle class, leading to an important feature of Chinese ethnicity: class distinction. Even among the total population of Chinese, including those racially mixed, class has become a feature important in the definition of Chinese ethnicity. Both economic and social factors are important in the construction of Chinese identity. Other social, historical, and cultural factors such as perceptions of familial history and kin affiliation are also significant to Chinese identity.

One hundred and fifty years after the first wave of immigration, there were over four generations of Chinese residing in Jamaica.[1] Many families included full Chinese parents, grandparents, and even great-grandparents. Even though younger members may not participate in the same Chinese traditions or speak the same dialects as native Hong Kong Chinese or those from the mainland, the fact that one's forebears are Chinese are indicators of Chinese identity and affiliation.[2] Yet, there has been biological as well as cultural mixing between Jamaicans and Chinese immigrants, and this has created a complex set of racial and ethnic distinctions. The factors pertaining to one's ethnicity are both objective and subjective (Hicks 1977; see also van den Berghe 1977). They are, at once, how the Chinese define themselves, e.g. self-ascription, and how they are perceived by others (Barth 1969).

The distinction between local-born and foreign-born Chinese is mirrored in the cleavages between Chinese social organizations.[3] The differences between the local-born and the foreign-born are also reflected in the linguistic differences.[4] Few Jamaican-Chinese speak any of the Chinese dialects, and the ones who do usually speak Hakka rather than the Cantonese spoken by the Hong Kong–born Chinese migrants of the twentieth and twenty-first centuries. These differences are also reflected in religious beliefs of Jamaican-Chinese, who are primarily Roman Catholic—the early immigrants converted from Buddhism to Catholicism because of the lack of facilities for maintaining Buddhist practices. Even though there are many underlying differences between the local-born and the foreign-born reflected in religion, class, and language, there remain connections among both. Therefore, the line separating the communities is blurred, which raises the question of whether Jamaica has one distinct Chinese community or many splintered ones.

Economic Factors: The Grocery Retail Trade

The growth of Chinese businesses in Jamaica began in the late nineteenth century with small retail grocery stores (Chang 1956:82) and remains a significant historical and current contribution to Chinese economic development. Most Chinese immigrants, after their arrival in Jamaica, left the field of agricultural labor and developed their own retail and manufacturing enterprises. As these businesses prospered, the types of ventures became more diversified.

Chinese involvement in retail grocery was well underway by the early 1900s. Although Chinese participation in the retail grocery trade has been dated to the post-1854 period (Yin 1953:55), there is no official confirmation. It was not until the final decade of the nineteenth century that official publications revealed the level of Chinese participation in the island's trading industry. By 1908, official interests in commercial activities of the Chinese had become more active. Government officials were eager to determine the extent to which this immigrant group had superseded other ethnic groups engaged in grocery retail.

Although the Chinese had considerable involvement in the retail sector, their interests did not constitute a monopoly. The number of

71

Chinese grocery shops becomes significant, however, when this figure is related to Chinese population numbers. The 1911 census reveals that the Chinese numbered 2,111 and represented only 0.3 percent of the population. One of every three Chinese was involved in retail grocery, and therefore, actual participation was quite high. As a perception of Chinese threat to Creole shopkeepers grew, public resentment also grew (Levy 1967:15). In a quote from the *Daily Gleaner* one Jamaican citizen complained, "Can the authorities do nothing to let Jamaicans feel that Jamaica is still their home, and strangers will not be allowed to elbow them out of what is theirs by right?"[5]

In the early 1900s, Chinese business activity expanded in part because of the economic boom that accompanied the First World War. As a result of this expansion, Chinese men sent for relatives to assist them in the shops. The number of grocery stores grew, and larger numbers of Chinese arrived in Jamaica. The prosperity in Chinese shops continued to grow well into the 1920s (Yin 1963:45).

In 1925, the number of trade licenses held by the Chinese had increased 28 percent from the previous year (Levy 1967:16). The Chinese population had also increased to 3,696.[6] This growth suggested that one of every two people was involved in retail grocery trade. Chinese participation in grocery retail was at its zenith until 1926, when Chinese business activities began to decline. The fall in business led to price cuts to undermine other competitors and resulted in some bankruptcies. Business continued to decline through the 1930s because of the Great Depression. At this time there were numerous cases of small shop owners, primarily non-Chinese, who could not afford to operate their shops all day and were forced to supplement their income by laboring in the fields. In response to the economic crisis, Chinese wholesalers added new fixed-weight quantities, such as twelve and a half pound weights, to facilitate sales to retailers who could not buy twenty-five pounds at a time, and also introduced quarter-dozen quantities at wholesale prices. Chinese retail shops that were surrounded by eight to ten such small non-Chinese shops competitively compelled smaller shops to relocate and drove others into bankruptcy. By contrast, the Chinese shops that faced the worst conditions between 1930 and 1938 had improved by World War II (Yin 1963:46).

Even though Chinese shops had faced periods of decline during the depression era, the Chinese continued to be regarded as "dominators" of the grocery shop industry. This myth grew to such an extent that the words "Chinese" and "shopkeeper" became synonymous (Levy 1967:16). In 1936, there were 9,265 trade licenses, and 1,543 were owned by Chinese.

Between 1945 and 1954 a general trend of business prosperity emerged. By 1954, the Chinese represented 8 percent of the grocery retail trade (Chang 1956:82). Despite evidence to the contrary that could be found in official and public sources, popular belief persisted that the Chinese had ousted all other ethnic groups from any significant involvement in the trade (Levy 1967:17). Although Chinese-owned grocery stores represented one out of every eight around the mid-1950s, carrying 90 percent of the total retail grocery business until 1970, their percentage of the retail business had dropped to 40 percent by the 1990s.[7] According to Jamaicans, both Chinese and non-Chinese, there was a general population decline after 1972, resulting from the threat of the parliamentary government turning communist. Most upper- or middle-class people, including Chinese, migrated to the United States or Canada.[8]

Overall, precise numbers for retail grocery stores are not given in the census data. According to Chang's figures, in 1954 there were 12,178 business establishments related to grocery trade. About one-tenth (1,250) were owned and operated by the Chinese, who then represented less than one percent of the total population. Of the 1,250 Chinese-owned businesses, 1,021 were retail grocery stores, and of this number one-third (336) were concentrated in the Kingston metropolitan area (Chang 1956:82–85). In downtown Kingston during the 1950s, Chinese groceries could be found at nearly every street corner. Most often these grocery stores would serve as the residence of the Chinese owner and family. Downtown Kingston, which had been a prime residential area for the Chinese in the early 1900s, had become nearly all non-residential by the end of the century.

Two types of grocery establishments developed in the Kingston Metropolitan Area, small grocery stores and company-owned chain supermarkets. The small grocery shops began as a combination of food markets, five-and-dimes, and drugstores. Vendors sold a variety of goods, from provisions and hardware to perfumery and toys, although the bulk of their import business consisted of foodstuffs (Chang 1956:86). These stores were characteristically known for selling food-stuffs in small quantities. Since the bulk of their business was geared toward the poor Afro-Jamaican community, Chinese shops were a great value for the majority of the Jamaican population. "People could normally not afford to buy in great quantity . . . and they did not have refrigerators, and therefore could not buy things [to store] in great quantity. [Shops] sold such things as a quart of milk or a quarter pound of butter in the morning then [customers] would come back around noon and ask for another quarter of a pound."[9] In the families operating these kinds of grocery stores, each member was expected to work in some capacity. One owner had worked and lived in a shop house for 29 years, nearly all of her life. She explained, "The shop was in the front and the house was behind. It was owned by my parents. It was a lot of hard work. Most shops are run by the family. It is a tightly knit, family-run organization. We never hired help. It was run by my family. After the shop closed, we still had to chop and wrap fish. In earlier times we would close as late as 10 p.m. but now because of the crime we close earlier. Before one did not have to worry about stealing. They could leave products out in the open with customers present."[10]

Chinese shops sustained long operation hours, beginning as early as 6 a.m. and closing as late as midnight.[11] Generally, store operating hours alone could consist of ten- to fourteen-hour days. Another storeowner, a 62-old Hong Kong–born Chinese, confirming the long hours and hard work involved in running a grocery shop, explained that his day began at 6:30 in the morning at opening and continued beyond closing time at 8 p.m. The storekeeper's sons and a non-family worker, an Afro-Jamaican, also worked in the small shop. The owner explained that because of the long hours he worked there was little time for socializing.[12]

Many small traditional shops in the Kingston Metropolitan Area were gradually replaced by large chain supermarkets by the end of the 1990s.[13] These large stores were also family-owned and sometimes family-operated but the store's employee rolls generally consisted of Afro-

Jamaican workers. These larger stores often began as smaller operations that were expanded when the owners accumulated sufficient capital. Two of the largest chain supermarkets in Kingston were family-owned and operated by four brothers. One brother described how his family's business, which began as a small store and expanded to a large chain supermarket, gave them financial stability. The grocery shops had enabled the first generation of Chinese immigrants to become financially stronger. As a result, they were able to send a second generation of Jamaican-born children to receive formal education. Thus, the second generation was able to give the third generation, the four brothers in this instance, a better chance for education and greater financial stability. This particular family had been in the grocery business for more than thirty years. The four brothers had owned four supermarkets in different areas in Kingston at one time, but consolidated to two stores in the late 1980s, creating one of the largest supermarkets in Kingston. Despite the size, however, the brothers frequently interacted with customers. The youngest brother acknowledged the changing trends of the traditional Chinese grocery shop, explaining that "the ownership of grocery shops is changing from Chinese to non-Chinese. In addition, most stores [that] were run and operated by families on a small scale may be owned but not always completely operated by Chinese."[14] In most cases Afro-Jamaicans were employed in bagging the food or stocking the shelves whereas Chinese workers operated registers or managed the store. By contrast, the larger Chinese-owned chain supermarket in the Liguanea area of Kingston in the 1990s employed only Afro-Jamaicans as baggers and register operators.

The pattern of founding of small grocery stores that expand into supermarkets also developed among Afro-Jamaicans, but not as successfully.[15] In comparison, the Chinese represented only a small fraction of the trade but their volume was significant because the Jamaican-owned stores had very little capital, usually no more than £100, while the Chinese stores had much greater capital, usually £500 to £1,000 or more. As a result, the Chinese stores had more and better stock than the Jamaican-owned stores. Second, the Chinese storekeepers were able to give their customers better service, including free delivery and buying on credit, which the small Jamaican stores could not afford to offer. Third, the wholesale grocery business was controlled by the Chinese, and most of the Chinese retail stores enjoyed a relationship with the wholesale business that Jamaican stores did not. Thus, the Chinese stores could easily manipulate retail prices, while those owned by Afro-Jamaicans were rigidly controlled by a small margin of profit (Chang 1956:83–84).

The control of the wholesale grocery business by the Chinese is an influential factor in the retail grocery business mainly because they supplied the majority of retail shops in Jamaica, especially in the Kingston Metropolitan Area. In 1946, there were 14 leading wholesale provision merchants in Jamaica, 10 of which were Chinese. In 1954, there were 46 wholesale grocers on the island, 38 of which were Chinese (Chang 1956:85). In Kingston, Chinese wholesalers were located within a few blocks along Barry Street and Princess Street, areas once known as Kingston's "Chinatown."[16] Although Chinese residents moved away from downtown Kingston by the 1950s, many relocated to adjacent outlying areas in St. Andrew designated as part of the Kingston Metropolitan Area.

In addition to the wholesale sector, the Chinese businesses included manufacturing, a supporter of the retail business because it produced products such as bread, soft drinks, ice cream, soap, and margarine. These products were manufactured in Chinese-owned factories and sold in Chinese retail grocery stores. The baking industry is another major manufacturing business that was under almost total Chinese influence during the 1950s, especially in the areas of Spanish Town, Montego Bay, St. Elizabeth, Portland, and St. Mary (Chang 1956:88).[17]

The beverage industry, specifically soft drink bottling, also had a significant Chinese presence. Though they did not control the entire industry, the concentration of business remained with Chinese-owned companies, where almost half of the soft drinks sold each year during the mid-1950s were bottled in the five Chinese-owned bottling companies. The largest individual industrial enterprise was the Chinese-owned soap factory that manufactured soap, margarine, and edible fats and oils (Chang 1956:89–90). These expansions into the manufacture of various kinds of products and the wholesale grocery trade helped to further develop the Chinese grocery retail sector.

The Chinese resourcefulness in trade and import provisions contributed to their economic development. Chinese who migrated to Jamaica beginning in the mid-1850s preferred working in trade.[18] Many of the original immigrants were "farmers or the sons of farmers" (Yin 1963:55) from the Kwangtung province, where farming was the basic livelihood (Freedman 1958:9). Chinese participation in commercial pursuits in wholesale and retail trade is explained as a natural development from agriculture in southeast China. One shop owner explained, "it [Chinese grocery retail shops] originated in China. It's, like, in our genes."[19] Chinese immigrants in both the earlier and later waves of immigration had both some agricultural background and commercial background in trading. Therefore, Chinese participation in trade is neither coincidental nor accidental. For the original immigrants, trade was a familiar alternative (or supplement) to agricultural laboring. Chinese migrants from the area of the Kwangtung province, who spoke the Hakka dialect, were oriented toward trade (Levy 1967:3). The inter-regional migrations in China by the Hakka speakers were stimulated by many complex circumstances including the search for economic opportunity (Clementi 1915).

Popular literature and the media emphasize Chinese presence in grocery retail in Jamaica. From the perspective of the Jamaican society, the immigration of Chinese indentured servants was seen as an "invasion" and was commonly referred to as "The Chinese Invasion." Local official sources also reported a perceived control of the grocery retail trade.[20] Despite the impression the literature projects of Chinese dominance in grocery retail, however, it cannot be characterized as a monopoly. Levy states that the "so-called monopoly of the grocery trade of Jamaica on the part of the Chinese, is constituted not so much in the proprietorship of the majority of such establishments in the island, but rather in the volume of business enjoyed by the Chinese shopkeepers in comparison with that conducted by retailers belonging to other ethnic groups" (Levy 1967:18). The persistence of this myth is due to the fact that Chinese grocery retail shops tended to be more visible because they were concentrated in urban areas and because a large percentage of the Chinese population were involved in these kinds of business activities and other related businesses. The myth persisted, not because Chinese actually owned more stores than other ethnic groups, but because their businesses were more successful.

The success of Chinese retail grocery has been attributed to several factors. First, the Jamaican economy was in need of these kinds of services prior to the Chinese arrival but they had not been established hitherto by other Jamaicans or Jamaican immigrants (Levy 1967). The emancipation of slaves had effects that offered other employment. Trade increased because the ex-slaves now had to buy their food, clothing, and essential equipment. Also, they produced more for sale and export themselves, particularly of minor crops. All this meant openings for retailers, tally clerks, porters, boatmen, stevedores, and so forth (Angier 1961: 188). In addition, from the formerly centralized residence pattern of the pre-emancipation period, the dispersion of the population more evenly throughout the island increased the need for retail outlets (Silin 1962:16). Second, the Chinese had prior experience in petty trade and were therefore pre-adapted to the hard work required of a successful retail grocer. The Chinese were the only people who could stand the unbearable long hours of grocery stores. It was this generally unattractive occupation that gave the Chinese settlers their start in business (Yin 1963:45). The proliferation and success of Chinese shops are also attributed to the belief that the Chinese were hard workers who lived modestly[21] and followed Confucian concepts that dictated family interest as a priority over the individual (Levy 1967:21). Third, it was argued that the educated Colored class was seeking to emulate the whites rather than go into grocery retail. The majority of the educated Colored population channeled their interests into the professions and civil service in an attempt to emulate whites (Silin 1962:17). Therefore, the Chinese would not have gained control in the grocery trade so quickly if the educated colored people had not become committed to the professions and the civil service as status-bearing occupations (Broom 1954:125).

A final claim proposed a purported lack of competition because (a) "The whites were too few in number and too high in status to be willing to demean themselves by serving their former slaves, and they were unwilling to work the long, hard hours for small returns which shop keeping entailed" (Silin 1962:17) and (b) "The Africans were not acquainted with the ways of commerce and the scope of the work they actually participated in was limited in labour." It was claimed that Africans had "a carefree nature and did not like the hard grind of six in the morning to midnight which the shop life called for." (Yin 1963:45). Thus, it was contended, "Negroes lacked both the initiative and desire for work which required long hours, as well as patience." (Silin 1962:17).

However, while the initial success of the Chinese in grocery retail may have been attributed to prior experience and the island's needs for food provisions for trade, other sources claim there was indeed competition from established Afro-Jamaican businesses. Levy states that the Chinese did face competition but were able to eliminate local competitors who were already established in the retail trade (Levy 1967:5). The Chinese arrived in the mid-nineteenth century, during a period of significant expansion in the consumer market, which allowed them to capitalize with more alacrity and with greater efficiency than did potential traders within the local community (Levy 1967:5). Other sources illustrate that Afro-Jamaicans were involved in considerable numbers in grocery retail. The first official report compiled by the Collector General's Department in 1908 reveals that the Chinese owned 13 percent of the grocery retail shops whereas the Afro-Jamaican population owned 78 percent.[22] Given this fact, the question becomes, what factors were involved in enabling the Chinese to capture the consumer market in those areas that had the greatest volume of trade and consequently where operating a shop would prove economically beneficial?

During early periods of immigration, Chinese men who had migrated to Jamaica came alone and were much freer to travel. They had no local financial obligations because of domestic ties. Therefore, they could locate in areas that were most suitable for opening a shop, accumulate capital, and then send for family members. However, Afro-Jamaican entrepreneurs were said to be "limited in their attempts to accumulate capital by the demands of domestic commitments, and the restrictions imposed by social conventions" (Levy 1967:20). The

Afro-Jamaican tradesmen of Jamaica were said to be handicapped by the needs of relatives and friends while the immigrant Chinese found in trade the one field of economic endeavor in which their status as single tradesmen was an asset rather than a liability (Lind 1958:154).

Single status may have proved beneficial for early tradesmen; however, family membership for the Chinese came to play a significant role in the success of these shops. Since their businesses were family-run, additional hiring costs could be avoided and families lived and worked at the same place, also saving money. This character of Chinese shop lifestyle influenced the growth of grocery retail shops. As capital was acquired, owners sent for family members, and as immigration increased, agnatic ties became useful for obtaining credit. Family members who had already resided in Jamaica would assist new residents by providing information for ideal locations for shops as well as capital to begin a business.[23]

The economic success enjoyed by the Chinese, as well as the impression of a closed, family-based trading community, contributed to an atmosphere of anti-Chinese discrimination. Because the Chinese grocery shops were mostly family-centric, it was believed that they denied others employment opportunities and were concerned only with the Chinese family's continued economic success. Native Jamaicans accused the Chinese of being overly concerned with material wealth. In an article in the journal *Spotlight,* one writer echoed accusations of parasitism leveled at Chinese communities across the colonial and post-colonial world: "Stop giving the impression that you are interested in grabbing and scraping all you can out of the island to take back to China. Forget about China."[24]

During the early and middle decades of the twentieth century, press references toward the Chinese were often derogatory, using labels such as "Celestial" or "Chinaman." In a letter to the *Star,* one writer claimed that ". . . the reason for the apparent discrimination is not racial but economic, because these small concerns are profitable only when operated on a family basis. These concerns pay no salaries and money is withdrawn only for the . . . operation and living expenses. Consequently, the meager profits accumulate and the capital grows until it is sufficiently large to provide a good standard of living for the operators."[25]

The public letters cited social factors as well in their criticism, charging the Chinese community with being socially exclusive and isolating. In a 1952 article in *Spotlight,* one writer stated, "The Chinese take full advantage of all the facilities the community offers, yet such facilities as they have as a group are reserved for Chinese only. Examples: only Chinese are employed in Chinese business; only Chinese kids are accepted in the Chinese public school; only Chinese are admitted to membership in the Chinese Athletic Club . . ."[26] As Chinese business organizations and social organizations developed, negative media attention increased, spreading anti-Chinese rhetoric.

Social Factors: Organizations and Networks

Chinese organizations[27] were developed to facilitate social and economic networks. They helped to promote social cohesion for and to foster economic conditions within the Chinese community in Jamaica. Organizations created schools in an effort to sustain Chinese cultural traditions, teach Chinese language, and strengthen ties within the community. Organizations also provided information about ideal locations for setting up shops, helped locate available housing, and offered financial assistance for businesses. This type of networking throughout the island created social and economic interdependence between members of the Chinese community—and independence from the larger Jamaican community. It fostered an image of the Chinese as deliberately "isolating" yet also gave rise to positive results such as a strong Chinese economy and coherent Chinese cultural identity.

Toward the end of the twentieth century, social organizations served less as locations for economic networking, especially as the workforce grew more diversified, becoming instead social gathering places for elder populations. One organization member explained how this significantly impacted the economic independence and success of the Chinese community, especially in comparison to the Chinese in other countries. He stated, "When you go to Toronto, the Chinese there have a complete economy, in any profession. They are actually like a small country, like Hong Kong. They have all type of services.

They are completely independent. They don't have to rely on any non-Chinese. Whatever, you need to look at what they have. As opposed to here. They are able to retain more cultural background. We were not able to retain as much as they. I can see one or two reasons. One of which is because we do not have a full economy we have to rely on outside people. You need to communicate or do your things in a non-Chinese way in order to achieve it. Because Chinatown in the U.S. and Canada is so big they can afford to have training, and because of that they can retain more of the Chinese tradition. Also population, they are in constant flux of new immigrants who will bring in news, the down to earth culture."[28]

While some Jamaican-Chinese expressed a preference for maintaining this kind of networking system in order to preserve "Chinese tradition" as expressed above, others did not. The differences in attitude are partly due to the differences between local-born and foreign-born Chinese.[29] These differences are also reflected in the different types of organizations to which the local Chinese belong and their members' views of maintaining and furthering Chinese schools, language, and culture. Some organizations actively seek to preserve Chinese traditions, while others seek to be more integrated within the larger community of the island. However, the ultimate goals—safeguarding the future of the younger generation and the Chinese community in Jamaica—were the same.

Identity and Interethnic Relations

The diversity among Chinese populations across the globe, and even throughout the Caribbean, raises critical questions as to what exactly constitutes a "Chinese" community. The Jamaican-Chinese community is primarily determined by membership within the network of local-born Chinese and foreign-born Chinese. Demographics have strongly influenced the development of the Jamaican-Chinese community and its interaction within the larger multi-ethnic community of the island. The Chinese community has tended to be small in number even though it is the third largest group after the Afro-Jamaican and East Indian populations. The first Chinese immigrants—mainly male since few Chinese women were imported—initially affected demographics through common-law unions with Afro-Jamaican women. These women were often helpers in Chinese shops. Although this form of "marriage" became very common, the parents of the young male did not generally accept it. However, it was uncommon for Chinese women to marry Afro-Jamaican men, and as the pool of Chinese or mixed Chinese women grew, to marry someone Chinese or half Chinese became preferable. Young, Jamaica-born, full Chinese men were expected to marry a woman of at least the same economic status. Even the young mixed Chinese women were frowned upon because they tended to be children born of Negro women out of wedlock and they tended to come from a lower economic status.

Patterns of intermarriage changed partly because of the demographic shifts within the Chinese populations—increase among Chinese and mixed Chinese women—and also because of increasing acceptance of interracial unions. Mixed unions were once preferred with women who were "red-skinned," "clear-skinned," or "light-skinned" since skin color has a correlation to class status. The earlier bias toward lighter skin is purported to be a matter of preference for skin lightness rather than on the basis of whether one is "Afro-Jamaican."[30]

By the end of the twentieth century, intermarriage between Chinese women and Afro-Jamaican men was still a rare occurrence even though interracial dating was increasing amongst the younger generations. It was more common for a Chinese man to enter into a union with an Afro-Jamaican woman, and legal marriages were rare. Families did not approve of interracial dating, but interracial marriage elicited the greater protest. Racial mixtures would be viewed negatively when they were obvious, and families also attempted to conceal the knowledge of racial mixing in the family.

The relations between the Chinese and the Jamaican communities outside of dating and marriage near the turn of the twenty-first century became more amiable and did not reflect the kind of anti-Sinitic aura that existed prior to 1965. Public comments before 1965 were mainly influenced by the economic prosperity of the Chinese but expanded to include other areas as the Chinese were charged with being "clannish," "isolating" and "close-knit" despite the increasing occurrence of interracial marriage."[31] Their social and business organizations were resented and their successes in economic ventures were targeted.

Jamaica had three significant anti-Chinese riots. The first riot, in 1918, was initiated by the two-day disappearance of an Afro-Jamaican police officer that was blamed on a Chinese shopkeeper. Angry Afro-Jamaicans in the parishes of St. Mary and St. Catherine, and even others outside these communities, looted and destroyed Chinese grocery shops. Although there were shops owned by other Jamaicans, Chinese shops were targeted (Johnson 1983:2). The hostility was attributed to the jealousy aroused by the commercial success of the Chinese community sparked by the alleged abduction, which was quickly determined to be a rumor (Johnson 1983:3). The Chinese at this time were viewed as aliens and outsiders (Johnson 1983:3) and the extent of their economic activity made them very visible at the local level. In addition, the 1918 riot occurred during the late stages of World War I, a time of scarce resources, which increased the likelihood that such an event could escalate (Johnson 1983:6).

The second riot, in 1938, was the culmination of widespread anti-Chinese bias that resulted in island-wide looting and rioting in December of that year (Silin 1962:63). Again the rioting has been attributed to the economic conditions of Jamaica at that time. The Jamaican economy was hit hard by the depression of the 1920s and 1930s, and under such conditions, the Chinese, because of their economic standing, became the target of Afro-Jamaican antagonism (Silin 1962:64). Chinese shops tended to do well during periods of war when prices for goods soared.

The riot of 1965 occurred in the downtown area of Kingston, referred to at that time as "Chinatown," after a Chinese proprietor of a bakery was accused of beating one of his Black female employees. As with the earlier riots, the Chinese bakery and other Chinese establishment were attacked. The looting of Chinese shops during this riot has also been associated with bad economic conditions (Lyn-Shue 1979). Chinese shops were located in poorer Jamaican communities, and as such were seen as prospering at Jamaican expense. This was especially the case during economically depressed times. However, the fact that it was only Chinese establishments that were looted, even in areas where "Creole" shops existed, indicates that regional and national antagonism toward the Chinese community also played a role in the looting.

As the preceding discussion shows, Afro-Jamaicans are often cited as the source of anti-Chinese antagonism (Levy 1967, Morrow 1972, Johnson 1983). The reason given is that Chinese prosperity in grocery retail is believed to have threatened and displaced members of the larger community. In the *Daily Gleaner*, one article read, "the Chinese are very enterprising in their methods of trade, and hence they have ousted the native shop-keeper. Owing to their success, the Chinese are regarded jealously; and the warping effect of this jealousy, made the villagers of Edwarton (and other places) foolishly ready to believe that Constable McDonald had been murdered by the Chinaman."[32]

While Chinese business owners in retail grocery were perceived as a threat to the native shopkeepers, numerically they did not monopolize the grocery market; their numbers were, in fact, quite small compared to those of Afro-Jamaicans. Rather, it was their visibility and location in urban areas where they catered to the poor that accounted for their high profile and possibly contributed to their perception as a parasitic monopoly. The Chinese shopkeeper is the middleman, a position that puts him in a precarious position. In one newspaper article the Chinese shopkeeper is described as "an essential economic link between the village community of peasants and outside world. As a result, he is often in the community, but he is seldom really of it. Economically he is a member, but culturally he is not, and it is this, which lies at the root of the peasants' ambivalent and often violent, attitude toward him. The peasant needs him, but dislikes him."[33]

In another statement made in the *New World Fortnightly* one writer claimed that "the Chinese retailers are at one and the same time the grocers and bankers for many of the working people. They supply daily bread and provide much-needed credit. They act partly as a social security system, partly as an unemployment relief agency. For all these services they have to be paid—covertly, by way of high retail margins. But their high retail margins do not endear them to their customers."[34]

Hostilities escalated during the first half of the twentieth century, with Chinese immigrants being treated as aliens. While they were accused of lacking allegiance to Jamaica, they were also denied recognition as Jamaicans. The Chinese were the targets of other forms of discrimination. They were charged with being deceptive and dishonest. "It is true he seldom gets into the poor house, but on his account somebody else gets there. He will sell you less: he adulterates everything even champagne...His success is due to the fact that he sells to people who cannot detect, it is not because he has sharp business intellect, but that it is sharpened by the fact that he knows no bound—the sin in China being not to steal, but being caught. He sells any putrified stuff because he does not eat it himself, but buys beef, pork and chicken at the expense of the poor people who have to eat his nasty products. He has forced some of our best people out of shopkeeping, besides he is very immoral and on this account alone, ought to be kept out" (Johnson 1983:4).

Hostility toward the Chinese ranged from large riots and attacks on Chinese settlements to individual confrontations, though attacks were few in number. No major hostile uprisings against the Chinese have occurred since 1965, although many people point to more subtle forms of discrimination toward individuals. For example, a Chinese person in Jamaica, whether Jamaican-born or foreign-born, would be commonly referred to as "Ms. (Mr.) Chin" even when the correct family name is known.[35] Chin is a common Chinese name in Jamaica because many of the first immigrants were given this name on arrival.

While some have claimed that the antagonism toward the Chinese arose from the friction between the Chinese shopkeeper and his customers or by competition with Afro-Jamaican retailers, others have claimed a different source. Many of the deep-seated anti-Chinese sentiments of the late nineteenth and early twentieth centuries were not held by the majority of the population but rather were confined to a small white minority who resented the economic success of the Chinese. (Silin 1962:64). Given some important facts, this hypothesis has some validity. The first official documented report of the commercial activities of the Chinese was compiled in 1908 by the Collector General's Department, on the activities of grocery retail trade by ethnic groups. The Chinese were reported as participating in 13.2 percent of the trade with East Indians and Syrians, holding 7.1 percent and 1.4 percent, respectively. The native population had the majority of 78.4 percent, according to the report. Although the Chinese holdings of only 13.2 percent of the grocery retail market could not be designated as a monopoly, by 1910 a general impression had been created that the Chinese were a serious threat to Creole shopkeepers (Levy 1967:15).

The media, owned by the elite, were largely responsible for the creating an image of national criticism of the Chinese. The spread of this news brought widespread resistance to the continuation of unrestricted Chinese immigration. During the first century of Chinese immigration, beginning in the mid-1850s, strict guidelines were set by British officials to make sure that Chinese immigrants would remain only a short while on the island. The fact that few women and children accompanied the men and the fact that poor laborers were preferred as indentured servants illustrates that the colonial government intentionally set guidelines to avoid a large influx of Chinese migrants that would settle as permanent residents.

Laws restricting Chinese immigration into Jamaica stated that "(1) All Chinese immigrants must be registered with Immigration authorities upon entry into the island; (2) All Chinese immigrants must procure a guarantee from a reliable concern (sic) stating that the immigrant was a law abiding person and would not become a public burden; (3) After landing all Chinese immigrants must register their address with the concerned authorities" (Yin 1963:8). These laws became more restrictive as the economic prosperity of the Chinese grew.

In 1910, the newer laws stated that (1) All aliens entering Jamaica must make a deposit of 30 pounds; (2) Before landing, all immigrants must pass a language test, which consisted of oral and written tests in English, French or Spanish; (3) All aliens must pass a physical examination, which barred anyone with infectious diseases from landing (Yin 1963:8–9). For the next 40 years, immigration laws continued to be restrictive. In January 1931, the Hong Kong government received notification that no passports were to be issued to Chinese bound for Jamaica. This virtually ended all Chinese entry into Jamaica, except for school-age children under 14 with student permits. In an edition of the *Daily Gleaner* in 1932, a column read: "We are not actuated by racial feelings when we ask: Why should Jamaica open her doors wide to Chinese immigration, when but few of her sons and daughters can migrate to nearby countries to enter larger fields of industry? Why should Chinese . . . be allowed to over-run this country to an extent which has placed the retail grocery trade in the hands of persons from the former Flowery Kingdom?"[36]

As the number of trade licenses issued to the Chinese in the retail grocery trade increased, so did the legal restrictions. In 1936, there were 9,265 trade licenses issued, of which the Chinese received 16 percent (Levy 1967:17). In 1940, all Chinese, except for diplomatic officers, tourists and students with permits, were barred from entering the island (Yin 1963:9). In 1947 the Chinese were allowed an annual quota of 20 immigrants to enter the island. It increased by 20 more the following year. However, in 1956 this additional quota was banned. At this time, surveys taken by the *Daily Gleaner* indicated that the majority of shops were operated by "Creole" proprietors and not by persons of Chinese descent (Levy 1967:17).

The myth of the Chinese population as monopolizer of the retail grocery trade has initiated a great deal of friction between the Chinese and Afro-Jamaicans. However, it is unclear whether the source came from the general Jamaican community or the few privileged elite. In fact, there have been positive relations between Chinese shopkeepers and their customers because shopkeepers often "[gave] their customers better service, including free delivery and buying on credit" (Levy 1967:22). In some cases the prosperity of Chinese businessmen has been viewed in a positive way, implying that it is thrift and hard work that contribute to the success of Chinese retail. The Chinese grocer popularized the notion of selling the smallest quantities of goods for correspondingly small denominations.[37] Some shop owners claim that the reluctance of others to do the same detracted from their own success. There was even a tendency for Afro-Jamaicans to purchase from Chinese shopkeepers rather than other Afro-Jamaicans[38] because the Chinese shopkeepers seemed more willing (and able) to sell products more cheaply or on credit (Levy 1967; Chang 1956).

The character of the shops—the fact that they kept long hours, sold small quantities, provided a wider and better range of products, were visible in urban areas, sold on credit and gave better bargains—created conditions on which many Afro-Jamaicans depended. Therefore, relations between Chinese shopkeepers and their Afro-Jamaican customers may not always have been strained, as newspaper articles and official reports suggested. Finally, the cautionary steps taken by British officials indicate that the official government had some initial unrest about the future of these immigrants. Subsequent immigration restrictions enacted by the colonial government were evidence of their growing concern of the Chinese presence in Jamaica.

Articles printed in the local newspapers sustained negative portrayals of Chinese shopkeepers. A frequent allegation was that the Chinese avoided paying taxes and recorded their sales ledgers in Chinese to deceive tax collectors. At other times they were accused of exploiting bankruptcy laws in order to avoid paying their creditors (Levy 1967:25). An early report in the *Daily Gleaner* stated that ". . . a Chinese shopkeeper doing business at Montego Bay will spend the next three months in jail for not keeping proper books of accounts as required by law. The debtor went into bankruptcy a short time ago, and it is said that his liabilities amounted to an enormous sum. The only books that were produced were some small pass books written in Chinese" (Levy 1967:26). Ideas such as this did not take into consideration that many Chinese were unfamiliar with the country's laws and customs, and therefore recorded the information in a manner manageable for the shop owner. Much of the antagonism expressed by the general Jamaican community was directed in response to the perceived threat of the image of the affluent Chinese created through media and legislation.

After the decline of Chinese businesses in the 1970s, negative images of the Chinese in the media decreased and relations between the Chinese and the larger Jamaican community did not reflect the belligerent feelings that had once existed. The changes were also attributed to the continual contact between Afro-Jamaicans and Chinese-Jamaicans and to Jamaica's national campaign to create an independent and united country reflecting the motto "Out of Many, One People."

Conclusion

In summary, the character of Chinese-owned retail grocery shops helped to foster economic success and consolidate Chinese ethnic identity. These economic establishments assisted the growth of an emerging Chinese community by creating social and economic networks through which members could encourage relations and community assistance. They also facilitated the rise to the middle class, an important feature of Chinese identity. The economic activity in the retail grocery trade also contributed to antagonistic relations between ethnic groups in Jamaica as evidenced through media portrayals, stricter immigration laws, and riots during economically difficult periods. The perceived Chinese dominance of the grocery retail industry, however, may be understood as a myth arising from the location and high visibility of the shops, their large volume of business, and the high level of involvement among the Chinese population.

This examination of Chinese ethnicity and Sino-Jamaican relations in Kingston, Jamaica, illustrates how economic and social factors have been instrumental in the construction and maintenance of Chinese ethnicity and interethnic relations. The success of the Chinese, particularly in the grocery retail industry, contributed to some marginalization. However, the interaction between Afro-Jamaicans and Chinese Jamaicans—rather than isolation—facilitated the process of ethnic group formation. Ethnic identity is created with interaction, based on a perceived shared sense of origin and descent and maintained by social and economic networks.[39] The Chinese did not come to Jamaica as a group (Patterson 1988)[40]; rather it was the social and economic conditions that affected the construction of a group from a category and influenced patterns of interethnic relations.

PART II
Cuba

When the ship finally reached
Regla, across the bay from
Havana, Chen Pan climbed to
the top deck to get a better view.
. . . When Chen Pan tried to
stand on the dock, his legs slid
out from under him. Others fell,
too. Together, he and his ship-
mates looked like a spilled barrel
of crabs.

—Cristina García, *Monkey Hunting*
(New York: Alfred A. Knopf, 2003), p. 20

CHAPTER 5

"One Brings Another": The Formation of Early-Twentieth-Century Chinese Migrant Communities in Cuba

Kathleen López

In March of 1923, eight Chinese vegetable cultivators returned from a morning of selling their produce in Cienfuegos, Cuba, to discover that the door to their residence had been broken. Bundles of money in the amounts of $120, $38, and $18 were missing from a case. The local newspaper—in addition to reporting their misfortune—noted the following: "On Santa Clara and Esperanza Streets the industrious Asians Antonio Gong, Fernando, Manuel, Alfonso, Mario, Benito, Ramón, and Martín, all of the surname Jhon, have a magnificent vegetable garden and dedicate all the hours of the day to extract what is necessary to live and to save 'a little something' for when they go to Cantón."[1] This report provides a glimpse into the everyday, lived experiences of Chinese migrants in Cuba. These men, who most likely came from the same village in Guangdong province, formed part of a network of support for housing and employment in their Cuban environment. They saved their earnings, however meager, for a return trip to their village in China, where these networks would be renewed. This essay examines the development of Chinese merchant communities in early-twentieth-century Cuba and the transnational ties Chinese migrants maintained with home villages.

The Power of Sugar: Indenture, Early Chinese Communities, and the Second "Wave" of Chinese Immigration to Cuba

The first major migration of Chinese to Cuba began in 1847 with a massive scheme to import indentured laborers for Cuban sugar plantations prior to and during the period of gradual abolition of slavery in the Spanish colony. Approximately 142,000 men, mostly from southeastern Guangdong province, left for Cuba between 1847 and 1874. The coolie trade ended after a Chinese imperial commission investigated abuses in the system in 1874. Enforced recontracting ensured that most Chinese who survived their first term of indenture continued to serve for another eight years. After the end of the coolie trade, the population of Chinese in Cuba declined through secondary migration to the United States and other parts of Latin America and the Caribbean, a relatively small return migration to China, and deaths.[2]

As early as 1858 some former coolies had established themselves as small entrepreneurs in the *barrio chino* or Chinatown in Havana and by the 1870s in other Cuban cities. Chinese settlements were further buoyed by the arrival of an estimated 5,000 Chinese from California and Mexico to Cuba between 1860 and 1875.[3] Most former coolies in the late nineteenth century continued working as day laborers on sugar plantations. Under the *cuadrilla* system, a Chinese contractor recruited and organized free Chinese into work gangs for plantations, construction, and shipyard docks. Besides day laborers, Chinese became truck gardeners, domestic servants, shopkeepers, cigarmakers, itinerant peddlers, charcoal burners, and launderers. By 1899, official census data reported 8,035 Chinese laborers in Cuba (8,033 males and 2 females), 2,160 Chinese domestic servants (including 6 females), and 1,923 Chinese merchants in Cuba.[4] Some Chinese targeted American employers in Cuba for household positions, as exemplified in the following advertisement: "Chinaman cook wants position in American or English family, either in city or country. Makes good pastry. Address No. 139 Campanario Street."[5]

After 1899, Chinese labor immigration to Cuba was restricted, but re-initiated in response to a demand for agricultural labor to boost sugar production during World War I. During the twentieth century, the greatest numbers of Chinese migrants entered Cuba from 1917 to 1930.[6] (See table 5.1 for official census data.)

Table 5.1
Chinese Population of Cuba according to
Official Census Figures, 1861–1970

Census	Total	Males	Percent	Females	Percent
1861	34,828	34,771	99.83	57	.17
1877	40,327	40,261	99.84	66	.16
1887	28,752	28,694	99.80	58	.20
1899	14,863	14,814	99.67	49	.33
1907	11,217	11,166	99.55	51	.45
1919	10,300	10,016	97.20	284	2.76
1931	24,647	24,445	99.18	202	.82
1943	15,822	15,657	98.96	165	1.04
1953	11,834	11,350	95.91	484	4.09
1970	5,892	5,710	96.91	182	3.09

Source: Baltar, *Los Chinos de Cuba: Apuntes etnográficos*, 90.

By the early twentieth century, Chinese had formed bustling communities in Havana and other provincial towns. The six major blocks of Havana's Chinatown were lined with small commercial establishments such as restaurants, bodegas, laundries, shoe and watch repair shops, bakeries, photography studios, and pharmacies. There were also theaters, four newspapers, a cemetery, two bilingual schools (one Catholic and one Presbyterian), a hospital, and a residence for the elderly. According to contemporary sources, Havana's *barrio chino* became one of the best-known in the Americas, where Chinese in the United States spoke of these streets, even in Spanish.[7] Chinese shopkeepers generally lived in their workplaces with family members and co-workers.[8] Shops became centers for informal gatherings of immigrant men, providing remittance and letter-writing services and informal public space for discussions of business, circulation of hometown news, and socializing. Unlike the majority of coolies from the previous century, these migrants were better able to maintain links with their hometowns in China.

The Power of Networks: Chinese Occupational Niches in Cuba

As scholars of Chinese overseas have noted, members of the same dialect groups in China tended to settle in the same regions and occupations overseas. They facilitated migration of others from the same surname group by providing housing and employment support in the foreign environment. Most migrants to Cuba were from the Pearl River Delta of Guangdong Province. The *san yi* (three counties) Chinese were from Nanhai, Panyu, and Shunde Counties, more urbanized areas located closer to the city of Guangzhou (Canton). In twentieth-century Cuba, they became import merchants, grocers, butchers, and tailors. Chinese from Jiujiang, Nanhai County, represented the economic elite of the Chinese merchant community, dominating the powerful Chinese Chamber of Commerce in Havana.[9] The *si yi* (four counties) Chinese were from the overwhelmingly agricultural Taishan, Xinhui, Kaiping, and Enping Counties. They mostly began as laborers but rapidly moved into other occupations. Between 1920 and 1930 the majority of Chinese came from these areas and neighboring Zhongshan, with more than half from Taishan. By 1942, 40.77 percent of the 18,484 Chinese registered with the Chinese Consulate were from Taishan, and only 43 were from outside of Guangdong province. These trends continued through the 1950s and are reflected in a 1980 census taken by the Casino Chung Wah of the remaining elderly Chinese population in Cuba.[10] (See table 5.2).

Table 5.2

Chinese Residents in Cuba according to Home District, 1980

County in China	Residents in Cuba
Taishan	1,736
Xinhui	974
Enping	445
Kaiping	394
Nanhai	452
Zhongshan	301
Total	4,302

Source: Baltar, *Los Chinos de Cuba: Apuntes etnográficos*, 92.

According to the chronicler of the nineteenth-century Chinese "colony" in Cuba, Antonio Chuffat Latour, the Taishanese sold fruits and vegetables and worked on sugar estates, and migrants from neighboring Xinhui had shops in the city of Havana and elsewhere worked as confectioners, cooks, vendors of meat and fish, and as "itinerant peddlers that we find daily on our streets." He emphasized that the Xinhui Chinese never had luxury goods shops for perfume, household wares, and silk.[11] Although migrants from Taishan and Xinhui generally formed the lower socioeconomic strata in Cuba, the actual patterns of occupational mobility were much more fluid than Chuffat proposed.

One of these Xinhui migrants in the early twentieth century was Lü Fan, known as Francisco Luis in Cuba. In 1918 at the age of 18 he migrated to Cuba with fellow villagers also surnamed "Lü." Like many Chinese throughout the diaspora, Lü Fan initially worked on a sugar plantation for a brief period before becoming a vendor of fruits and vegetables in Cienfuegos. Peddlers typically carried two baskets on a bamboo pole balanced on the shoulders or pulled them in a cart. Before dawn Lü Fan went to the local market to purchase fresh produce from truck gardeners. Carting it through his neighborhood, he maintained a regular supply of Cuban customers.[12] Peddling fruits and vegetables required comparatively little capital. Unlike shops, restaurants, inns, and pharmacies, only access to truck gardeners and a loyal customer base were necessary. Although he was not one of the wealthier merchants in Cienfuegos, Lü Fan generated enough income through his small business to support families on both sides of the ocean and to fund several return trips to Lü Village.

Return trips were a goal even for lower-income Chinese in Cuba, who guarded savings in cases or under floorboards. Others depended on a stroke of good fortune. For example, in April of 1934 the front page of a Cienfuegos newspaper reported that after winning the national lottery, "two humble Chinese" from Rancho Veloz gave their fruitstand to "a fellow countryman" before they embarked on a train to Havana and from there continued on a journey back to China.[13]

Remittances and Return:
The Significance of Migration for Guangdong Villages

By the first part of the twentieth century, Chinese migration to Cuba had become a dual-sided, network-driven process.[14] Men working abroad maintained strong ties to their home villages through remittances, investments, and return visits. Economic and social achievement for Chinese in Cuba was in large part defined by the maintenance of these transnational links to home villages in China. With enhanced wealth, expertise, and social standing, some formerly marginal Chinese who had worked as laborers or merchants abroad became increasingly influential when they returned. They were often hoisted on a chair and escorted through the village. Some became local political leaders, school principals, and newspaper editors.[15]

In Guangdong and Fujian provinces, *qiaoxiang*, or emigrant hometowns, had developed where returned overseas Chinese and their dependents were (and are) concentrated. Recent scholarship has focused on the "transnational" aspects of the international migration process. However, like other movements of people past and present, migration from Guangdong province to Cuba can perhaps be more accurately described as "translocal." The patterns of Chinese transnationalism were based on sustaining ties with specific *qiaoxiang*.

Within one administrative unit in China, different villages were affected by different chains of migration overseas. Several villages in Taishan and Xinhui Counties historically sent the majority of their men to Cuba (rather than the United States or Southeast Asia) in the early twentieth century. Today, village elders in Guangdong aptly describe the network-driven migration process with the phrase "one brings another" (*yi ge dai yi ge*). Sons followed fathers and uncles and brothers followed each other. For example, from 1919 to 1930, over 700 men from the town of Dulian in Xinhui County went to Cuba to work in sugar production and road construction. During this period almost every family in Dulian had one relative in Cuba.[16]

Given the expense of return trips, letters and remittances were the primary means of maintaining transnational ties to China. Most remittances from Cuba were managed unofficially by shops and associations on both sides of the ocean.[17] For this reason, detailed records are sparse for the 1920s and 1930s. To ensure against fraud, Chinese migrants always included the amount of the remittance in their accompanying letters. An existing record from the Guangdong post office during the Nationalist era reveals who sent remittances from Southeast Asia and the Americas and who received them, county by county, town by town. Chinese who sent money home had settled in towns throughout Cuba. In addition to Havana, where the largest number of Chinese were concentrated, remittances also came from Matanzas, Cárdenas, Jovellanos, Colón, Cienfuegos, Santa Clara, Remedios, Camagüey, Bayamo, and Santiago de Cuba. The majority of the remittances from Cuba sent through the post office were from Chinese of Jiujiang, Nanhai County (75 out of a total of 137).[18] Although migrants from the "four counties" of Taishan, Xinhui, Enping, and Kaiping were numerically stronger, they sent fewer remittances that year than migrants from Nanhai. This imbalance is most likely a reflection of the predilection of the wealthier, more urbanized Jiujiang Chinese for using official government remittance services. These official government numbers do not include the thousands of remittances sent annually through traditional immigrant organizations.[19]

In addition to sending remittances to families, Chinese in Cuba also shaped local Guangdong society through the building of railroads, hospitals, schools, ancestral temples, and houses and the establishment of modern banks, mining ventures, land reclamation projects, and steamship lines. Today, Chinese in the town of Shadui in Xinhui County point out the two- and three-story houses built by returned Chinese from Cuba in the early decades of the twentieth century. Towering above the rest of the village and incorporating Western architectural traits, these houses are typical of Guangdong *qiaoxiang* in the 1920s and 1930s.[20]

Besides remittances, information and goods traveled to China via migrant circuits. Migrants from Dulian filled letters with news about business, wages for manual labor, and safety conditions abroad. They sent Western-style suits, vests, and hats to their relatives back home (which the Dulian village elders today still proudly wear).[21] Men from neighboring Meige worked on sugar plantations and in restaurants in Cuba in the 1920s. At times, along with letters and money, they sent a coarse, white sugar back home.[22]

Although Chinese migrants lived in "bachelor societies" in the Americas, the majority of them were married or intended to marry upon their return to China. The general pattern in the late nineteenth and early twentieth centuries was for women to remain in home villages in China. This cultural norm, combined with the lack of Chinese females imported for prostitution in Cuba, produced a migration that was almost exclusively male.[23] "Split-household families" developed from long-term separations between Chinese migrants and their wives. In a typical scenario, Chinese men working overseas provided financial support through remittances and ensured continuation of the family line through return trips. In an inversion of the traditional view of patriarchy, Chinese women who remained in their villages often became heads of household. Specifically, they tended to the fields, raised livestock, performed chores, engaged in cottage industries such as weaving and silk spinning, and were responsible for the education of the children. Often facing loneliness, alienation, and hardship, these women displayed flexibility and endurance in adapting to south China village life without their husbands.[24] The following accounts illustrate some facets of life among *qiaojuan*, or "overseas Chinese dependents," in Guangdong.

A "lifelong widow" and her son: the Liu family of Guanghai

Laishui Village in Guanghai, Taishan County, is a typical *qiaoxiang*, in which the majority of households depend on remittances from relatives overseas. Laishui consists of a total of 30 households. Of these, 11 sent men to Cuba, four to the United States, four to Burma, three to Canada, three to Hong Kong, two to Australia, and one to India. Thus, 93% of the village was formed by overseas Chinese households, and 37% of households had relatives in Cuba. The coastal region of Guanghai provided a convenient point of departure for emigrants, who proceeded through Hong Kong or Macao to board foreign ships destined for the Americas.

A meeting in Laishui with a scholar of Taishanese overseas history,

Liu Chongmin, uncovered the experiences of a typical "lifelong widow" and her son. Liu Chongmin recorded extensive interviews with his elderly mother, surnamed Ling, who died in 1995 at the age of 104. Mrs. Ling had remained in her Taishanese village, passing on oral history from three generations of her husband's family to her son.

In 1911 (well before immigration restrictions were officially lifted in Cuba), Liu Kongjiu went to Cuba at age 18 along with three brothers. In 1926 Liu Kongjiu made his first return trip to Laishui, building a new house adjacent to the family house and marrying. Mrs. Ling was acutely aware of the difficult life her husband led in Cuba. She described the harsh treatment received by Chinese in Cuba at the hands of sugar estate foremen and, later, her husband carrying laundry on his back until after midnight.

After their child died at a young age, Liu Kongjiu and his wife adopted the six-year-old Liu Chongmin. Long-term absences of immigrant men made producing heirs back home difficult. Thus, adoption became a viable—although not ideal—strategy for maintaining the family line. In this case, the adopted son (and only heir) Liu Chongmin remained in China with his mother. He developed an especially close relationship with her based on mutual dependence in the absence of his father. As the only son, Liu Chongmin said that he and his mother "leaned on each other" (*xiang yi wei ming*). Like many other women in Guangdong emigrant communities, Liu Chongmin's mother had lived most of her life without her husband. She was referred to as a "lifelong widow" (*shou sheng gua*), as opposed to a "chaste widow" or woman who does not remarry after the death of her husband. Out of the 11 men that went to Cuba from Guanghai, only two were able to reunite with their families at an old age.[25]

Life without father: The Lü sisters of Xinhui County

Distance and long stretches of time without communication had the potential to devastate transpacific family relations. Madeline Hsu states, "Even when letters and money crossed the Pacific at regular intervals, years of separation distanced husbands from wives, and children grew up ignorant of the contours of their fathers' faces. In the worst cases, Gold Mountain guests disappeared into the unknown wilds of the United States and abandoned wives remarried other men in Taishan."[26] The Lü family, divided between Xinhui County in Guangdong and the town of Cienfuegos in Cuba, offers a vivid portrait of the ability of a Chinese migrant and his descendants to maintain relations, despite the difficulties. Lü Fan (Francisco Luis) of Lü Village in Daze, Xinhui County, sold fruits and vegetables from a cart in the town of Cienfuegos. He returned to China three times. Following typical immigrant patterns, during his first return trip he built a new house, and on his second return trip in 1928, he married. All of the residents of Lü Village were invited to the extravagant wedding banquet. Lü Fan departed again for Cuba before the birth of his first daughter, Baoqin. In 1932 when Lü Fan made his third return trip to China, he stayed for one year, long enough to see the birth of his second daughter. He gave her a "Western" name, "Mali" or Mary. Lü Fan generally remitted funds once or twice each year. For special occasions, such as the marriage of one of his daughters or the birth of a grandchild, he sent more money than usual.[27]

On several occasions Lü Fan asked his wife in China to join him in Cuba to help with cooking, cleaning, and the tasks of domestic life. She refused, being unfamiliar with the Cuban lifestyle and the Spanish language. She also wanted to remain in China to care for her elderly mother. This refusal to join her husband abroad indicates another reason behind the skewed gender ratios in Chinese migration: women's ability to make decisions based upon their own self-interests.

After returning from his third and final visit to China, Lü Fan formed an unofficial union with a Cuban woman. He eventually informed his family in China that he had a Cuban "wife" and two daughters, Lourdes and Violeta (to whom he also gave Chinese names, "Guiguí" and "Guipó"). When Lü Fan's wife in Cuba abandoned him and the children after three years, he assumed full responsibility for raising his two Cuban daughters.

Lü Fan promoted communication between his daughters in China and Cuba by having them write letters to each other. He sent photos and wrote letters on behalf of his two Cuban daughters to their so-called "cousins" in China. From the beginning, his Chinese daughters referred to them as "Third Sister" and "Fourth Sister." Through this process of naming, the Cuban daughters were given the status of "full" sisters.[28] After Lü Fan died in 1975, fellow villagers emphasized that the Lü women needed to depend on themselves, and communication between them and their Cuban sisters ceased (until recently).[29]

Associational and Community Life in Cuba and the Maintenance of Hometown Ties

Even while maintaining hometown ties through remittances, investments, and return visits, Chinese became increasingly settled into the daily routines of life in their new environment. Pivoting between hometown issues and those particular to the Chinese in Cuba, Chinese associational organizations served a dual function within one space. By the early twentieth century, a plethora of home district and clan associations had been established in Havana and other provincial towns. *Huiguan* were regional associations that provided mutual aid, assisted with employment, extended credit, maintained hostels, mediated disputes, represented the Chinese "colony" in the non-immigrant community, and initiated and coordinated fund-raising and charitable projects. In addition to their important social function in Cuba, these associations helped Chinese maintain connections with their native communities, whether it be assisting with return passage or sending remains of the deceased home for proper burial.

As in other parts of the diaspora, the Chinese community in Cuba produced an umbrella organization known as Casino Chung Wah (Zhonghua Zonghuiguan, equivalent to the Chinese Consolidated Benevolent Association in the United States). It was established in 1893 under the influence of Chinese diplomats and acted as an auxiliary consulate, facilitating procedures for Chinese returning to China. The Casino Chung Wah engaged in Chinese charitable, welfare, cultural, and educational missions. In 1902 Chinese Consul General Tan Qianchu purchased the *huiguan* building for U.S. $40,000. Branches of the umbrella organization were established throughout Cuba, and representatives of the merchant community and various associations assumed leadership on the board of directors.[30] By the early decades of the twentieth century the need arose for a residence to provide for the aging Chinese community. In 1915 with over U.S. $33,500 the Casino Chung Wah built a care facility (*yiqiaoyuan*) in the Havana suburb of Regla for elderly overseas Chinese who were over 60, poor, and without family.[31]

In addition to native place, social relationships in China were underpinned by mutual clan and surname. Accordingly, clan and surname associations were established overseas. The Jiang Le An Tang of Cuba was an association of natives of Xinhui named "Jiang." Its purpose was to strengthen common surname ties and provide mutual aid for those seeking employment in Cuba. It was active throughout the twentieth century, with frequent mention of its activities in the daily Chinese language newspapers.[32] Out of necessity, smaller clans merged with other surname groups in Cuba. Association membership requirements were fluid once migrants were overseas, and considerations of mutual assistance overshadowed those of common surname or home district.[33]

The Jiujiang Overseas Chinese Merchants Hospital (Jiujiang Qiaoshang Gongyiyuan), called Quinta Benefica de Kow Kong in Cuba, was founded in 1924 by the wealthy Chinese of Jiujiang, Nanhai County. Members, who came from all areas of Guangdong, paid monthly dues of $1.05 for treatment, and non-members who were unable to pay also received free treatment if their status was corroborated by the Chinese association. Nestled in a serene setting in Havana, the hospital housed departments of dentistry, pulmonary tuberculosis, bone grafting, autopsy, internal and external medicine, examination, pediatrics, and women's health.[34]

The associations' management of "bone repatriation" or secondary burial of Chinese who died overseas was an important manifestation of transnational ties. In the late nineteenth century the Chinese cemetery (Zhonghua Zongyishan) was established under the Consul General, who purchased land with donations from members of the Chinese "colony."[35] Burial plots and mausoleums were arranged according to home district and clan or surname associations. Bones from "La Reina" Cemetery in Cienfuegos were sometimes transferred to this cemetery in Havana or to Hong Kong. For example, in November of 1916, the Chinese José Jhulay was authorized by the local sanitation headquarters to exhume the remains of the "asiático" Alfonso Pons for transport to

Hong Kong. José Jhulay was a leader in the Chinese community who in 1924 founded the Sociedad "Long Kuan (Gran China)" in Cienfuegos. It is likely that José Jhulay and Alfonso Pons were connected through shared workplace or social circles, as Pons was a common surname among the association's members.[36] Although the Chinese cemetery in Havana was initially considered to be a temporary resting place, its importance was highlighted during the eight-year period of Japanese occupation of China (1937–45), when sea transport was cut off and there was no means of transporting the remains of deceased Chinese.[37]

Chinese migrants also organized on the basis of mutual interests in occupational guilds, sworn brotherhoods, and political parties. In 1897 the first Chamber of Commerce for Chinese merchants in Cuba was created under the direction of the Chinese Consulate (in the same manner that the Casino Chung Wah had been established).[38] On a more local level, occupational, money-lending, and rotating credit associations assisted Chinese immigrants with beginning a business. For example, in November of 1926, ten Chinese employed in the cultivation and sale of fruits and vegetables met in a building on No. 157 Santa Clara Street, the site of two existing Chinese associations, to form the Asociación Cienfueguera de Agricultores Chinos (Cienfuegos Association of Chinese Agriculturalists) for the defense of the members' collective and individual interests. It was dedicated to the development of agriculture and systems of cultivation as well as the facilitation of contracting.[39]

Throughout Cuban cities the Partido Republicano "Chee Kung Tong" (the Triads or Zhigongtang, later known as the Hongmen Minzhidang) and the Partido Nacionalista de China (the Nationalist Party or Guomindang) enjoyed the largest membership, alternating in leadership of the Casino Chung Wah in Havana. The Triads, who operated in the southern provinces of China, were secret societies that advocated the overthrow of the Manchus and the restoration of the Ming dynasty. Triad lodges became the best-known fraternal organization in the Americas, as they were often considered to be adept at dealing with the needs of migrants in their new settings. Rather than sharing an organization, what Triad lodges everywhere—in China and the Americas—had in common was that members of these sworn brotherhoods underwent an elaborate initiation ritual underpinned by a rhetoric of fraternity and comradeship.[40] Responding to the call to organize from the North American Zhigongtang, the Triad organization known as the Hongmen Sanhehui in Cuba became the Partido Republicano "Chee Kung Tong" (Zhigongtang) in 1902.[41] Despite its label "partido" in Cuba, the Zhigongtang was not a political party and did not develop detailed political programs for China (other than advocating the overthrow of the Manchu government).[42]

In Cuba, Triad members generally came from among the lower strata of merchant society. In the Cienfuegos branch, founded in 1924, both members and officers were small traders, itinerant vendors, launderers, tailors, barbers, gardeners, and employees and operators of fruit stands and small restaurants. Vegetable vendor Lü Fan (Francisco Luis), who was one of 15 members with the surname "Luis," was a founder and treasurer of this branch.[43] The president of the Cienfuegos branch stated that the association had over 10,000 members in Cuba in 1928.[44]

China in Cuba: The Development of Overseas Chinese Nationalism

Toward the end of the nineteenth century, Chinese reformers and revolutionaries called for the modernization along Western lines of government, commerce, education, and the military. This intellectual momentum spilled beyond China into Chinese communities overseas. However, the Chinese in Cuba (and elsewhere) first had to imagine themselves as part of the Chinese nation before they could fully participate in the movement. Most immigrants had initially maintained loyalties to their families and native place rather than to a broader construction of "China."

As in Southeast Asia and the Americas, Chinese "nationalism" was promoted in Cuba by three groups with different agendas for building a strong, modern nation-state: the late Qing imperial state, reformers, and revolutionaries. Deviating from a tradition of disinterest and suspicion toward Chinese overseas, the Manchu Qing government

106

(1644–1911) in the late nineteenth century established consulates abroad and bestowed honors and titles upon merchant community leaders overseas in order to retain their loyalties. The imperial reform movement under exiled leader Kang Youwei (1858–1927) initially had stronger support in Chinese overseas communities than the revolutionary movement. Kang and his associates advocated the formation of a constitutional monarchy.

Although Sun Yat-sen (1866–1925) did not personally visit Havana, his revolutionary message reached Cuba through diasporic networks. In Havana, the revolutionary leader Huang Dingzhi and his Three Principles of the People Study Society (Sanmin Yuebao She) were predecessors to the Nationalist Party branch.[45] Huang regularly composed essays advocating revolution and sent news to be published in the San Francisco newspaper *Young China Morning Post* (*Shaonian zhongguo chenbao*), launched in 1909 for nationalist propaganda dissemination. He appointed a fundraising commission that raised over U.S. $10,000 for Sun Yat-sen's revolutionary efforts in China. Branches of the revolutionary Three Principles of the People Association (Sanmin Tuanti Hui) were established in Guantánamo and Remedios.[46]

In July of 1911 a small contingent of Chinese revolutionaries in Cuba launched a demonstration against a Qing naval mission stopping in the Havana harbor. What is interesting about the incident is how it was remembered by later generations of Chinese nationalists. A 1950 community record describes the incident as an example of Chinese "overseas compatriots" in Cuba delivering the revolutionary message through leaflets and speeches to Qing subjects aboard, successfully urging them to renounce their Manchu rulers.[47] But in his 1936 memoir of the Chinese Nationalist Party in Cuba, revolutionary leader Huang Dingzhi (who witnessed the event first-hand) describes it as an example of good luck for the movement in Cuba. Cuban newspapers, including the English-language *Havana Daily Post*, had mistakenly interpreted the chaos caused by the demonstration as support for the revolutionary cause.[48] After the successful overthrow of the Manchus in 1911 and the installation of Yuan Shikai as the first president of the Chinese republic, the press drew parallels between Sun

Yat-sen and Cuban revolutionary leader José Martí, a discourse that has continued in Cuba to this day.

In the first half of the twentieth century, Chinese in the Americas provided havens and logistical support for the broader nationalist movement in China. In 1915 Chinese parliamentarian Lin Sen, accompanied by the editor of the San Francisco newspaper *Young China Morning Post*, traveled to cities in the United States, Canada, and Cuba to increase support for the republic.[49] Both Havana and Cienfuegos were part of the circuit. On January 10 this anti-Yuan Shikai propaganda commission visited Cienfuegos, accompanied by two representatives of the Triads in Havana (known as the Partido Republicano Chino), President Simeón Chiu and Secretary Cristino Pérez Lani. In Cienfuegos they were greeted with a banquet at the illustrious Hotel Unión and visited the Chinese association, and two days later they departed for Remedios.[50]

Overseas branches of the Nationalist Party became especially important during the period of regional warlord rule in China, after the death of Yuan Shikai in 1916 until the establishment of the Nanjing government under Chiang Kai-shek in 1927. The U.S. General Branch in San Francisco had jurisdiction over Nationalist Party affairs in the United States, Hawaii, and Central and South America, claiming a membership of over 15,000 in the Americas. During the 1920s, when the Nationalist Party was still defining and organizing itself, this process spilled over into branches in the Americas. As in other cities, the Nationalist Party did not initially dominate the Chinatown in Havana. Instead, it competed for leadership with conservative merchant groups and the Triad lodges, who were allied with the existing regime in Peking.

When the Nationalist Party in China reorganized from 1923 to 1924, it formed a coalition with the Chinese Communist Party (still in its formative stage) for the shared purpose of national reunification. Furthermore, the central committee established a special department to guide party activities in Chinese overseas communities. Cuba had originally been under the jurisdiction of the powerful San Francisco branch. As party headquarters in Guangzhou (Canton) extended its reach, other territories in the Americas came under its direct authority: Hawaii in 1924, Mexico in 1924, Cuba in 1925, and Peru in 1927.[51] Combined with its daily newspaper and regular meetings, Nationalist Party branches in towns throughout Cuba became an important propaganda and fundraising mechanism. By participating in these political activities, the Chinese in Cuba were becoming part of a diasporic community that transcended several national boundaries.

When the Nationalist Party finally consolidated rule of China under Chiang Kai-shek in Nanjing in 1927, it sought to further enlist the wealth, expertise, and, above all, loyalty of Chinese abroad. The Nationalist Party purged Communists and their sympathizers, reducing the number of Party members both in China and overseas. As a result, left-leaning Chinese formed Marxist political groups in the Americas.[52] Former left-wing Nationalist Party members became involved in the Communist Party in Cuba and began publishing a weekly newspaper. The Alianza Protectora de Obreros y Campesinos (Defensive Alliance of Workers and Peasants) was founded in 1927 by left-leaning Chinese in Havana, with some of its principal leaders joining the Communist Party of Cuba between 1928 and 1929.[53]

Publications and loyalty to the homeland

Publications linked with associations in both China and Cuba played a key role in the development of transnational communities. Loyalties to a migrant's hometown and transnational ties were strengthened through *qiaokan*. These magazines geared toward Chinese overseas were published in home areas and distributed globally.[54] In addition to hometown news, they contained articles on immigration restrictions, discriminatory policies, government protection of Chinese overseas, population statistics, development of communities abroad, education, unemployment and economic difficulties, and remittances and investments. These magazines also appealed for contributions to native place, and advertising pages fostered diasporic business networks.

Four major Chinese newspapers were published in Havana in the twentieth century. These included the merchant community's *Huawen shangbao* (Chinese Commercial Newspaper) founded in 1914, the Triads' *Kaiming gongbao* (Enlightenment Gazette) founded in

1920, the Nationalist Party's *Minsheng ribao* (People's Voice Daily) founded in 1921, and later the Communist Party's *Guanghua zhoubao* (Bright China Weekly).[55] These Chinese dailies translated news obtained from Spanish newspapers and news from China received by cable.[56] In addition, they reported events pertinent to Chinese in Cuba and at home, such as the names and villages of those whose remains were being sent back from the Chinese cemetery in Havana.[57]

In order to launch the Nationalist Party newspaper, the board of directors solicited support from the wealthier merchants of the Chinese community. They called for investors to rally around Sun Yat-sen and the 1911 Revolution, writing:

> We, in the name of the Three Principles of the People, summon patriotic comrades. It has been over 10 years, yet there is not much evidence of many overseas Chinese realizing them. It is not that their ideological inclination is not as noble as that of their overseas Chinese brothers of North America, Canada, and Southeast Asia. It is really because our party does not have a comprehensive organ for discussion to bring into full play these Three Principles of the People. Almost 80,000 Chinese people are now in Cuba. Those that follow upon their heels come in a continuous stream, and thus there are numerous overseas Chinese. Now that they have departed from their homeland and come to Cuba for labor and commerce, they want to learn of affairs in China.[58]

Uniting against Japan

The Japanese occupation of China from 1937 to 1945 was the catalyst whereby the Nationalist Party attained control of Chinatowns in the Americas.[59] The occupation had severe repercussions for Chinese communities overseas and their relatives in China. On the one hand, communication and transportation were largely cut off, with a devastating effect on family members who were dependent on remittances. Women whose husbands were abroad became especially vulnerable.[60] Liu Kongye's wife, like many in her Taishan County village, remained in China. During the Japanese occupation she resorted to begging for subsistence and died prematurely.[61] Similarly, life was difficult for the Lü family in the adjacent county of Xinhui when the Japanese invaded. In the absence of a male head of household, the Lü women were "bullied" by others in the village.[62]

On the other hand, Chinese overseas were pulled closer to their homeland through a series of broad-based anti-Japan resistance movements. Many Chinese abroad had suffered racial discrimination and ill-treatment. They feared that their compatriots would suffer the same fate if China's status were reduced to that of a colony under Japanese domination. Within Chinese overseas communities, a high degree of inter-regional cooperation distinguished the anti-Japanese mobilization from the earlier anti-Manchu movement before the Chinese Revolution of 1911.[63] Paralleling the situation in China, factions were united through public fundraising events. The Cuban Overseas Chinese Association for Aiding the Resistance against Japan had 59 branches throughout Cuba for fundraising and the sale of Chinese government bonds. An umbrella organization in the U.S. (United China Relief) channeled the efforts of the myriad of smaller groups throughout the Americas, resulting in greater fundraising success. During the eight-year period of Japanese occupation of China, Chinese in Cuba donated a total of U.S. $2,400,000.[64] The rhetoric of patriotism was accompanied by intense social pressure to donate funds for resistance to the Japanese invasion.[65]

Chinese Communities in Republican Cuba

The maintenance of these transnational ties to China did not preclude desire for integration or collective action to defend against anti-Chinese sentiment in Cuba. Beginning with the birth of the Cuban republic that followed the wars for independence from Spain (1868–98), the Chinese became part of a discourse of national identity in Cuba that paved the way for their integration into Cuban society. Whites, blacks, mulattos, and Chinese participated side by side in the Cuban struggles for independence. The Chinese have been valorized in Cuban national memory and historiography for their role in these wars, and a monument was erected in Havana inscribed with the famous words of Gonzalo de Quesada: "Among the Chinese soldiers there were no traitors or deserters."[66] This monument, in a sense, redeemed the image of the Chinese as oppressed, racialized coolie laborers by layering over it one of heroic "*chinos mambises*" (freedom fighters). However, despite the formation of a Cuban republic in 1902 after the struggles for independence from Spain and the first U.S. occupation, racial divisions from the colonial era persisted, and with periods of political turmoil and economic hardship, new anti-Chinese prejudices surfaced.

Murder in the barrio chino *and the hardening of racial lines*

In the mid-1920s, before the Nationalist Party had consolidated its rule in China (and in Chinese overseas communities), it competed with the Triads for leadership of Havana's Chinatown. The shaky hold that the Nationalist Party had over Chinese communities overseas is evident from events in the *barrio chino*. A May 7, 1926, article in *El País* reported continuing problems in the Casino Chung Wah caused by a pro–Nationalist Party faction of the board of directors. In disregard of established procedures, the faction had approved the sending of funds to "revolutionary troops" in China to fight against the recognized government in Beijing. Several members of the association and board of directors who were not affiliated with the Nationalist Party protested to the Provincial Government of Havana, demanding that the association's funds be used to assist Chinese in need, as stipulated in the regulations. The Provincial Government intervened, declaring the actions of the board of directors illegal.[67]

Tensions escalated when the wealthy and controversial Chinese merchant Andrés Chiu Lión, a Nationalist Party member, and his Cuban wife were gunned down by a group of Chinese in front of his Havana residence on August 16, 1926. Chiu named as his perpetrators members of the Zhigongtang, including its president, before dying two days later. The board of directors of the Nationalist Party requested that Cuban authorities take measures to neutralize the threat of their rivals.[68] The Cuban Ministry of the Interior advocated that the Triads be declared "illicit and immoral," citing their irregular procedures and "secret code" as examples of infringement of the Cuban association laws.[69] A spokesman for the Zhigongtang defended his organization in a letter of September 8, 1926: ". . . truthfully we only dedicate our activities in Cuba to the mutual protection of our members . . . ." He reiterated that the organization opposed Soviet ideas[70] (alluding to the Nationalist Party's recent alliance with Communists).

In the wake of Chiu's murder, police increased vigilance in the *barrio chino* of Havana, and the provincial governors were ordered to close branches of the Triads. An investigation was launched into not only all Triad lodges, but all Chinese associations in Cuba. On September 23 the Provincial Governor of Havana suspended the Triads, and authorities began official investigations in Matanzas, Santa Clara, Cienfuegos, Ciego de Ávila, Morón, Camagüey, Cueto, Santiago de Cuba, and Guantánamo.[71]

These events prompted a wave of negative commentary in the Cuban press that condemned the rivalry between the Nationalist Party and the Triads and tied the latter to blackmail, gambling, opium, and immigrant trafficking. Historically, Triad lodges in the Americas possessed both the connections and infrastructure for smuggling, and the importance of recreational vices in Chinese "bachelor" societies helped to sustain such fraternal organizations in Chinese overseas communities.[72] In 1920s Cuba, the scrutiny of the Chinese community by Cuban authorities extended beyond concern with the activities in the associations to questioning the very existence of Chinatown itself.[73]

Two days after the murder, the Chief of National Secret Police sent to the Minister of Sanitation a chart of the principal artery of the *barrio chino*, "where the Asians live in complete overcrowding and lack of hygiene," and a list of the commercial houses of "third order" in the neighborhood.[74] (See tables 5.3 and 5.4, pp. 114–16). A campaign of sanitary inspection resulted in 25 proprietors being fined for maintaining "true nuclei of infection" by permitting from eight to 10 Chinese to share small rooms in their buildings. On September 11, 1926, a Cienfuegos newspaper reported more than 70 Chinese in Havana who were "undesirable and should be expelled from the national territory" for different offenses, especially drug trafficking.[75]

113

Table 5.3
Chinese Residents of Principal Artery of the
Barrio Chino of Havana, 1926

Street address	Floors	Divisions	Name of principal renter	Number Chinese
Zanja 5 (by Rayo)	2	26 rooms	Pilar Palmeiro	67
Zanja 11	1	1	Enrique Li	10
Zanja 179 (by Nicolás)	1	2	Lin Kay Chang	9
Zanja 17A	1	1 living room, 2 rooms	Manuel Li	15
Zanja 17B	1	1 living room, 2 rooms	Jai Tung Fung	19
Zanja 17C	1	1 living room, 2 rooms	Roberto Chin	4
Zanja 17D	1	1 living room, 2 rooms	San Su Yi Fong	15
Zanja 18	3	3 living rooms, 6 rooms	[blank]	73
Zanja 41 upper	1	4 rooms	Roberto Chao	45
Zanja 45 upper (society) San Yit Tong	1	[blank]	Miguel Jo	46
Zanja 47 upper (society) Won Wun Sankon Son	1	[blank]	Luis Choy	36
San Nicolás 85	2	13 rooms	José Chong	45
San Nicolás 87	1	6 rooms	Donato Bon	30
San Nicolás 91	2	12 rooms	Alfonso Martínez	54
San Nicolás 95	1	[blank]	Antonio Chang	20
San Nicolás 122	1	9 rooms	Luis Vidal	35
San Nicolás 114	1	[blank]	Martin Chong	17
Dragones 70 (by San Nicolás) Poo Sig Tong	1	[blank]	[blank]	[blank]
Dragones 31 (by San Nicolás)	1	1	Luis Chi	15
Campanario 101 (by Zanja)	1	[blank]	José Aquin	25
Manrique 81 (society) Sum San Ton	1	4	Rafael Eng	25

Continued on next page

Table 5.3, continued

Street address	Floors	Divisions	Name of principal renter	Number Chinese
Rayo 15 upper	1	6	Fernando Llí	16
Rayo 24	2	9	Juan Lan	37
Rayo 26	2	9	Juan Lan	38
Rayo 30 lower	1	21	[blank]	60
Rayo 34	1	10	León Tan Lau	35
San José 25 upper	1	12	José Cortin	35
San José 33	1	1 living room, 3 rooms	Bernardo Asusta	[blank]
San José 33	1	7	José Ka	20
San José 38	1	4	Fernando Li	18
San José 40	2	12	Ratura Lan	30
San José 42	1	2	Antonio Wong	18

Source: Archivo Nacional de Cuba, Secretaría de la Presidencia, Legajo 25, Expediente 51, 28 August 1926.

Table 5.4
Businesses of Third Order of Principal Artery
of Barrio Chino of Havana, 1926

Street address	Establishment	Owner
Zanja 10	inn	Santiago Bú
Zanja 18	tailor	Andrés Li
Zanja 22	tinsmith	Jok Mon Lluke
Zanja 22	carpentry	Julio Jun
Zanja 32	tailor	Can Wa
Zanja 17	bodega	Guillermo Lin
Zanja 19	tailor	Chiún Chin
Zanja 23	eatery	Juan Lang
Zanja 25	shoe store	Wa Chen
Zanja 27	bodega	Sun Ma Wo
Zanja 37	shoe store	Antonio Chung

Continued on next page

Table 5.4, continued

Street address	Establishment	Owner
Zanja 37	tailor	Julio Chin
Zanja 111A	tailor	Fo Con
Zanja 41	fruit stand	Manuel Wong
San José 35 (by Zanja)	photography	Lai Lan
Campanario 101 (by Zanja)	shoestore	José Aquin
Rayo 36	café	León Tan Leu
Rayo 19	chop suey	Chin In Lan
Rayo 11	chop suey	Alfonso Wong
Rayo 21 and 22	eatery	Chang Tin
Rayo 24	miscellany	Weng Chen
Dragones 54	inn	Alfonso Lúi
Dragones 66	shoe store	Juan Chen
Dragones 66	fruit stand	Mario Lujo
Dragones 29	eatery	Ley Pin
Dragones 27	fruitstand	Domingo Lain
Manrique 81B	shoe store	Gustavo Wong
Manrique 100	tinsmith	Antonio Lai
Manrique 100	tailor	Luis Chí
San Nicolás 108	eatery	José Chang Claat
San Nicolás 114	fruit stand	Martin Chong
San Nicolás 85	fruit stand	Juan Chen
General Casas 1	fruit stand	Cué Long
General Casas 3	tailor	José Chi
General Casas 5	eatery	Mi Giam Chi
General Casas 7	eatery	Chan Chon
General Casas 9	fruit stand	San Sen Lung
General Casas 79 and 81	fruit stand	Quong Cheon Long
Zanja 17 (by San Nicolás)	eatery	Yat Pon San
Zanja 17 (by San Nicolás)	fruit stand	Chung Son

Source: Archivo Nacional de Cuba, Secretaría de la Presidencia, Legajo 25, Expediente 51, 28 August 1926.

The anti-Chinese sentiment can be explained only in part by the accusations of illegal gambling, opium, and immigrants. As in other places in the Chinese diaspora, Chinese racial identities became "hardened" during times of political transition and social upheaval in Cuba. In the 1920s and 1930s, a politically conservative, anti-immigrant nationalism developed in Cuba, reinforced by decades of North American– and European-dominated capitalist expansion since the founding of the republic.[76] In August of 1922, a front page article in a Cienfuegos newspaper reported that Washington had requested that Cuba adopt measures preventing the immigration of Chinese and "undesirable" Europeans (namely, Communists and Bolsheviks), proclaiming that they came to Cuba only in order to enter the United States surreptitiously.[77]

New prejudices against Chinese as foreign labor also surfaced, and the press denounced continued illegal immigration of laborers. Even before the second major migration of Chinese laborers to Cuba, the English-language newspaper *The Havana Daily Post* encouraged the immigration of European families. An article of October of 1913 implored, "Cuba needs immigrants who come with the intention of becoming citizens and who will conform to the laws, usages and reliable customs of the country, and not those who come to merely get work and return to their homes with the fruits of their toil."[78] An August 19, 1926, article from *El Sol* reveals the sentiment behind these negative opinions toward the Chinese. A high government official declared, "Those Chinese, besides their unruly and false character, are a terrible competition to commerce in the capital and to native workers. As they live grouped by the hundreds and eat delicacies as eccentric as they are cheap, rats, lizards, dogs, shark fins, and rice seasoned with strange gelatins, their expenses are the lowest and they can be therefore a ruinous competition to merchants and to Cuban and Spanish workers."[79]

Throughout the twentieth century, the Chinese were able to organize and challenge perceived discrimination. In 1915 a commission of Chinese merchants complained to the editorial office of *El Republicano* and to the Chinese Consul that the sanitation authorities of Cienfuegos were imposing measures almost exclusively against the

Chinese. The director of the newspaper was sympathetic to their complaints.[80] From 1922 to 1923 the Spanish newspaper *Diario de la Marina* ran a series of anti-Chinese articles. In response, a Chinese overseas representative assembly was convened to coordinate and improve diplomatic relations.[81] In 1926 the Chinese of Cienfuegos pushed for modification of reentry restrictions on Chinese merchants who were absent from Cuba for more than 18 months and spoke against the deportation of illegal residents in Cuba.[82] In the wake of the murder of Andrés Chiu Lión in the *barrio chino*, Antonio Chuffat Latour (translator and interpreter for the Nationalist Party) published an article in a Cienfuegos newspaper defending Chinese merchants "de valor" and describing the numerous dialect groups of the Chinese in Cuba.[83]

Depression and economic tensions

Unemployment in Cuba was exacerbated by the world-wide depression of 1929. The economic crisis provided a ripe atmosphere for the passage of the 1934 Nationalization of Labor decree that mandated that 50 percent of all employees in industry, commerce, and agriculture have Cuban nationality. The Cuban nativist labor movement was directed against Haitians and Jamaicans in agriculture and Spanish, Jews, and Chinese in commerce. Although the main target in retail trade was Spanish immigrants, Chinese small businesses such as restaurants, laundries, and truck farms were also affected by the movement. According to Chinese Cuban Napoleón Seuc, "The Nationalization of Labor law was not applied and many times we evaded its application."[84] Chinese merchants took advantage of legal loopholes to evade the law. Through an arrangement sanctioned by the commercial code (a vestige from Spanish colonial times) whereby Chinese workers for a firm were made limited partners, they were not considered "employees," and therefore not subject to the "law of fifty per cent." Furthermore, depending on the political climate, for much of the time that the decree was in existence, it was not strictly enforced.[85] Nevertheless, many Chinese during this period returned to China when economic opportunities in Cuba dried up. Others, like many Spaniards, applied for Cuban citizenship in order to meet the new legal requirements.[86]

In the first part of the twentieth century a commercial rivalry played out in Havana between Spanish and Chinese owners of bodegas. According to testimony from Chinese, consumers preferred the cheaper prices and home delivery offered by Chinese shops. Due to pressure from Spanish merchants, a presidential decree of 1934 established a minimal distance of 100 meters between bodegas (excluding those already in existence). As legal consultant to the Chinese community, Napoleón Seuc argued that the regulation was unconstitutional (according to the Constitution of 1940), and the decree was eventually annulled.[87] In 1936 the Chinese Chamber of Commerce in Cuba joined two Cuban national commercial federations, after which anti-Chinese incidents by Spanish merchants decreased.[88] When the Chinese Chamber of Commerce in Cuba investigated all Chinese businesses, its President Li Kunyu (Li Kent) submitted a report to the Bureau of Overseas Chinese Affairs in China, the arm of the Nationalist Party that had a vested interested in capturing the loyalty—and financial support—of Chinese merchants overseas. In 1936 there were 3,889 Chinese business establishments in Cuba, valued at $3,924,677. These included 1,808 grocery stores, 799 fruit and vegetable stands, 656 laundries, and 312 restaurants.[89]

The Nationalization of Labor law was enforced more rigorously beginning in 1944 under the administration of Cuban President Ramón Grau San Martín, leading to the unemployment of 400 to 500 Chinese. In August and September of 1944, members of the "Cuban Front" incited rioters and disturbed Chinese restaurants. Their actions were directed at the Chinese strategy of making nonequity partners out of workers and aimed for the immediate hiring of Cubans. According to a Chinese community record, "Day after day they [members of the "Cuban Front"] carried slogans in their hands and gathered at Chinese restaurants, clothing shops, general stores, fresh fruit stands, etc., shouting and causing disturbances."[90] The restaurants organized an occupational league to handle the incidents. Furthermore, the Chinese Chamber of Commerce in Cuba established a federation of occupational organizations to assist consular officials and promote the welfare of Chinese in Cuba. The federation represented six Chinese occupational organizations (Chamber of Commerce, Garment Association, Federation of Industrial and Commercial

Products, Fruits Association, Agriculture Association, and Restaurant Association), three newspapers, and the Casino Chung Wah. It advocated "people-to-people" diplomacy and reconciliation through meetings with powerful Cuban government authorities and commercial magnates.[91] Common economic interests had the potential to foster cooperation between Chinese and other merchants. For example, in April of 1934 Cuon Chong Long and Cong Gen Long, joining prominent non-Chinese importers, petitioned for the reestablishment of direct ship service between the port of Cienfuegos and New York.[92]

Adaptation, Integration, and the Second and Third Generations

Racial democracy as envisioned by independence leader José Martí and "transculturation" or *mestizaje* as formulated by anthropologist Fernando Ortiz have been the basis for a conception of *cubanidad* or "Cuban-ness" that incorporates Europeans, Africans, and Asians.[93] However, most Chinese historically sought to identify with whites and be officially classified as *blanco*. Well into the twentieth century, much like blacks and mulattos in Cuba, Chinese endeavored to elevate the social status of their children, through legal means if necessary. For example, in 1945 the Chinese José Wong Lam successfully appealed the lower court in Cienfuegos to have his son's birth registry changed from *mestizo* to *blanco*. Although it was declared that the child was the son of a Chinese man and white woman and that the color of his skin was white, he had been registered as *mestizo* or "mixed" at birth. The lower court judge in Cienfuegos denied the claim, stating that "*mestizo* is no more than one born of parents of different races; and in this case the registered is the son of a yellow father and a white mother." However, a reversal by the Ministry of Justice cited a 1943 census law that classified the races of inhabitants of Cuba as *blanca, negra, amarilla,* and *mestiza* (white, black, yellow, and mixed). In the reversal, a detailed discussion of *mestizo* reveals that the category was intended for children of whites and blacks, Chinese and mulattos, and Chinese and blacks, but not for children of Chinese and whites.[94] The ambiguous label *mestizo* or "mixed" had appeared in Cuban censuses since 1899 and was associated with a distancing from being categorized as "black."[95] Although they had more opportunities to bring Chinese wives and children to Cuba in the 1940s, Chinese men still formed unions with white, *mulata*, and black Cubans, and the hope was for their children to be considered part of white society.

Even while striving to become integrated into Cuban society, Chinese Cubans sought to maintain language and other elements of Chinese culture. In the twentieth century, some Chinese merchants maintained ties to China through the education of their children. On October 1, 1936, the Colegio Chung Wah was inaugurated in Cuba by the Casino for the education of children of Chinese, both male and female. Another school was established on the far eastern end of the island, in Santiago de Cuba. By 1950 the Colegio Chung Wah had over 100 students, also attracting Cubans who wanted to learn Chinese. However, the Chinese school in Havana was constantly plagued by insufficient funds and facilities. In general, given the degree of integration by the mid-twentieth century, Chinese overseas education in Cuba was described as "undeveloped" by chroniclers of the community.[96]

Chinese male children born in Cuba were also sent to China for education. Often, one son remained in Cuba to learn the business and another was sent to Hong Kong or Guangzhou for education.[97] In Guangzhou, the Canton Christian College housed a separate school "for the education of those youths who being born and brought up in a foreign land still desired a knowledge of their mother country, its language and customs."[98] The Overseas Chinese Students Association of the school was founded in 1921. In an English-language article entitled "Why Should We Come Back to China to Study," the president of the association states, "Of course we know why we are sent here to School. We want first to understand Chinese, our own language, without which our education will never be complete." In a passionate, patriotic plea, he further advocates Chinese overseas youth returning with their expertise to develop commerce and industry in China.[99] Students at the Canton Christian College were grouped by overseas region for photo day, with eight boys in uniform from "Cuba and Central America" in 1923.[100] Through education in both Cuba and China, the potential for an "overseas Chinese" (*huaqiao*) identity was thus fostered among some members of the second generation.

Churches also aimed to meet the varied needs of Chinese families in Cuba. Chinese in Havana who participated in institutionalized religion belonged to either the Presbyterian or Catholic church. A Presbyterian church in the *barrio chino* held religious teachings in Cantonese and Spanish on Sundays at 3 p.m. and evening Chinese classes for children. It became known as the "Chinese church," and the interior is adorned with an image of Guanyin, the Buddhist goddess of mercy. Baptism ceremonies and godparentage forged important social ties between Chinese and non-Chinese in Cuba.[101]

In the early 1940s a "crisis" of Chinese theater in Havana ensued, when many Chinese actors departed with traveling troupes from the United States. As a solution, music teachers founded the Ópera Chung Wah and three other theater companies in Havana. In an effort to preserve this element of Chinese culture, "mixed" female descendants from age eight to 28 who did not speak Chinese were trained to sing Cantonese opera. They memorized a phonetic pronunciation that was written next to the Chinese characters in the libretto. Also, according to informants, some participants "were not Chinese nor children of Chinese, but *apadrinados* [godchildren] of these, although the cases were minimal."[102]

Besides schools, churches, and opera, Cuban-born Chinese youth also participated in Chinese associations. The Nationalist Party formed a youth corps for Chinese men and women to study the principles of Sun Yat-sen.[103] The organization represented an attempt by the Nationalist Party to extend its reach to Chinese youth in Cuba and develop potential full members.[104] Even mixed descendants of higher economic strata were also admitted to participate in some of the associations, including the Nationalist Party and the Triads. These associations promoted musical bands, dance groups, and martial arts teams formed with "mestizos."[105] The Asociación Nacional Chino-Cubana (Chinese-Cuban National Association), located in Havana on the upper level of 170 San Lázaro Street, operated from 1943 to 1953. Its aim was "the realization of charitable and cultural works among its members, always propagating better understanding and friendship between the members of the Chinese colony in Cuba and their family with Cubans. . . ."[106]

Chinos Cubanos

A common theme in scholarship on Chinese Cubans is that "culture" is transmitted through Cuban mothers, with their dominant role in the upbringing and education of children.[107] Biethnic children were socialized into Cuban domestic culture by mothers, aunts, grandmothers, godmothers, and other children. Thus, with Chinese men remaining bachelors or uniting with Cuban women, Chinese cultural markers such as language faded among the second generation. While this phenomenon *has* largely played out among the children of Chinese in Cuba, there are some exceptions and nuances, especially in cases of Chinese fathers who were in charge of raising their children. The assumption that cultural transmission is determined by Cuban mothers is inadequate for an understanding of the Chinese Cuban biethnic experience. A similar phenomenon is noted by anthropologist Karen Isaksen Leonard in her examination of marriages between women of Mexican descent and men from India's Punjab province who came to work in California agriculture in the early-twentieth century. Leonard finds that her original hypothesis about Punjabi male dominance and ethnicity of children is undermined by evidence that Mexican women developed a sense of individuality and kinship networks of their own.[108] Similarly, Chinese men living in "bachelor societies" in the Americas maintained strong kinship networks that impacted child rearing.

Napoleón Seuc was born to a Chinese father and one of the few Chinese women in Cuba in 1924. During the depression Seuc's father lost his fruit-stand businesses, and in 1929 his mother and his three younger siblings embarked for her family house in Guangdong, utilizing subsidized passages from the Chinese consulate. Because of the Japanese invasion of China and the onset of World War II, she was unable to return until 20 years later. Napoleón Seuc and his older brother Armando remained in Cuba and did not see their mother again until after the Chinese Communist victory in 1949. Seuc recalls growing up in his father's stores surrounded by his uncles and other neighborhood men. He states in his memoir, "In my childhood I never had skates or a bicycle, I did not know—in a Chinese home and environment—who the Three Kings were and why they came; a lady cus-

123

tomer and friend of my parents gave us our first toys."[109] Although Seuc grew up without a Chinese mother, he learned to speak Chinese. "I was born and raised Cuban. I was a Cuban citizen. I was considered Cuban. I was not considered Chinese. But I think Chinese was my first language," Seuc said.[110] Today, Napoleón Seuc embodies the complex, multifaceted identities of Chinese Cubans in the United States: simultaneously a Spanish-speaking Cuban exile living in Miami and a Chinese-American, with relatives spread over Havana, Miami, New York, and Xinhui City in Guangdong.

Imagining China: The legacy of Pastor Pelayo

Oral testimony from descendants of Chinese also testifies to the imaginative links to an ancestral homeland created among descendants who have never been to China. Blas and Santiago Pelayo Díaz are the grandsons of a Chinese indentured laborer. In 1859 at age 15, their grandfather Pastor Pelayo (Tung Kun Sen) arrived in Cuba from Dongguan County, Guangdong for work on a sugar plantation. Pastor Pelayo's life history is representative of both "images" of the Chinese in Cuba, as he made the transition from coolie laborer to small entrepreneur. After fulfilling his original and recontracted term of indenture, Pelayo worked for wages in a gang on several estates in Cienfuegos and eventually became a contractor himself. He purchased the freedom of a black slave who worked as a domestic on Rosario Estate named Wenceslaa Sarría, as well as that of two of her brothers, and together he and she had nine children.[111] Pastor Pelayo moved between rural and urban settings. He was named the first Chinese Consul in Cienfuegos after the visit of the Chinese Imperial Commissioner Chen Lanbin in 1874, and he became the first president of the Chinese Association "La Gran China" in 1884.[112] In 1885, after being denied permission to build a Chinese theater, he constructed a small one on the association patio, where a theater company rehearsed during the evenings.[113]

In March of 1999, strolling down the dusty streets of the former Chinese neighborhood in Cienfuegos, Blas and Santiago Pelayo shared their family history with me.[114] The dilapidated skeletons of Chinese shops and associations highlight the stark contrast between the tourist-oriented "revitalization" of the *barrio chino* in Havana today and the reality of the former Chinese communities throughout smaller Cuban towns. We proceeded to "La Reina" cemetery where Pastor Pelayo was buried in 1913, now overgrown with weeds and inundated with water from the adjacent bay. Blas Pelayo has "poco a poco" (little by little) raised money from family members to refurbish his grandfather's grave and erect a memorial plaque. Extremely proud of his Chinese heritage, Pelayo has researched his family tree, learned elementary Cantonese (as opposed to the Mandarin that is currently being emphasized in the *barrio chino*), and is writing a novel based on the life of his grandfather.

In her analysis of children of Punjabis and Mexicans in California, Karen Leonard states, "When descendants talk about being Hindu or East Indian today, they do not mean objective criteria that link them to India or the Punjab, attributes such as an anthropologist might list. They have few or no experiential links to Punjabi and Indian culture and are non-speakers of Punjabi. But they possess a sense of place and history that is distinctly Punjabi nonetheless."[115]

Matthew Frye Jacobson similarly suggests that a diasporic imagination and attachments to the homeland are linked by a "cultural thread" to descendants of early-twentieth-century Irish, Polish, and Jewish immigrants in the United States.[116]

Blas Pelayo possesses such an imagination. Following is an excerpt from an essay Pelayo wrote for the Chinese Cuban community chronicling the visit of China's President Jiang Zemin to Havana's Chinatown in 1993. He compares the official visit to the imperial commission that came to Cuba over 100 years earlier to investigate the abuses in the coolie trade. The essay expresses the sense of connectedness a descendant of a Chinese migrant experienced with his own family history, with the Chinese Cuban community, and with the remaining elderly native Chinese. The significance of President Jiang Zemin's visit varied for different segments of the population: for Cubans, it held the promise of improved diplomatic relations and material goods in a time of scarcity; for Chinese in Cuba, it was a connection with a homeland that had been severed for nearly half a century; and for descendants of Chinese, it may have been a "cultural thread" linking their past with the present.

> I only await the next day, which promises to be filled with emotions because of the economic and political significance of the visit of the president for our country; once again, as when the first time a state leader from the former Celestial Empire came to Cuba . . . Chen Lanbin, with the specific mission to learn about the problems from the mistreatment and abuses of the Chinese coolies. . . .
>
> The moment is significantly emotional: the native at my side yells immediately in Cantonese "Forever China!" Even though I do not know that language, perhaps out of ethnic instinct and solidarity, I repeat it in Spanish.
>
> In another very old native, I was surprised to see his tired eyes filled with tears of emotion and joy. . . .[117]

Watersheds in Migration: Decline and "Revitalization"

Migration trends are intimately linked with global forces. Migration to Cuba had dropped significantly during the depression and after World War II, when the United States eased restrictions on Chinese entry. The adaptive and network-based nature of migration is reflected in the movement patterns of the Chinese of Dulian, Xinhui County. When sugar prices dropped precipitously after World War II, the network patterns changed, and the Dulian Chinese followed each other from Cuba to pursue work in the oil industry in Venezuela. They even called the Venezuelan town in which they settled "New Dulian," underscoring the shifting of hometown attachments from one foreign land to another.[118] After 1949, a brief resurgence in immigration to Cuba occurred as Chinese fled the political upheaval in the aftermath of China's Communist revolution. In the years following the Cuban Revolution of 1959, which nationalized Chinese-owned businesses, a significant secondary migration of Chinese Cubans to Miami, New York, and Toronto was part of the larger exodus. The Chinese who remain in Cuba are elderly men, most of whom came to Cuba in the

1950s. With little new immigration since 1959 and the loss of private businesses, the *barrio chino* fell into decline.

Today, the Chinese Cuban community is composed of two major groups: the *chinos naturales* or "native Chinese" and the children, grandchildren, and great-grandchildren of Chinese, most of whom are descendants of a union between a Chinese father and Cuban mother. In addition to the few hundred elderly native Chinese that remain, it is these mixed descendants that form contemporary Chinese Cuba.[119]

With the end of subsidies from the former Soviet Union, a severe economic crisis in the early 1990s forced Cuba into reforms resulting in a "mixed socialist economy" and the legalization of the U.S. dollar. The Havana Chinatown Promotion Group (Grupo Promotor del Barrio Chino de la Habana), an organ of the Cuban government, was formed to "recover" Chinese culture, customs, and traditions for the Cuban community. Its projects include a center for Chinese arts and traditions, an evening language school with native Mandarin speakers, a martial arts club, a clinic for traditional Chinese medicine, a residence for the elderly, celebrations of festivals, food stands and Chinese restaurants on the pedestrian walkway (Calle Cuchillo), and the publication of a magazine.[120] This ongoing revitalization project in Havana's Chinatown coincides with the Cuban government's efforts to develop tourism as a solution to its economic problems and to attract foreign investment. The priority (as stated in the Promotion Group's literature) has been to transform the historic *barrio chino* into a tourist attraction.[121] In part as a result of these efforts, Cubans continually join the Chinese Cuban community, discovering they have an ancestor who was Chinese.[122]

In January of 2001, Lü Fan's Cuban granddaughter, Mitzi Espinosa Luis, located two "uncles" at Chinese New Year's celebration in Havana's Chinatown. They were 96-year-old Felipe Luis and 67-year-old Santiago Luis, both surnamed "Lü" and from the same village in China. Both were former bodega owners living in the *barrio chino*. In a display of "fictive kinship" for compatriots from Lü Village on the other side of the ocean, they recognized Mitzi as a granddaughter, continuing Lü Fan's legacy of fostering familial relations between his Chinese and Cuban families.[123]

Felipe Luis during his younger days in Havana

CHAPTER 6

◆

Si tú pleguntá,
a mi gusta hacé cuento.
"If you ask, I'll be happy to tell you":
Felipe Luis narrates his story

Mitzi Espinosa Luis
Translated by Kathleen López

Translator-Editor's Introduction

Mitzi Espinosa Luis is the granddaughter of Lü Fan, a first-generation Cantonese immigrant who worked as a vegetable vendor in Cuba until his death in 1975. As a descendant of a Chinese immigrant, Espinosa has become increasingly involved in the activities sponsored by the Havana Chinatown Promotion Group (Grupo Promotor del Barrio Chino). In January of 2001 at a Chinese New Year celebration in Havana, she discovered two elderly Chinese with the same surname and from the same village as her grandfather. As she developed a relationship with Santiago and Felipe Luis, she was able to further explore her own Chinese heritage.

Felipe Luis came to Cuba in 1926, and his nephew Santiago Luis followed in 1952. Among the few remaining Chinese with the surname Lü, the two men lived together in Havana's Chinatown. Both had long since retired, and Santiago maintained the house and cared for the bedridden Felipe until his death at the age of 99 on September 7, 2003. According to Espinosa, who was with him at the time, Felipe simply stopped eating when he realized that Santiago, plagued by recent health problems, would not be able to care for him as in the past. In the short time that Mitzi cared for her "grandfather" Felipe, she gleaned from him many anecdotes about his life in China and as a Chinese immigrant in Cuba. While far from a complete chronicle of Felipe's experiences, Espinosa Luis' retelling of his story not only reveals details of Felipe's journey but also allows us to explore, through Espinosa, issues of race, ethnicity, and identity from the perspective of a Cuban woman of Chinese descent.

The following essay is a compilation of transcripts of Espinosa's conversations with Felipe from January and February of 2003, with his nephew Santiago occasionally chiming in. Given his heavy Cantonese accent, outsiders often had difficulty comprehending Felipe's speech. But, with patience and persistence, Espinosa has recorded his life history, observations, and thoughts as a Chinese in Cuba. Direct quotations have been translated into English, with Espinosa's rendering of Felipe's non-native Spanish following in brackets. Chinese family names and words have retained the transliteration used by Felipe himself, a Cantonese speaker. Espinosa also preserved the heavy accent of Felipe's Spanish. There is a tradition of this type of rendering of Chinese speech patterns in Cuban historiography and folklore, demonstrating how native Cubans have perceived Chinese immigrants both as an integral part of the Cuban national experience, but also as something exotic. This ambiguity is reflected in the folk song, "El chino comerciante," the humor and rhymes of which are built on "typical" Chinese pronunciations of Spanish words.   —KL

"If you ask, I'll be happy to tell you"

My stay of just over one month in Havana to care for Santiago, a relative of mine undergoing surgery, permitted me to get closer each day to his 99-year-old uncle Felipe Luis. Felipe came to Cuba at the age of 23, when the construction of the National Capitol building had just begun.[1] He always links his arrival to the island with this fact, rarely mentioning the exact year, 1926.

Hunched, dragging himself around the house with a walker, and silent (he speaks only to ask for what is necessary), Felipe is typical of the Chinese immigrant who left family and country in search of economic improvement with which to help his relatives and eventually return. Recently he told me that he would die in Cuba, knowing for certain that return to China was impossible. Nothing has been easy for me about speaking with this grandfather or "*akón*," as all of the little boys and girls called him (even though they were not his grandchildren). At times he seems distant and refuses to speak, perhaps thinking of things in his long and laborious past. When he talks, he does so with a voice deep and stammering, and when exclaiming, his tone and gestures return so energetically that they reveal the youth he once was.

The passing of the years has affected Felipe's hearing, and neighbors or pedestrians below his house can hear the raised voices of those inside trying to communicate with him. In this manner and drawing myself close to his ear, I have woven together fragments of my conversations with Felipe. Some stories he spontaneously told me, while others were at my initiative, as on many occasions he has repeated to me, "If you ask, I'll be happy to tell you." [*Si tú pleguntá, a mi gusta hacé cuento.*]

Vanished Chinese customs

Lui Cuan Chong (Felipe's Chinese name) was born in Xinhui County, Guangdong Province, on December 14, 1903. One of his first memories was his mother's atrophied and bandaged feet. This painful practice was intended to keep the feet of Chinese women extremely small, considered a measure of feminine beauty. Foot-binding dates from the tenth century, and one of the first reforms after the establishment of the Republic in 1911 was its eradication. Fortunately, Felipe's sisters did not suffer this torture, and their feet grew freely. Felipe expresses, "Before when a Chinese woman did not bind her feet, no people, no men married her. Now all feet are big. Already 100 years passed. They don't bind the feet, and they cut the braid." [*Ante cuando una china si no marrá la pie, no hay gente, no hay hombre casá con ella. Ahora to' lo pie son grande, ya pasa 100 años, no ta' marrá ya lo pie y cortá la moña.*] Felipe further explains that in China many men wore long braids (queues), and their heads often became filled with unpleasant insects. He immediately clarifies that he did not wear a queue.[2]

Dragons are like a snake with horns

On one occasion Felipe noted that both in China and Cuba the skies are blue and there is sunshine and rain. However, in China a dragon winds between the clouds, darkening the sky and producing heavy rains. When I asked Felipe if he believes in dragons, he responded, "That's a story, nothing more. I never saw one." [*Eso son cuento na' má, nunca visto.*] He added that the only ones that existed in China were similar to an enormous thick-bodied snake with horns. I look at my surroundings, and delicate teacups, large vases, and splendid plates of the purest and whitest porcelain return to me painted images of the mythological monster. The dragon had become a symbol of the Chinese emperor, with its image adorning imperial clothing, building facades, and works of art.[3]

Roof corners turned upward

Grandfather Felipe recalls that the houses of his native village were like those of Cuba, some of wood and others of masonry, with mud houses belonging to the poor. One difference was that the corners of the roofs turned upward. Felipe's family's house was large and of masonry, simply furnished. It had tables, chairs, and beds, but not like the fine furniture of his current home in Havana. Food was cooked in a large frying pan over a wood and straw stove that blackened the walls and ceiling. They ate quite well . . . fish, eggs, pork, cundeamor, rice without salt, and bananas, among other things. In Cuba Felipe ate plantains (*plátanos machos*) for the first time, boiled and fried, green and ripe. In China he had not known this variety of banana, which he finds delicious. Rather than being a daily food for the poor, chicken was only consumed on festival days. To sleep he used a kind of pillow of wood called a "*chong hau*" placed under the nape of the neck. These pillows were also made of straw or ceramic. His bed was of wood, covered by a thin mat. In comparison, he finds the bed he uses now to be soft and comfortable.

Felipe's leg was attacked by insects

The dark brownish-gray color of Felipe's left leg attracted my attention. He tells me that in his village, as an adolescent of thirteen or fourteen years old—in addition to carrying 120 pounds of dry rice in two baskets hanging from a bamboo pole—he cultivated it. He would harvest up to three crops during a single season. Rice needs abundant water for its growth, and in the paddies lived insects that sucked blood through wounds or scratches on the skin. They did not dislodge until satisfied, causing pain and itching. To cure Felipe's leg, fresh herbs were applied directly to the bites and afterward it was bandaged, a process that took about three months.

Felipe knows medicinal plants that were used fresh, dried, or powdered and stored in bottles. But he does not tell me their names, emphasizing that I will not understand. "A lot of herbs, herbs and also roots, a lot of herbs over there in China. In China it came from the mountains. Herbs for curing. A lot of medicine in China and here in Cuba. There are dried herbs, saved. When you have a cold, you take it out and cook it," he says. [*Mucha yerba, hay yerba, hay raí también . . . mucha yerba allá en China, allá en China salió de la montaña, yerba pa' curá, mucha medicina en China y aquí en Cuba, hay yerba seca, guardao, cuando tú tiene catarro, saca y cocina . . .*] When there were illnesses in his family, at times they consulted a doctor or expert on the properties of plants. Then I tell Felipe what I learned from reading about Chinese medicine; for example, the use of infusions of young doe horns, ginseng roots, and grasshopper wings for fever and the beneficial properties of soy.[4]

Hope of a happy return with pockets filled with money

Felipe decided to come to Cuba because Santiago's grandfather, Lui Wo or Lui Sui Kao, who already lived on the island, wrote him a letter urging him emigrate. Remaining in Guangdong were his wife and two small children, a girl named Lui Fung Hei and a boy named Lui Chau Ling. Felipe endured the bitter separation through the hope of a happy return with pockets filled with money. His son tried his luck at emigrating in 1948, and the two became reacquainted. Known as Evelio Luis, Felipe's son lived in Cuba until 1979, when he returned to China.

The letters between father and son, frequent at first, suddenly stopped arriving from China. Felipe still does not know that his beloved son died in the year 2000. On Qingming Day, celebrated on the fifth day of the third month of the lunar year, relatives in China pay their respects at the tombs of their ancestors, tidying up, removing weeds, and sweeping away leaves. This custom was also practiced in Cuba beginning in October of 1893, when the General Cemetery of Chinese in Havana was inaugurated. When I asked Felipe if he wished to return to China, he responded, "Yes, but I can't. It's very expensive to return . . . by plane, for dollars." [*Sí, pero no pu'e, muy caro pa' regresa, por avión por dolá.*]

He lost hair on the journey

The passage from the Celestial Empire to the Greater Antilles was by boat from Hong Kong to Havana, a trip that took about forty days. Felipe remembers suffering from terrible seasickness, and touching his head, he told me that he even lost clumps of hair. Pigs were raised on the ship to feed the passengers. But traveling in the "poor class," Felipe was usually given old, hard chicken, while those of greater economic status would eat it tender. Felipe does not remember the name of the boat, but like his fellow immigrants who only knew Chinese, he identified it by the Arabic numbers when he embarked. "About 200 Chinese came on the boat. When the Chinese left, they didn't know English or Spanish." [*Venían como 200 chino en el barco, cuando lo chino salió no sabe americana ni españó.*]

Felipe's first residence in Cuba

When Felipe first arrived in Cuba, he lived in the Chinese association on No. 15 Cuchillo Street for immigrants of the surname Lü. He explains, "Each one arrives and enters the society of his surname, rents a room, and is given a name." [*Cada uno llega y entra a la sociedad de su apelli, alquila y pone el nombre.*] Fellow countrymen decided upon a Western name for him. When I asked him if he likes his name, he quickly responded, "It doesn't matter. Anyway, they named me Felipe." [*Da iguá, de toa manera me pusí Felipe.*] Discussing Cuban writer José Lezama Lima's 1966 novel *Paradiso*, Yamilet García Zamora provides background to the role of the associations in the development of the *barrio chino*: ". . . in the 1870s what was known as the

Chinatown of Havana began to take shape, situated on Zanja and Dragones. Around these streets the Chinese began to group together, founding associations to reunite emigrants by surname or region of origin. With the savings they had accumulated through years of fatiguing work, they associated among themselves and established small businesses. Under these conditions, the Asian colony continued to develop until it became an important commercial zone of groceries, restaurants, shops, pharmacies, etc. At the end of the nineteenth century it had already reached a notable peak and in the first half of the twentieth century, its maximum splendor."[5]

Felipe related that when he arrived in Cuba, Zanja Street was like a river with abundant mosquitoes.[6] Opium smoking took place in some associations. Through this business some of the most prominent members of the Chinese community got rich, in many cases relying on police favors. He says, "That was in the past. Before on Zanja and Cuchillo there was a lot of opium. Me, no! Wherever . . . upstairs, third or fourth floors . . . downstairs no. Yes, other Chinese smoked opium, paid the police so that they did not see it or speak of it . . . that was before." [*Eso es antiguo ya, ante aquí Zanja, Cuchillo, hay mucho opio, ¡ yo no!, dondequiera, casa alto, tercer piso o cuarto piso, abajo no. Si hay otro chino fumá opio, pagá a la policía, pa' que no vea y no hablá, eso ser ante.*]

Vendor of fruits, ice cream, and fried food

In Cuba, Felipe engaged in the sale of vegetables, fruit, ice cream, and fried foods. He owned his own establishment, first on San José and San Francisco from 1926 to 1927, later on Jesús del Monte, and finally in the neighborhood of Lawton. In the Havana neighborhood of Víbora he grew garlic, beans, onions, watercress, and cundeamor, with seeds he brought back from China. Felipe most enjoys talking about his businesses. His loquacity on this matter is not surprising, if one keeps in mind that he dedicated the majority of his life to work and little to diversion.

Often using gestures to substitute difficult words, Felipe elaborated on the fruit ice creams of mamey, mango, and banana, not forgetting the delicious mantecado. He used a *sorbetera* for the mixture of fresh and condensed milk, sugar, fruit, and water. He separately prepared chunks of ice and granular salt for chilling and hardening the ice cream, a fatiguing task.

The many times I insisted that Felipe reveal the details that made famous the ice cream of the Chinese in Cuba, he said that only by observing how it is made can one learn. On one occasion his nephew Santiago intervened, saying that the secret of the best ice cream is in the combination of all types of milk: condensed, evaporated, fresh, and powdered. He relates that the most delicious ice cream in Havana was made in the cafeteria of the theater "America," and the owner, who was Chinese, confided in him this secret. Felipe's son had worked there during the 1950s. Santiago narrated an anecdote from this era. One time a regular customer told the cafeteria owner that he had tried better ice cream in "el Norte." The owner immediately boarded a plane for the United States and returned with a sample of ice cream. When the customer in Havana asked for his preferred flavor, he noted that it was not the ice cream that he was accustomed to eating. Upon tasting it, he shouted some obscene words to the Chinese, complaining about the flavor of the ice cream. With a triumphant air, the owner said, "Eat and don't object, for you are eating the best ice cream that exists in the United States!" In this way, he had salvaged the well-earned fame of his product.

Besides ice cream, Felipe prepared fried foods with flour, eggs, and fillings of meat or fish. Others were of fresh corn with sugar. Many of his customers were Jamaicans who painted the houses around his food stand. Business was broadened with the sale of pastries of beans and green plantains or potatoes. To grind the beans, Felipe used a wooden mill called "*tsia bo*" that was acquired from China. It cost him $100 and weighed 200 pounds. At one time he also sold pork rinds.

With the exception of the years of the Japanese occupation of China (1937–1945), Felipe always sent a portion of his earnings to his family in China, with whom he maintained frequent correspondence. Remittances were deposited in a bank in Havana and from there to another in Hong Kong. When business was going well, he sent money two or three times a year to help his relatives with food and clothing. After the Cuban Revolution, Felipe concentrated on the sale of select fruits and refrigerated juices, which customers consumed in his establishment or brought home.

He learned Spanish little by little

Felipe learned the language of Cervantes on his own, little by little. Each day he incorporated a new word into his limited vocabulary, essential for his social and commercial relations. Listening to Felipe, I remember a burlesque version of speech of these immigrants. It was recreated through humor in the following poem, "El chino comerciante" by Lico (a pseudonym)[7]:

> *Señor?, quién es ese chino*
> *Que se me pasa delante?*
> *Este chino vende mucho,*
> *Este chino es comerciante.*
>
> *Chinito qué vendes tú*
> *Que yo te quiero comprar,*
> *Y dime lo que tú vendes*
> *Para oirte pregonar*
>
> *Yo lleva galletica Santo Lumingo*
> *Cuculate, panitela*
> *Cucolonga,*
> *Uá, uá, úa...*
>
> *Yo lleva nalanja de china,*
> *Caña de la tiela,*
> *Platanito mansango,*
> *La milonga de agua*
> *Úa, úa, úa...*
>
> *Yo lleva butifala catalana*
> *Churisa lan uimeña*
> *Putage lan gallego*
> *Fabada lan tuliango*
> *Úa, úa, úa...*

Yo lleva buniato sancuchagua
Bacalao leflitu,
Salina gallega,
Abincón con hueva
Y se cabú, uá, uá, uá...

Relaxing on Sundays

On Sunday afternoons in Cuba, when Felipe rested from the week-ly grind, he would go swimming. After paying one *peso* to enter the beach, he moved far from the shore and into the depths of the blue ocean. Afterward, he entered a hut "with clean water to bathe with" [*con agua limpia pa' limpiá*.] Felipe alternated swimming with attending cockfights, another of his favorite diversions. He remembers the fences on Aguas Dulces at the corner of Tejas, and another in the countryside. He says, "I spend one *peso* to enter, but I don't play. A lot of people, a lot of Chinese. When the rooster fights, I don't pay one *peso*, others pay five *pesos*." [*Yo gasta un peso pa' entrá, pero no juega, mucha gente mucho chino, cuando el gallo pelea, yo no paga un peso, tú pagá cinco peso.*] Felipe told me that in China people also liked gam-bling, but more so in the city. In the countryside the poverty was such that the more reasonable action was to eat the rooster before losing it in a bet. Upon returning from the beach or betting, Felipe would go to any one of the many *bodegas* to buy some refreshments, such as sand-wiches and Coca-Cola.

Master of his throne

At the end of the staircase leading up to Santiago and Felipe's home is a painting welcoming visitors with beautiful Chinese calligraphy sig-nifying "Happiness." Because a hip fracture prevents him from walk-ing all around the house, Felipe has converted his bed into a genuine throne. From there, with his index finger—when he is not using the cane that allows him small maneuvers—he orders doors and windows opened and lights turned on or off. The doctor who visited him to take his pulse and blood pressure was amazed at the firmness of Felipe's abdominal muscles. Of course, the doctor had no idea of the multiple acrobatic postures Felipe adopts in bed to avoid stiffness and fatigue.

Not even the most seasoned practitioner of tai chi does it better!

Putting into practice Confucius's maxim of filial piety, Santiago dutifully brings Felipe daily meals from the residence for the elderly in the *barrio chino*. Felipe still conserves his good appetite and marvelous digestion. He devours *café con leche*, bread, hot oolong tea without sugar, chicken seasoned with soy sauce, fish in sweet-and-sour sauce and rice, occasionally guava paste with white cheese, and a dose of vitamins and minerals that reinforces his frail body.

A preoccupation of Felipe's is to constantly find out and compare the prices and quality of different products from over fifty years ago with those of the present, always concluding that those in the past were better and cheaper. The rewards for this activity lay in simply recollecting the past, often the dearest time for the elderly.

A passion for reading

Felipe attended school in China through fourth or fifth grade. He loves reading, and nothing printed with characters escapes him. In the house are piles of Chinese newspapers and magazines. Most of these are old, but from time to time, he rereads them for entertainment. He is a regular reader of *Kwong Wah Po*, the official newspaper of the Chinese association Casino Chung Wah. He also remembers the other newspapers he used to read, such as the merchant newspaper *Wah Man Sion Po* and the Nationalist Party newspaper *Man Sen Yat Po*.

An old book of divination

Of the Chinese-language books preserved in the house, my attention was drawn to an extremely old copy that Felipe cares for with great zeal, despite the fact that he can barely read it. The book is written in an ancient, enigmatic language and filled with symbols that he does not know how to interpret. I consulted Sun Zhong Chen, a professor of Chinese language in the *barrio chino*. Upon reviewing the strange booklet, he explained that it is a divination text consisting of poems and 60 hexagrams, resembling the *I Ching* (Book of Changes). The original manuscript was discovered by English and French troops after they burned the "old" Summer Palace (Yuanmingyuan) in Beijing in 1860. The published version of 1867 contains a prologue in

English that informs us that the manuscript deals with "the rise, the fall, the tranquility, and the turbulence of China" and that it was prohibited by the emperors of past dynasties.

Guan Gong is San Fan Con

One afternoon as I sat next to Felipe recording his stories, my gaze was directed toward a painting in the room. I asked him the significance of the three figures represented in the scene. He explained, in his way, the legend of Guan Gong.[8] He tells me that the three friends lived many years ago. Liu Bei, Guan Yu, and Zhang Fei were brave men who knew how to fight. But missing from the painting is Zhao Zilong, another courageous soldier who was the youngest of them. Felipe tells me that "Guan Yu is the Cuban San Fan Con," adding that I should not ask him more about the story, as it is very old and he does not remember it well. What Felipe neglected to mention is that the three friends, although of different families, swore to be brothers and provide mutual aid in all moments of life—danger, war, fortune, love, and above all, in the service of the emperor and common people. The declaration of the three heroes is known as the "oath of the peach garden."[9]

A sculpture of Guan Gong or San Fan Con sits on a shelf in the living room. The figure, reading a book, has a long, black beard and reddish purple face. At times, Santiago lights incense sticks that scent the air. I imitate him and with devotion invoke the venerated ancestor Guan Gong, as demonstrated to me by Leandro Pérez Asión (Chiu Pan), treasurer of the Long Gang association that groups together descendants with the surnames of the four famous and loyal friends (Liu, Guan, Zhang, and Zhao).

Manuel Luis, a relative of Felipe

One of the members of our Chinese family in Cuba was Manuel Luis (1914–1968), a notable revolutionary fighter and comrade in the struggles of Blas Roca Calderío and Carlos Rafael Rodríguez. He was president of the Chinese Socialist Alliance in Cuba (Alianza Socialista China en Cuba) and merchant of the town of Regla, where he resided. He died in Beijing on October 21, 1968, where he had been representing the Chinese association Casino Chung Wah. To perpetuate his memory a plaque has been placed at his house on No. 363 Martí Street.

Attending Chinese opera

Felipe liked the cinema and theater. He still remembers the "Águila de Oro" (Kam Yen or Golden Eagle) and a theater on Zanja Street, gone for some time. He attended performances of Chinese operas with actors from Hong Kong or mainland China. As José Baltar Rodriguez states, "Independently of its manipulation by wealthy Chinese, the traditional opera, through its characteristics and representation, constituted for the immigrant a form of enjoyment that kept him in contact with his original culture."[10]

It occurred to me to inquire of Felipe his opinion on Cuban women. Mischievously and with an oblique gaze he responded, "I don't know anything, I don't look at anyone," and laughing, told me, "It doesn't matter . . . white, Chinese, *jakuey*,[11] mulatto . . . it doesn't matter." [*Yo no sabe ná, yo no mirá nada. Da iguá, blanca, china, "jakuey," mulata, da iguá.*]

Felipe shows his treasures

My conversations with Felipe had a surprising culmination. He directed me to open a small display cabinet. I opened it. Its interior emitted an odor of incense, herbs, and menthol. I extracted a small cardboard box and another of metal, containing treasures conserved by Felipe with zeal throughout the years.

The images of his mother, sisters, children, grandchildren, and great-grandchildren, at weddings and at play, came alive as the old photos passed before my enthralled eyes. I looked at Felipe. His eyes had recovered their faded brilliance as he introduced me to his loved ones. He also showed me the certificate of recognition for residing more than 50 years in Cuba awarded to him by the Havana Chinatown Promotion Group in 1999. I also observed the distinctive seal (chop) from the Chinese Chamber of Commerce, to which he belonged.

Among the photos was a recent one taken of Santiago, Felipe, and myself. On the reverse Felipe had written the characters for Kuan Yi, the Chinese name he had given me after thinking about it for many days. He told me that in China the name is considered to have a nice sound. This gesture moved me profoundly, and I consider it proof of the preferential place that I already occupy in the heart of grandfather Felipe.

I know that the history of Felipe is incomplete, and I have failed to mention many of his experiences. At 99 years of age Felipe is tired, and although he is still lucid, I cannot force the many other memories, foggy from time, to reemerge from his past. I have collected and ordered what he has told me in his peculiar Spanish, and I have added some observations from my research to complete his ideas without distorting them.

The history that Felipe narrates is the same or almost equal to that of other Chinese in Cuba. What is interesting is not the singularity of his case, but its universality for understanding the experiences of Chinese immigrants living in the same time and place. The present story is a demonstration of affection toward my Chinese family through one of its oldest members, as well as respect and admiration for the humble coolies who arrived in Cuba beginning in 1847 and all the others afterward. They added the more than 4,000 years of their civilization to our people, also the product of Spanish and African blood. The contributions of the Chinese are, without doubt, an indissoluble part of Cuban nationality and culture.

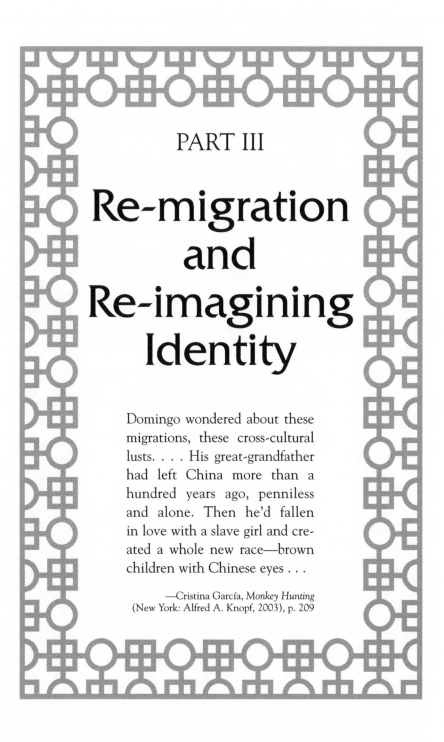

PART III

Re-migration and Re-imagining Identity

Domingo wondered about these migrations, these cross-cultural lusts. . . . His great-grandfather had left China more than a hundred years ago, penniless and alone. Then he'd fallen in love with a slave girl and created a whole new race—brown children with Chinese eyes . . .

—Cristina García, *Monkey Hunting*
(New York: Alfred A. Knopf, 2003), p. 209

CHAPTER 7

Anatomy of a Craze:
The Tangled Roots and Twisting
Branches of the History of
Cuban Chinese Restaurants in
New York City

ANDREW MEYER

Residents of the U.S. are raised on the image of our nation as a melting pot. The teeming masses from many lands pouring into crowded ports are a staple of novels, movies, and textbook accounts. No North American city bears more claim to this legacy than New York, site of the Statue of Liberty, with its famous beckoning inscription, and Ellis Island, where so many arrived from afar. Thus it is perhaps understandable for visitors to New York's Chinatown to be amused at the sign marking the Cuban Chinese Benevolent Association overhanging a window on East Broadway. Many are prone to wonder how many "Cuban Chinese" there could possibly be. The blithe acceptance of a hodgepodge tapestry of cultures in New York City does not extend to foreign shores; U.S. citizens will not necessarily grant other cultures and places the heterogeneity they themselves take for granted. While the thought of a Chinese person resident in New York or San Francisco seems natural, a Chinese person resident in Havana seems

My gratitude to the owners and staff of La Caridad 78 and Dr. Evelyn Hu-Dehart for their aid in my research.

odd, exotic, and even funny. In this regard, it is ironic that history brought Chinese people to Havana before they arrived in New York. It is doubly ironic that now more Cuban Chinese live in the U.S. than in Havana.

This sense, however, that "Cuban Chinese" (be it a person, object, or dish) must be exotic and strange helps explain a cultural phenomenon that New York City experienced in the 1980s—the burgeoning and (for a while) explosive popularity of Cuban Chinese restaurants. During the late 1970s and 1980s a spate of Cuban Chinese restaurants were launched, such as "Asia Numero Uno" or "La Dinastia China." Like these examples, most had names in Spanish that suggested the blending of Latin and Sinic cultures. Signs in the entrance or window announced "*Comidas China y Criollo.*" Like the menu at "La Caridad 78" restaurant, most of these Cuban Chinese restaurants offered a selection divided between "Spanish" and "Chinese" dishes. Chop Suey and Carne Guisada were (and are) both mainstays.

The cachet of and high demand for these restaurants did not last long, though a dozen or more Cuban Chinese restaurants remain open throughout New York City. Though this culinary fad was a brief and perhaps insignificant chapter in the broad cultural history of New York, it does shed light on some interesting issues. A search for the historical roots of the Cuban Chinese restaurant craze speaks to questions of cultural perception versus historical reality and demonstrates strategies immigrant groups employ in creatively adapting to exigent circumstances in host communities. At the same time, the story of the Cuban Chinese themselves reveals how global history can radically and at times tragically affect the local lives of individuals and communities.

Despite the conventional perception that a Cuban Chinese New Yorker must be some form of anomaly, in reality the Chinese diaspora in the Americas began in Cuba. The Cuban Chinese community, now decimated in the aftermath of the Cuban Revolution, is the oldest Chinese community in the Western hemisphere. The same forces of global market capitalism that engendered the Opium War (1839–42) drew the first Chinese workers to Cuba, though the specific timing of events was an almost preternatural coincidence. In the mid-1840s the

Spanish colonial regime in Cuba faced an expanding demand for labor on its commercial sugar plantations coupled with a shrinking pool of slave labor due to the spreading abolition of slavery and the slave trade throughout the Atlantic. At that very moment, the British victory against imperial China in the Opium War, with its subsequent expansion of the British commercial and official presence in southern China, created the opportunity to develop and exploit a new, cheap labor source—Chinese "coolie" labor. It is a testimony to the driving power of market capitalism that, despite the daunting logistical challenges of geography and culture, by 1847, only five years after the signing of the Treaty of Nanjing that allowed European commercial penetration of China's port cities, ambitious entrepreneurs brought the first Chinese workers to Cuba. During the subsequent 27 years of *la trata amarilla* ("the yellow trade"), more than 125,000 Chinese laborers arrived in Cuba.[2]

The first encounters between these Chinese migrants and their new home were heavily laden with tragedy. Thousands died in passage between China and Cuba, thousands more died from hunger, disease, and overwork on the sugar plantations. Discriminatory laws limited their freedom of movement and sought to create conditions of inescapable economic dependency. Many who survived their sojourn in Cuba returned to China. Yet others stayed, settled, and married (some to other Chinese, some to native Cubans). These ultimately formed the first and, for a while, the largest Overseas Chinese community in the Americas. In a pattern familiar among Chinese immigrant groups in other parts of the world, the Cuban Chinese established roots in the urban commercial economy of their adopted homeland. In Havana and other Cuban cities, Chinatowns evolved, filled with small businesses (restaurants, laundries, groceries) owned by Cuban Chinese entrepreneurs. By the early twentieth century the Barrio Chino of Havana was thriving, occupying an area of more than forty blocks square with an estimated population of thirty to forty thousand residents.

The Cuban Revolution of 1959 brought this era to an end. Though the Castro government declared an end to racism and discrimination of all kinds, the pervasively *petit bourgeois* nature of the economy of the

147

Barrio Chino placed it at odds with the ideological vector of the new regime.[3] The Castro government undertook a massive nationalization of the private economy, effectively dispossessing the majority of Cuban Chinese citizens. This radical dislocation drove the Cuban Chinese community away in droves, most (along with their *criollo* émigré compatriots) to cities in North America. At the height of the Cuban Chinese restaurant "craze," an estimated five thousand Cuban Chinese lived in New York (in contrast to current-day Havana, where the Barrio Chino has perhaps one thousand residents of Chinese ancestry).

Against this backdrop, the Cuban Chinese restaurant craze can be viewed in several different lights. The most basic (and in many ways perhaps the most accurate) characterization of this trend is as a common stage in the social and economic trajectory of a new immigrant group. Cuban Chinese first began to arrive in the U.S. in large numbers in the late 1960s and early 1970s. Thus the simultaneous opening of these small businesses corresponds neatly to the end of the first decade after entry. This is quite comparable to the personal history of many immigrant families, including my own. For many families arriving in the U.S. from overseas, opening a small business was the first step toward middle-class status in a multi-generational strategy of social advancement. Typically the first generation builds up wealth through small-scale commercial activities, which subsequent generations then invest in either education or real or commercial capital.[4] Thus the closure of many Cuban Chinese restaurants in the last five to ten years represents the transition between the first and second generation of Cuban Chinese-Americans. The children of the first Cuban Chinese to immigrate have traded upon their parents' small business success and pursued greater prosperity and higher social status, seeking careers in professions such as medicine and engineering or in larger-scale industrial and commercial enterprises over that of restaurateur.[5]

Yet these sociological and economic factors alone do not account for the Cuban Chinese restaurant craze. Cuban Chinese émigrés could have opened any kind of business, and even if only a percentage of them opened restaurants, their choice to market themselves as *specifically Cuban* Chinese (as opposed to Cantonese, Hunanese, etc.) is significant. The volume of Cuban Chinese restaurants (given the other alternatives open to Cuban Chinese immigrants) can only be understood in light of some intrinsic appeal to either the producer or the consumer.

Thus another context against which to examine the Cuban Chinese restaurant phenomenon is the experience of Overseas Chinese more generally. The Cuban Chinese represent an intriguing case in the history of the Chinese diaspora in that their "Chinese" identity does not, on the surface, seem to be completely fungible in the transition from Havana to New York. In Cuba they were Cuban Chinese. In the U.S. they do not become Chinese-American, but Cuban Chinese-American.

The question naturally arises as to why the Cuban Chinese identity should remain so enduring and coherent, and if this fact should make us view the Cuban Chinese as exceptional among Overseas Chinese as a whole. On the one hand one could argue that this must be the case, otherwise we would see a "Malay Chinese Benevolent Association" and a "Costa Rican Chinese Benevolent Association" alongside that of the Cuban Chinese in downtown Manhattan. Yet this line of reasoning fails when one compares the actions of the Cuban Chinese to those of other Overseas Chinese communities both in New York and elsewhere. The persistence of a regional identity and the formation of regional and kinship societies among Chinese immigrants are common wherever Overseas Chinese have laid down roots.

This phenomenon can be amply attested by reference to a different (and for the most part, more recent) group of immigrants to New York's Chinatown, the Fujianese-Chinese. Coincidentally just below the window of the Cuban Chinese Benevolent Association in Manhattan is a statue of the Opium Commissioner Lin Zexu, the Chinese official who in 1839 commanded the destruction of foreign opium stockpiles in Canton that set off the Opium War. Most Chinese histories view Lin Zexu as a nationalist hero, a lone voice of integrity who stood up to foreign imperialism. A statue of Lin could even be perceived as vaguely anti-American, since American traders were included among the owners of the opium that Lin Zexu destroyed in 1839. Yet the inscription on the statue in New York's Chinatown does not call attention to foreign imperialism, American commercial avarice, or Chinese national pride, but reads "Pioneer in the War on Drugs." The statue of Lin Zexu, who was in fact Fujianese, was erected by a consortium of New York's Fujianese-Chinese, to combat the (supposed) popular perception that Fujianese-Chinese are engaged in drug trafficking. This is definitely a new use of the historical image of Lin Zexu. The vast majority of Chinese would view Lin as a national icon rather than a model of regional pride. Yet this radically narrow (and rather anachronistic, since the "war on drugs" in Lin's time and place is not wholly comparable to what is transpiring now in the U.S.) employment of Lin's image testifies to the lengths to which Chinese immigrants will go in defending and promoting their regional identity.

One could argue that the status of "Cuban Chinese" is a regional identity nearly indistinguishable from that of "Fujianese-Chinese." The fact that Cuban Chinese (as opposed to the Malaysian or Costa Rican Chinese) express a common bond similar to that of immigrants from Fujian may reflect the fact that like the Cuban Chinese, the Fujianese arrived in large numbers, with similar speed, and under similarly difficult economic circumstances. Thus the tendency to group coherence and action might represent a typically "Chinese" response, and not be a product of the group's uniquely "Cuban" experience.

Yet one might contend that, on further analysis, this portrait does not fully explain the phenomenon. After all, there has yet to be a "Fujianese-Chinese" restaurant craze. Moreover, if "Cuban Chinese" is to be compared to the regional identity of Chinese immigrant groups, we are faced with the problem that virtually all Cuban Chinese already had one prior to immigrating to the United States. The Cuban Chinese themselves come, almost exclusively, from the same home region of Canton (or Guangdong) Province in China. As the experience of other Chinese-American immigrants attests, the regional identity of Cantonese Chinese has a very powerful influence on the self-perceptions and collective activities of Overseas Chinese who share it. In Cuba this was definitely true: Cuban Chinese formed societies dedicated to commemorating their shared origins in villages and regions of Canton. Yet upon transposition to the U.S., the sway of "Cantonese Chinese" as a mark of collective identity was seemingly less powerful than that of "Cuban Chinese." Moreover, "Cuban Chinese" restaurants are not the only unique cultural product to emerge from the Chinese experience in Cuba. Wilfredo Lam became an internationally celebrated artist through the exploration of his Cuban Chinese and Afro-Cuban identities. Thus it remains possible that the Cuban Chinese experience is in some way unique, creating an enduring cultural amalgam out of disparate elements.

Even so, the picture may be further nuanced. If we look deeper into the activities of Cuban Chinese restaurateurs, one might argue that they are following a strategy or strategies practiced by Overseas Chinese the world over. Examining other Overseas Chinese communities in other times and other places, one observes common recurrent methods employed by people forced (or alternatively determined) to inhabit the margins of the societies in which they reside. One such strategy is the search for patrons among the "host" community within which an Overseas Chinese group resides. Andrew Wilson has documented this tendency with respect to the Chinese community in the late-nineteenth- and early-twentieth-century Philippines. Local elites in those communities sought to establish ties with the Spanish and American colonial authorities, adopting measures such as converting to Catholicism or applying for Spanish or American citizenship.[6] In this light, the Cuban Chinese purveyance of "Comidas China y Criollos" could be seen as a similar plea for patronage from the Cuban-American community. If so, this would of course be intriguing, as it represents a search for "patrons" among a group who may themselves be perceived as "clients" of a host society. Alternatively, perhaps what we see among the Cuban Chinese is an attempt to maintain pre-existing patron-client networks that precede their departure from the Caribbean.

Investigation further complicates the picture, however. When I undertook to visit some Cuban Chinese restaurants still operating in New York, I found that the ties of their owners and employees to Cuba were very variable. At "La Caridad 78" I spoke with three Cuban Chinese waiters. Each man told me a similar story. They had all been born in Guangdong Province and moved to Cuba in the 1950s. All had sojourned in Cuba for fifteen to twenty years and come to

151

America, where they had entered the restaurant business (two had previously operated their own restaurants in different parts of New York City). What struck me most prominently was that none of the three men had married or raised families in Cuba. All had waited until immigrating to the United States to marry. Moreover, *all three* men had returned to Hong Kong to find wives. One need not impeach these men's feelings for Cuba or the "authenticity" of their claim to be Cuban Chinese. Yet certainly one could argue that their ties to Guangdong remained at least as strong as those to Cuba and Cuban culture. What then of the idea of "Cuban Chinese?" At the very least one must acknowledge that this identity is quite elastic. Global forces have been impelling the movement of people, goods, and cultural artifacts between Cuba, China, and the U.S. for more than 150 years. The imprint this dynamic has made on specific individuals cannot be reduced to some enduring essence, but exists within a broad range of potential human experience.

This observation forces us to reconsider (or at least refine) the notion of the Cuban Chinese restaurant as a plea for patronage. If Cuban Chinese experience and identity is so variable and elastic, the patronage ties (particularly pre-Revolution ties) that Cuban Chinese enjoy with other Cuban-Americans must be equally so. In this light, the impetus (at least in part) for the Cuban Chinese restaurant craze might be sought not in the social and economic dynamic of the Cuban Chinese themselves, but in the dispositions of Cuban-Americans. Cuban-Americans might, after all, be the first natural clientele that a Cuban Chinese restaurant might seek to serve.

Here we North Americans (particularly residents of the U.S.) must confront some of our most deep-seated assumptions about the experience of dining out. Dining at a Chinese restaurant has become a kind of pop-cultural cliché, a common point of reference around which jokes, idiomatic expressions, and entire popular entertainments can and have been constructed. The episode of the television comedy *Seinfeld* set entirely in the foyer of a Manhattan Chinese restaurant[7] (the characters never actually get seated) is perhaps the ultimate expression of this phenomenon. The episode is intended to resonate with the experience of the viewer—it is funny because "we" have all been there. At the same time, the viewer is invited to share in (or at least recognize) an inside joke . . . the range of "we" is not all-inclusive. The setting is presented as specific to America, even more particularly to New York, and especially so of Manhattan.

What many Americans might fail to realize is that the experience of dining at a Chinese restaurant is just as common and modular in other parts of the world and at other times. This would have been especially true in pre-Revolutionary Cuba, with its thriving Barrio Chino. For U.S. residents (depending upon their age and geographic location) certain items or details are classically evocative of the experience of dining in a Chinese restaurant, despite the fact that these details are particular to the U.S. and have little if nothing to do with Chinese cuisine—fortune cookies, duck sauce, and chow mein are three examples. If the menus of Cuban Chinese restaurants in New York provide any standard by which to judge, the experience of dining in the Barrio Chino was marked by similarly distinctive sights, tastes, and smells, such as *chicharrones de pollo* (fried chicken crackling) and *arroz amarillo* (yellow rice). This is perhaps the most appealing service that a Cuban Chinese restaurant can afford its non-Chinese Cuban-American patrons—the re-creation of a dining experience redolent of pre-Revolutionary Cuba. The senses of taste and smell are the greatest triggers to memory; thus for Cuban-Americans what others might take for granted as "ethnic cuisine" could attain a much more profound significance. A meal out can become an evocation of a lost world.

This sense is implicit in the writing of the Cuban-American author Cristina García, whose first novel, *Dreaming in Cuban*, explored the complexity of a persistent Cuban identity in exile. Her second novel, *Monkey Hunting*, continued these same themes through a fictional account of the Cuban Chinese. Midway through the novel, we encounter Domingo Chen, a Cuban Chinese New Yorker:

> The dishwasher broke down in the middle of the dinner rush, and so Domingo had to wash everything by hand. He couldn't work fast enough to please the waiters, irascible old Chinese men like his father who'd left Cuba after the

Revolution. "*¡Mas platos! ¡Mas cubiertos!*" Domingo scraped and rinsed plate after plate of house specials— breaded steak with onions, fried rice, and *tostones*—until his stomach flip-flopped with disgust.

After work, he headed downtown to see Ray Barretto's late show at the Village Gate. Domingo knew it drove his father crazy that he spent all his money on concerts and clothes. But what was he supposed to do? Save for retirement?. . .

The nightclub was jammed, but Domingo talked himself into a seat up front, next to a washed-out little nurse with a mole on her cheek. El Watusi Man was hitting the skins like a dialect freaked by thunder. Smoke-sounding *rumbero*. *De otro mundo.* Domingo felt the *timba* as if the Man were playing his own bones. *Ashé olu batá.* He closed his eyes and let loose, felt the groove, a deep reverie, the pulse of his own peculiar birth.

"Hey where you from?" the nurse asked him when the music finally stopped.

Domingo wanted to answer her, to say that his blood was a mix of this and that. So how was he supposed to choose who he wanted to be?

"Cuba," he said. "I'm from Cuba."[8]

Domingo's dilemma and its ultimate resolution distills García's theme. Confronted with the challenge to answer where he is from, he can only answer "Cuba." Domingo is (and through him, all Cuban Chinese are) portrayed as embodying the Cuban condition. His mixed ancestry, his blending and straddling of different cultures, even his confusion over how to "choose who he wanted to be" can be construed as the common legacy of all Cubans. Particularly, the filaments and personal rhythms of his life are an invocation of pre-Revolutionary Cuba. In his food, music, and sexual flirtations he exemplifies the materialism, sensuality, and exoticism which were so much a part of the reputed Cuban character and which have been driven from Cuba's shores as thoroughly and comprehensively as the Cuban Chinese themselves. Under García's pen, Domingo's assertion "I am from Cuba" can be read as a kind of manifesto. If Domingo himself is both authentically Cuban and wholly excluded by the Revolution, his dilemma is redemptive of the whole Cuban community in exile. A Cuba that has no room for Domingo Chen is a Cuba alienated from its own soul.

Cristina García's artistic imagination is very powerful, but one must of course be extremely cautious in examining the Cuban Chinese restaurant phenomenon against the poignancy of her novel. One can only imagine what the response of the waiters I interviewed at La Caridad 78 would be if asked whether their own life stories could carry the same symbolic freight as that of Domingo Chen. The fact that a Cuban Chinese dining experience can be vividly evocative does not preclude its inception being driven by commerce. Many of those who own or work in Cuban Chinese restaurants may be small businessmen seeking any edge in a climate of cutthroat competition. But this does not delegitimize either Cristina García's prose or the motives of even the most "marginally" Cuban Chinese restaurateur. It only under-scores the fact that any cultural expression is the product of a complex negotiation between all those with any interest in either its creation or appreciation.

If in fact Cuban Chinese restaurateurs are trading upon a special nostalgia for Cuba, this is another way in which they comply, at least provisionally, with the common strategies and cultural patterns appar-ent in other Overseas Chinese communities. Nostalgia has always been a stock-in-trade of Overseas Chinese elites, going back to long before the Chinese diaspora in the Americas. Carsey Yee has shown, for example, how Vietnamese Chinese intellectuals created a total dis-course of nostalgia through the production of Ming (1368–1644 C.E.) loyalist poetry during the eighteenth century in Vietnam.[9] This might seem a world removed from the evocation of a Caribbean milieu, as the Vietnamese Chinese were, after all, expressing yearning for their "homeland." But their paeans to the Ming dynasty (during the second century of Manchu rule) looked to a world no more real, immediate, or recoverable than pre-Revolutionary Cuba is today (indeed, arguably less so). One could assert that the choices of the Cuban

155

Chinese have been conditioned by the chance confluence of the Overseas Chinese's conventional expression of nostalgia with the interests and tastes of their "host patrons."

Yet if Cuban Chinese cuisine in New York is the product of a complex negotiation between disparate but converging interests, it is folly to assume that Cuban Chinese and non-Chinese Cuban-Americans are or can be its only participants. In fact, the greatest success story in "Cuban Chinese" cuisine involves entrepreneurs who are neither Chinese, nor Cuban, nor any combination thereof. The chic, celebrated, and astronomically expensive Asia de Cuba, with locations in New York (the original), Los Angeles, San Francisco, and London, is a collaborative venture initiated by restaurant impresario and Philadelphia native Jeffrey Chodorrow. His restaurants offer exotic "Sino-Latino" dishes in interiors designed by Phillipe Starck within hotels established by Ian Schraeger. Thus the saga of the Cuban Chinese has produced an ambience that is itself modular, commodifiable, and commercially lucrative across two continents.

A final caveat to any reductionist account of the history of Cuban Chinese restaurants is afforded by my "fieldwork" in researching this essay. I visited one restaurant on the Upper West Side of Manhattan that is among the oldest Cuban Chinese restaurants in New York and always listed in guidebooks as an example of "authentic" Chinese Cuban cuisine. The young man who now owns and runs the restaurant is Chinese Latino, but he is from Ecuador, not Cuba. He bought the restaurant from its Cuban Chinese founder ten years ago; that man has retired to Connecticut. When I asked about his clientele, he replied that while many of the former patrons might have been Cuban, his customers now represent the changing makeup of the neighborhood. They mainly include non-Chinese from the Dominican Republic, Mexico, and Central America. This is reportedly so at many Cuban Chinese restaurants still in operation. The Cuban Chinese might have been the first to explore this niche in the culinary market, and its first flourishing might have fed on all the forces outlined above. Yet the persistent appeal of these restaurants does not rest in poignant nostalgia or the siren song of exotic "fusion cuisine." Rather, it seems to tap in to a pan-American dining culture of which most *yanquis* are unaware. Dominican-Americans and Mexican-Americans might patronize a Chinese restaurant simply because, like the Chinese restaurants they frequented in the land of their birth, it affords the opportunity to have a side order of *plantanos* with one's lo mein or yellow rice instead of white. In other words, virtually all Americans who migrate to the U.S. come from places with significant Chinese communities. This is perhaps the most prominent lesson to draw from the history of Cuban Chinese restaurant culture. The presence of Overseas Chinese and the cultural influence they exert on the communities in which they are embedded is a pan-American experience and a shared pan-American legacy, not one that is exclusive to the United States.

CHAPTER 8

Migration Stories: Serial Migration and the Production of Home and Identity in Transnationalism

LOK SIU

Why should Chinese in Panama be considered part of the larger Chinese diaspora in the Caribbean? Although Panama is not formally considered part of the Caribbean, it is very much influenced by Caribbean cultural and social flows. Bounded on the north by the Caribbean Sea and on the south by the Pacific Ocean, Panama, like most of its Central American neighbors, is culturally divided between the Anglophone-influenced Caribbean side and the Hispanic-dominated Pacific side. In addition to its proximity to the Caribbean, at least two factors link Chinese in Panama to the larger diaspora in this region.

First, Chinese in Panama must be understood within the larger framework of nineteenth-century Chinese migration to the Caribbean (and the Americas). Like the rest of the region, the first large group of Chinese that arrived in Panama in the mid-1800s came in response to labor demands. They migrated as indentured male laborers and worked on the trans-isthmian railroad. After 1874, with the end of the "coolie trade," Chinese migration consisted primarily of free men who went into farming, fishing, trading, and shopkeeping. It was not until the 1920s that women began to immigrate to Panama in large numbers. This pattern of Chinese migration was more or less consistent throughout the Caribbean. Second, the history of intra-regional migration links Chinese in Panama to the rest of the Caribbean. As soon as they arrived, the Chinese began traveling and migrating throughout this region. Some were indentured laborers who were sent from one country to another; others were free men who sought work opportunities in different locales. Indeed, one of the most striking factors about Chinese migration to Panama (and I suspect it is not unique to Panama alone) is that diasporic Chinese came not just directly from Greater China[1] but also from different parts of the Caribbean and the Americas.[2] These migratory movements between Panama and Asia and within the New World are often circular and part of a series of migrations. And from these travels emerge not only intricate webs of kinship and social networks that link diasporic Chinese to China and across the Americas but also a distinct regional form of diasporic consciousness and identity.

While extensive research has documented the circular migration of diasporic Chinese between China and their adopted homes in the New World,[3] Chinese migration within the Caribbean and the Americas is less known. This essay hence focuses on the trans-American (in which I include the Caribbean) migrations and examines how they inform diasporic identity formation. An investigation of these intraregional migrations will extend our understanding of diasporic Chinese subject formation beyond the current convention of focusing on the binary relationship between homeland and diaspora. I argue that, in addition to homeland-diaspora relations, practices of trans-American travels and migrations have shaped diasporic Chinese consciousness, sense of belonging, and ideas of home.

Drawing on four migration narratives, this paper examines how diasporic Chinese make sense of their "serial migration" in constructing notions of home, identity, and belonging. I propose the term "serial migration" to describe the process by which people migrate to a series of places over a period of time. While it resonates with James Clifford's discussion of "itinerary,"[4] serial migration describes a more profound engagement with dwelling places. If traveling connotes a transitory mode of moving across space, migration represents a more prolonged and meaningful interaction with place. Indeed, scholars have used terms such as step migration,[5] remigration, or secondary and tertiary migration[6] to describe one specific movement within the phe-nomenon of serial migrations. While each term refers to a singular migration from one place to another, serial migration describes the overall, cumulative process of engaging in multiple migrations across different national borders. In other words, rather than examining each migration separately, serial migration situates each border-crossing experience as part of a more extended and open-ended migratory process. It treats migration as a process of subject formation and seeks to understand the concomitant effects of multiple migrations on con-structions of home and identity. How are people shaped by serial migration, and how do they make sense and narrate their migrations in relation to home, identity, and community? Could serial migration be a strategy of extending and multiplying the possibilities of "home" in diaspora? Can analysis of serial migration reveal continuity along-side disjuncture?

Mapping a set of intricate detours and returns, the narratives con-vey three important aspects of diasporic Chinese subject formation. First, they show the diversity of diasporic Chinese as they practice migration under a variety of sociohistorical circumstances and contin-gencies. They illustrate the significance of sociopolitical forces shap-ing migration circumstances as well as the creativity of diasporic peo-ple who use migration as a strategy of survival, self-determination, and social mobility. Second, they illustrate how migratory experiences construct notions of identity, home, and belonging in diaspora. A most surprising aspect of these narratives is the mundane manner in which people speak about their trans-Pacific and trans-American migrations. In effect, it suggests the very ordinariness with which they approach and treat migration as social practice and calls into question the assumption that migration is solely about ruptures and disjunc-tures. And third, the four narratives, taken together, reveal an imag-ining and mapping of the Americas and China as a fluid and con-nected terrain. They articulate a diasporic identity that draws on con-nections not only to the Chinese homeland and the Panamanian nation-state but also to the Americas more broadly. Indeed, from these narratives emerges a trans-continental "Chinese of the Americas" identity.

Migration, Diaspora, Transnationalism

Discussions of transnationalism and globalization have inspired a plethora of research on global migration and the various manifestations of transnational communities. While some examine relations between migrants and their countries of "origin," others study historical and cultural links that bind migrant communities in dispersed locations. While the former are more interested in the back and forth movements and social relations established by migrants between nation-states, the latter are concerned with the cultural production of identity and community that extends beyond the borders of the nation-state. These two approaches loosely constitute recent formulations of transnational and diaspora studies, respectively. On one side, the work of Basch et al. illustrates how transmigrants in the United States sustain social, economic, and political ties with their nations of origin.[7] Similarly, Roger Rouse describes the circular process by which Aguilillans link together their place of residence in California and their hometowns in Mexico.[8] Not to be lost is Aihwa Ong's discussion of Hong Kong elites, whose flexible citizenship enables them to travel back and forth between California and Hong Kong.

In addition to these studies on first-generation migrants, others have examined later descendants' relations with the homeland. For instance, both Karen Leonard's work on Punjabi Mexicans and Andrea Louie's on Chinese Americans show the complications that American-born generations face when connecting up with India and China, respectively.[9] Unlike their predecessors, whose sense of connection to the homeland is more immediate, the American-born descendents have a difficult time identifying with their ethnic "homelands." Both groups experience a sense of disidentification that forces them to rethink their connections to the homeland. Likewise, their counterparts in Latin America, such as Japanese Brazilians, also confront similar struggles when they return to Japan.[10] Together, these works explore the complex and varied relationships that migrants and their descendants sustain with their homelands.

Diaspora offers a different perspective. While definitions and uses of diaspora range widely, the general concept is based on the idea of people scattering from one "homeland" to many different locations.[11] Unlike transnational studies, it attends to the set of relations, discourses, and sentiments that bind not only migrants to their homelands but also migrants to co-ethnic communities dispersed in other locations. In the past two decades, no other scholar has influenced the way we think about diaspora as much as Paul Gilroy. His work on the "Black Atlantic" shifted the analytical focus away from the "homeland" to examine more closely the connections forged among communities in the diaspora. In *The Black Atlantic*, Gilroy provocatively traces the dynamic formation of diasporic identification among blacks dispersed in Britain, the United States, and the Caribbean.[12] Focusing on connections and ties among these communities, Gilroy challenges conventional notions of diaspora that tend to posit the "homeland" at the center as the all-powerful force that determines the activities, the loyalties, and the identifications of the diaspora. Whereas diaspora often has been represented by the metaphor of a tree, with its roots firmly planted in the homeland and its branches representing the diaspora, the black Atlantic is described as a transcultural, international formation that is fractal and rhizomorphic in structure. In his reformulation, diaspora is not a residual or imperfect replica of its homeland. It does not have one center, but rather many different centers and nodes of power. Indeed, the image of the rhizome suggests multiple localities and complicates the binary relationship between the "country of origin" and the "country of settlement" that dominates the migration and diaspora literatures.

In shifting focus away from the homeland as the central source of diasporic identification, Gilroy also problematizes earlier notions of diaspora as primordial or essential identities prescribed by ethnic lineage. Diaspora, for Gilroy, is historically situated and culturally produced. To create the Black Atlantic, diasporic Blacks communicate and reproduce common themes of identification through the continuous circulation of people, ideas, and black expressive culture.[13] Indeed, Gilroy's attentiveness to these flows and circulations provides the point of departure for this essay. His work prompts the question of how, for diasporic Chinese, does the practice of serial migration shape notions of identity, home, and belonging? Conversely, how do diasporic Chinese use serial migration as political resistance, social mobility, and cultural remapping of home and community?

While many earlier studies of overseas Chinese provide in-depth nation-based analysis of local communities,[14] recent writings have turned their attention to transnational flows, circuits, and subjectivities.[15] Nonetheless, following the established canon of overseas Chinese scholarship, the majority of these texts has focused primarily on the regions of Southeast Asia and the United States. It was not until a few years ago that explorations of Chinese in Europe, Africa, and Latin America began to gain more attention.[16] This essay contributes to the burgeoning literature of diasporic Chinese and employs ethnographic methods to provide close analysis of the perspectives and interpretations of diasporic subjects. It uses ethnography to illustrate how diasporic subjects understand their practices of serial migration in constructing notions of who they are, the meaning of belonging in diaspora, and the cultural geography of home and community in the Americas. Such an approach not only supplements the plethora of theoretical literature that already exists but also moves beyond the conventional binary relationship between "homeland" and "places of settlement." Instead, it opens up a new line of inquiry into regional identifications that are drawn from and generated by practices of serial migration. Indeed, what these narratives suggest is that, through the practice of migrating across the Americas, diasporic Chinese assert and perform a sense of belonging *in* the Americas as well as an identity of being Chinese *of* the Americas.

Fernando: The Adventures of Bob Montenegro

"Bob Montenegro.... Hello, my name is Bob Montenegro," Fernando* enunciates these words slowly, pauses dramatically, then continues again, "I just thought it was a cool name to use sometimes. It sounds so suave and cosmopolitan. I used to introduce myself that way at jazz clubs, when I was in college in Chicago. It was just for fun . . . the ladies liked it." He winks, and I smile in response, prodding him to continue his story. After knowing me for a few months and being in a

*Pseudonyms are used for all interviewees.

more relaxed setting—his son's thirtieth birthday party—Fernando seems much more comfortable talking to me.

We met for the first time at his home, which is located in a quiet, middle-class neighborhood of Panama City. After a brief informal introduction, he starts, "So, what is it that you want to ask me? What do you want to know?" From the very beginning, Fernando has been direct, honest, and straightforward. He wastes little time between questions and hardly hesitates to give his opinions and answers. Over the course of my year in Panama, however, I discover that despite his "no-nonsense" attitude, there is a playfulness about him. In his mid-sixties, Fernando had acquired a keen sense of humor and a talent for storytelling.

Being "part Chinese, part white, part black, and part indigenous," Fernando claims that he does not emphasize any one racial identity over the others. He confidently asserts his racially mixed identity. When asked, "How do you see yourself fitting into these different communities?" he responds rhetorically, "Is there a category for mongrels? If so, that's the category I fit into." With brown skin and wavy black hair, he does not possess obvious Chinese features. Even his name, Fernando Jackson, shows no hint of his Chinese background. Despite his mixed racial identity and refusal to define his ethnic identity as exclusively Chinese, both his active participation in Chinese social networks and leadership in a prominent Chinese organization effectively demonstrate his affinity with and identification as part of the community. Belonging in the Chinese diaspora, then, is broadly defined. It does not adhere to essential definitions of race or ethnicity. Rather, belonging in the diaspora is defined not only by self-identification but also through participation in diasporic activities. In other words, one belongs because one chooses to participate and to assert belonging.

It may be important to note from the outset that one important difference between the Chinese in Latin America and those in the United States (with the exception of Hawaii) is the historically high rate of interracial unions and family formation. Anti-miscegenation laws did not exist in Panama (and Latin American more generally), as they did in certain parts of the United States. To the contrary, the dominant ideology of mestizaje, or racial and cultural mixing, in most of Latin America encourages interracial relations. Moreover, the extreme imbalance in gender migration in the late nineteenth and early twentieth centuries was also a factor. For many of the early Chinese bachelors, marrying or cohabiting with local women was the only means of creating a family life in Panama. In fact, among the Chinese whose families have been in Panama for more than two generations, it is not unusual to be racially mixed. Not to be ignored, however, is the existing discrimination by both Chinese and non-Chinese alike. Among the Chinese community, there is a certain level of bias against non-Chinese speakers and racially mixed Chinese. Likewise, in certain circles of non-Chinese Panamanians, Chineseness is not a positive characteristic. In a sense, it may be easier for racially mixed Chinese not to assert any particular identity. Fernando's identification as racially mixed, then, reflects both the dominant ideology of mestizaje and his ambivalence about being Chinese.

The politics of naming is also noteworthy. In the case of Fernando, his paternal grandfather had migrated from China to Jamaica. To obtain a Jamaican passport, he adopted Jackson as his surname. In Panama, such a surname automatically indicates one's familial itinerary through anglophone Caribbean. Purchasing another person's documents and assuming his/her identity in order to immigrate was quite common in the nineteenth and twentieth centuries, and to a large extent they remain common practices today. In fact, many of my interviewees have two different names: an official name on legal documents and a birth-given or "everyday-use" name. The combinations vary. Some have Anglo and Chinese names (i.e. Jackson/Lee, Wilson/Chan), while others have two Chinese names (i.e. Chu/Wang, Chen/Lee). Rarely do I encounter people who have used Hispanic names for immigration purposes. Moreover, this practice is not exclusive to Latin America. One may recall the "paper son" phenomenon in the United States.[17]

In the context of Latin America, then, Fernando's biography is not extraordinary in any way. What is particularly interesting about Fernando is his prominence in certain Chinese social networks. In particular, he has been extremely active in Agrupación (Panamanian

Chinese Gathering) or Agrupa, as many members call it. The organization is primarily interested in promoting cultural and social events for Panamanian Chinese. Some of their regular activities include the Debutantes Ball, the Friendship Dance, and Mother's Day Celebration. His participation in this organization, as he has conveyed, has less to do with his sense of being Chinese and more with his choice of social networks. He explains, "Almost all the active members of Agrupa are my friends from years back. Setting up the organization was merely a way of providing a venue, an occasion for all of us to get together. There are no formal rules or bylaws to joining the organization. It's all done by word of mouth. People bring their friends, and they bring their friends, and that's how we deal with our membership. We don't make a big deal about it. Many of the people in Agrupa went to school with me in Colón (the main city on the Caribbean coast of Panama). We basically grew up together. In fact, we all got married at around the same time, and our kids were born within years of each other." Fernando walks into his library and returns with an old, black-and-white fourth-grade class photo in his hand. He begins naming all the faces on the picture, and sure enough, they are people I have met through Agrupa.

In response to my question of how he sees himself as part of the Chinese community, he comments, "I have no trouble identifying with the Chinese community. However, it's not so much because of my Chinese heritage. Most of [the people in] my social circle are Chinese in varying degrees. Therefore my wife and I tend to lean in this direction for our social contacts. However, I also move in other circles depending on the activity, for example, my theater group of contacts are mostly Caucasian. Unlike so many of my Chinese friends, I don't make a big deal—unless it suits me to do so—about being Chinese. I try to recognize what I am, as a full person, and leave it at that." Even within his social circle of Chinese Panamanians, there is a strong desire to maintain and affirm one's Chineseness. The general opinion is that marrying "Chinese" is preferred. They claim that there are certain Chinese values that they want to keep within the family, values like the emphasis on family, industriousness, and honesty.

Creating community, for Fernando, depends more on affiliation, a sense of connection based on social relations, than filiation, a sense of connection based on kinship relations.[18] His practice of community and understanding of identity articulate what Stuart Hall discusses in "Cultural Identity and Diaspora."[19] According to Hall, identity is not a stable essential self but a positioning, a politics of identification. As such, identity is a process and is created through memory, fantasy, and narrative. Fernando's story, as represented below, illustrates how memory and experience become sources for generating a diasporic sensibility and identity.

Our conversation on serial migration begins three generations back. As mentioned above, Fernando's paternal grandfather was Chinese and had immigrated first to Jamaica before remigrating to Colón, Panama, in the late 1800s. He married a black Jamaican woman and changed his surname from Cheng to Jackson in order to obtain a Jamaican passport. In Colón, this grandfather owned a grocery store. Fernando's maternal grandfather was Portuguese and his maternal grandmother was "a mixture of different ethnic groups including Chinese and Caucasian." They had emigrated from Guyana (previously called British Guiana) to Colón, where Fernando's mother was born.

At a young age, Fernando's father was sent to Jamaica for school, and after he finished high school, he came back to Panama and started working at the shipping division of the United Fruit Company in Colón.[20] His ability to speak English and his educational background no doubt helped secure this position.

Fernando was born in Colón and attended the only private boys' school in the area. It was there that he met most of his lifelong friends. After the fifth grade, Fernando was sent to a boarding school in Jamaica, where his father had studied; and after high school, he went to Chicago for his university education. Fernando elaborates, "At first I was attending a public school in Colón, but because I was getting into so many fights with other kids, my father decided to put me into a private school. From there, I went to Jamaica. My father wanted me to learn English well, so he sent me to Jamaica. Afterwards, I applied for college in the United States, and I was accepted. So, in a sense, I spent much of my childhood and young adult life outside of Panama."

When Fernando returned to Panama after college, he moved to Panama City instead of returning to Colón. He and his wife, who is also part Chinese, met through a social function sponsored by a Panamanian Chinese organization. All of their three children (two sons and one daughter) have finished college and are working in professional careers in Panama City. Two of them have married non-Chinese Panamanians, and each couple recently had their first child. Only one of Fernando's children speaks English fluently, and none of them went abroad for school.

Clearly, Fernando has migrated and lived in Panama, Jamaica, and the United States. Furthermore, his father and grandparents also have migrated a couple of times: his grandparents immigrated from China and British Guiana to Jamaica before settling in Panama. Three generations back and almost a hundred years ago, migrations between countries appear to be as common as remaining sedentary. As we think about transnational migrations today, it may be important to recall these historical practices of detours and returns, practices that are not altogether different from today's patterns of traveling and dwelling.

"Why did you return to Panama after graduating from the university? Why didn't you stay in the U.S.?" I ask. Taking a long sigh, Fernando replies, "I was offered a job [in the U.S.] upon graduation; however, after spending six years in boarding school and four years in college, I just did not feel like being away from home anymore. In reality my ties to home were not strong because [in my] four years of college I had been home just once. Nevertheless, I did not want to stay in the United States any longer. Perhaps there was an unconscious desire to re-establish roots in Panama. Who knows? I have often thought about 'what if . . .'? What would have happened if I had stayed there?" Fernando's return to Panama disrupts the assumptions underlying U.S.-based studies of transnational migration that assume a teleological movement from less developed nations to more developed ones. The United States, Western Europe, and Canada tend to be the assumed endpoints of these migrations. Instead, Fernando's return to Panama challenges this assumption.

On another occasion, Fernando discusses the racial discrimination and inequality he witnessed while in the United States. Reminding me that he was in the U.S. during the late 1950s, he recalls, "You know, I was in Chicago around the time of the Civil Rights movement. Racial relations were very different back then . . . I was once set up for a blind date with a girl from one of the 'better' sororities . . . when it was canceled, my friend was honest enough to tell me that the girl had seen me on campus and called the date off because I was 'brown.' This was the first time that I was directly and personally affected by racial bigotry."

When I ask him about his experiences of racial discrimination in Panama, he replies, "Racial discrimination was instituted in Panama by the United States during the construction of the Panama Canal. They created the Gold and the Silver rolls as a means of differentiating the white and non-white workers; they were basically synonyms for white and black. There were gold and silver communities, stores, schools, and even water fountains within the various establishments. After I returned from college, I taught school in what was then called the 'Latin American Communities,' which was another name for the silver roll or non-white communities. The people in it were predominantly black . . . I have not personally ever experienced racial discrimination here in Panama, at least not that I have been aware of, although I have seen bigotry at work in the old Canal Zone in terms of pay and benefits that favored the Americans."

Fernando suggests that racial discrimination in Panama was imported by the Americans who instituted their system of racial segregation in the American Canal Zone. Surely, Fernando's interpretation of race relations in Panama had been greatly influenced by his work experience in the Canal Zone, where inequalities between Americans and Panamanians, or between whites and blacks/mestizos, were blatant, institutionalized, and actively enforced. So strong was the structural racism in the Canal Zone that other forms of discrimination pale by comparison.

In contrast to Chinese immigrants who speak extensively about their experience of racial discrimination in Panama, Fernando, a third generation Panamanian Chinese of mixed race, does not share their interpretations. I can only speculate that his less than obvious Chinese features, his English last name, and his cultural and class background all contribute to how others have treated him. His racially mixed appearance does not automatically distinguish him from the mestizo majority of Panama. Moreover, his American university education and bilingual fluency in English and Spanish both grant him a certain level of cultural capital and access to social mobility. These factors distinguish him from the majority of recent Chinese immigrants, who are racially marked as not only different but also foreign and who lack the necessary cultural and economic capital that commands acceptance and respectability in Panama.

A few months after our interview, Fernando became involved in his annual play production of Neil Simon's "The Odd Couple." Since his retirement, he has been directing this same play every year, varying the script ever so slightly. It seems noteworthy that Fernando would choose to direct an American play, not a Panamanian one. This is yet another expression of how the United States—as geopolitical entity, colonial power, and cultural force—has permeated his life.

Marco: Rediscovering Chineseness Abroad

In his mid-20s, Marco is the youngest of four children and comes from a family that is quite well established and respected in the Chinese Panamanian community. As a fourth generation Panamanian-born Chinese, he has an extensive family network in Panama. His father and all his other siblings are in the medical field, but following in his mother's footsteps, he handles the financial and management aspects of the family business. Trained as an electrical engineer, he is a business entrepreneur at heart. Like most people of his social standing, Marco received his degree in the United States and speaks impeccable English. But these factors are not what make him unique. What distinguishes him from his peers is his unusual mix of talents and aspirations. He not only went to school in the United States, but also studied Mandarin in Taiwan. In his extended family, he is the only one who is fluent in all three languages.

I met Marco for the first time at the annual inauguration dinner of APROCHIPA (the Chinese Panamanian Professionals Association). His cousin and my good friend, Laura, introduced us; and immediately, we launched into a heated discussion about Chinese politics in Panama and the ins and outs of the Chinese Panamanian community. Within minutes, we became like old friends who had known each other for years.

Marco's family is considered to be one of the founding Chinese families in Panama City. His maternal great-grandfather was one of the earliest and most successful Chinese entrepreneurs in Panama. His great-grandfather had immigrated in the 1890s and had established both wholesale and retail businesses in Panama City's Chinatown. He married a Chinese woman who immigrated to Panama during the 1910s. I am told that Marco's great-grandfather was the primary distributor of dry goods to the Darien region of Panama. His company was among the three largest Chinese-owned operations of that time.

According to Marco's father, Marco's paternal great-grandfather and two great-granduncles had come to Panama around the 1850s. They had gone to California in search of gold, but with little success. They later came to Panama to work on the railroads, and after the completion of the railroad, they migrated to Peru for a short period of time before returning to Panama again. Marco's great-grandfather owned a shoe store in Chinatown, and he eventually married a Chinese woman and had seven children. Marco's grandfather was born in Panama City, and through an arranged marriage, he was sent to China to marry a Chinese woman. They came back to Panama together, had two sons together, and were informally divorced shortly afterward. Marco's grandfather remained in Panama City while his grandmother took the children with her to Colón and opened a cantina (bar). Like most first sons of the family, Marco's uncle was sent to China, and he did not return to Panama until the 1950s. Marco's father grew up in Colón, and when he decided to study medicine, he moved to Panama City and lived with Marco's grand-aunt and her family.

Marco lives with his parents and one of his brothers in a middle-class neighborhood of Panama City. The house is spacious with a swimming pool in the backyard. His sister is currently studying medicine in Mexico City, while his other two brothers live elsewhere in Panama City. His oldest brother married a (mestiza) woman from

Mexico and has two young children, and his second brother married a (mestiza) woman from the Dominican Republic. Both women hold medical degrees, although neither of them is presently practicing medicine.

Getting to know Marco's extended family is quite a challenge. It seems as though Marco is related to almost every Chinese Panamanian whose family has been in Panama City for more than three generations. For instance, on his paternal side, Marco's great-grandfather had five children. On his maternal side, Marco's grandmother comes from a family of seven, and his grandfather came from a family of five. With each generation, his kinship network grows exponentially, making it more and more difficult to maintain relations with everyone equally. From what Marco tells me, the extended family gathers only on holidays and special occasions. Most of the time, the family members only see one another in association meetings and other community activities.

Indeed, Marco is sharply aware of his location within both his extensive family networks in Panama as well as his larger kinship network spanning Asia and the Americas. Unlike most of his relatives, he has become very curious and knowledgeable about existing relatives in Taiwan, Hong Kong, Peru, and the United States. Shortly after I left Panama, he and one of his brothers traveled to Taiwan and Hong Kong to visit a couple of their uncles who are in the shipping business. On that same trip, they also visited Los Angeles, where another uncle and aunt reside. Marco is unique in that he truly situates himself within a global diasporic family network. The fact that he is trilingual in Spanish, English, and Mandarin facilitates his efforts to maintain ties with relatives dispersed throughout the world.

In contrast to his peers of similar class and social background, Marco has embraced his sense of Chineseness. He is actively interested in Chinese history, culture, and politics. Yet, I was surprised to learn that he has not always been that way. He recalls, "As a teenager, I never liked the fact that I was Chinese . . . But as I grew older, well, after I went to college in Miami and met some Chinese Americans, I came back to Panama with a new attitude. I wanted to learn Chinese and get in touch with my 'Chinese side.' I guess my Chinese American friends were so proud of their ancestry that they made me think about my own background. So, when I came back to Panama, I decided to go on this intensive language program sponsored by the Chinese Cultural Center. There were two other guys who went on the same program, who had scholarships to go study in Taiwan. I didn't have a scholarship, but I didn't care because I really wanted to learn Mandarin. I was determined to learn Mandarin. Living in Taiwan was quite an experience. I loved it . . . and I learned Mandarin." Since returning to Panama, Marco has tried to maintain his Mandarin by listening to language tapes and Taiwanese-produced music CDs. And whenever he encounters other Mandarin speakers, he lights up and enthusiastically engages them in conversation.

Interestingly, it was Marco's migration to the United States and subsequent interaction with Chinese Americans that sparked interest in exploring his own Chinese identity. His narrative not only illustrates the many different locations he and his family have traversed—California, Peru, Miami, Taiwan, Mexico, and Panama are only some of the places he has mentioned and that make up a larger mapping of where "home" has been—but also conveys how serial migration has shaped his sense of identity and redrawn the boundaries of family and community. Through every migration, he discovers a different aspect of himself, extends and re-establishes ties with dispersed relatives, and re-imagines the possibilities of home and belonging.

Pedro: Not Belonging Anywhere

Humidity has a way of draining your energy. After spending all morning wandering around Chinatown, I am ready to call it quits for the day. But somehow, the Chinese character on the exterior of the building catches my attention, and I feel compelled to walk in. The character is my mother's maiden name, and I suspect that the owner of the store must share that same surname. The building, with its clean white walls and newly remodeled exterior, stands apart from all the other stores in the area.

I step inside, and the cool temperature of the air-conditioned room makes me realize just how unbearably hot and humid it is outside. Compared to the other shops in Chinatown I have visited so far, the spaciousness of this place makes it appear semi-empty. Most stores are stacked with items from floor to ceiling and all around the walls, but the merchandise in this store is neatly shelved and carefully organized in its place. The white walls and floors all make it seem very clinical, cold, and sterile. Usually, there are hundreds of trinkets hanging all over the place, and bright colors of red, blue, and yellow radiate from every space of the wall. Often, walking into Chinatown stores is an all-body experience of sensory overload. What amazes me most about them is not how much merchandise is packed into tiny little spaces, but how easily and quickly the owners are able to locate that last can of Madras curry powder hidden behind the dried peppers and bags of egg noodles. This particular store is different; it is nothing like the others.

In Cantonese, I ask the man behind the counter where I can find Mr. Cho, presumably the owner of the store. In response, the clerk asks for my name, then walks toward the back of the store. When he returns, he leads me to a small office where a solemn-looking man is writing behind his desk. As I enter, I extend my arm forward to shake his hand, greeting him in Cantonese, "How are you, Mr. Cho." I quickly introduce myself as a doctoral student doing research on the Chinese in Panama and present him with my "business" card. He examines the card, then surprises me by asking in fluent English, "So, what can I do for you, Ms. Siu?"

Surprised by his flawless English, I proceed to give more details about my work. And after covering the usual formalities of exchanging brief family histories, he warmly invites me back for a longer conversation and dinner with his family. Certainly the fact that my mother and he share the same last name and that our families are from the same region of China help establish an immediate sense of connection. Happily, I accept his invitation.

When I began my research, I had suspected naively that Panamanian Chinese would speak either Spanish or Cantonese. These two languages made logical sense, given that Spanish is the dominant and official language of Panama and Cantonese is the most common Chinese language of diasporic Chinese. Yet, over and over again, my interviewees would surprise me by responding in fluent English. And

I quickly learned, through the process of interviewing, how profoundly American presence had influenced Panamanian Chinese. Speaking English was no coincidence but a result of colonialism and a strategy of survival and social mobility.

Pedro's family is one of the better-known Chinese families in Panama, partly because of his father's entrepreneurial success and his family's long-standing presence in Chinatown. I would say that every Chinese Panamanian knows or at least has heard of Pedro's store. It has become sort of a landmark in Chinatown. Furthermore, the store donates a lot of money to various organizations and community events. Hence, its name and logo can be found in newspapers, pamphlets, and posters.

In his late fifties, Pedro appears serious, contemplative, sometimes even sad. Although he seems at first to be a man of few words, he turns out to be quite intent on telling his story. He begins with his father, who at the age of sixteen boarded a cargo ship originally heading for Cuba. After the family rice fields in China were flooded in 1922, Pedro's father was sent to Latin America to help generate income for the family. Cuba became his destination simply because a fellow kinsman returned to their village that year, raving about the opportunities on that island of abundance. However, en route to Cuba, Pedro's father was detained at the quarantine station in Panama, where he met a Chinese Panamanian who convinced him to stay and helped him with immigration.

It was my uncle in Nicaragua who had first mentioned this quarantine station in Panama. He called it the "wooden house" and compared it to the immigration station at Angel Island, located off the coast of San Francisco, California. After a thorough search in the American Canal Zone, I was unable to locate the actual structure of the station or find any documentation that connects it to Chinese immigration to Latin America. Nonetheless, several of my interviewees who had immigrated to Latin American during the 1920s and 1930s vividly remember this "wooden house," the quarantine station that had served as an immigration processing point for Chinese going to various destinations in Latin America.

"In the beginning, my father worked at the public market, selling vegetables in carts. Later he advanced to working in a shop across the street from the market. He worked hard and saved every penny so that he eventually was able to send for my uncles." In the early 1930s, Pedro's father moved to the interior of Panama and married his mother, who is Panamanian-born Chinese. By the time Pedro and his brothers were old enough for school, the family relocated to Panama City's Chinatown, now popularly known as Sal Si Puedes.[21]

Chinatown stretches no more than two city blocks, and consistent with the older neighborhoods in Panama, the streets are narrow, and the buildings are next to one another with no space in between. Today it appears run-down and dirty, and I was warned repeatedly by both Chinese and non-Chinese Panamanians not to go there by myself and definitely not after dark. After my first excursion there with a friend, however, it seemed perfectly safe for me to go alone during the day.

Nostalgically, Pedro recalls, "Sal Si Puedes was very nice back then, it was clean, and it was a two-way street. [My family] used to live right across from our restaurant. My father started it when we moved to Panama City. It was one of the nicest restaurants then. Presidents used to dine there . . . and the Chinese school[22] was close to the sea, it provided classes in Chinese and Spanish."

He continues, "I guess my father must have considered himself prosperous or at least wealthy enough, because by 1947, seven years after we moved to Panama City, he decided to go back to China. We sold everything, and the entire family moved to Guangdong and into a very exclusive area. We started a textile company that made exercise outfits like t-shirts and sweats. Then, when the communists were approaching, our family sold everything again and came back to Panama. My oldest brother left first, followed by my father and another brother. My mother and I were the last ones to leave in 1950. We came back to Chinatown and bought back our old house and restaurant. Business was good in the 1950s; we had to expand the restaurant, adding two more floors.

"Then the government decided to close the traffic around this area, and shacks began to appear. So by the late 1950s most of the Chinese had moved away from Chinatown. Only some of the shops remained. We continued working at the restaurant until 1969, but the family started to go into the shrimping business. We invested in shrimp trawlers. At that time, shrimping was one of the biggest industries . . . From the late 50s to mid-60s, I went to school in Northern California and studied architecture. Three out of my four brothers went to California for college.

"I was in California from 1957 to 1966. After I graduated and worked for a little while in San Diego, I returned home to help with the family business. By this time, my father had gone into business with another Chinese Panamanian and had started building shrimp processing plants in Guatemala and Mazatlán. In Panama we would send the shrimp to a packing company and export it to the United States. In Guatemala we had our own packing company.

"To make a long story short, a big storm in 1968 badly affected the conditions for shrimping in Guatemala. The sand swallowed the ship within one month. After that, my brothers and I tried to start another plant in Nicaragua, but Somoza (then president of Nicaragua) owned the national packing company, ALINSA. They were very unfair with the prices and they treated us badly, so we returned to Guatemala, but this time, we didn't stay for very long. We eventually came back to Panama in the late 1970s.

"When we returned, we came back to Chinatown, and I started to look after the store. Well, I met my wife right here in Chinatown. We got married not too long after we met, and now we have three kids, two boys and a girl."

Curious about his multiple remigrations, I ask, "You've lived in so many places, where do you feel you most comfortable? Where do you feel you most belong?"

"Nowhere really," he responds, "I don't feel like I belong anywhere, not even in Panama. Sometimes I get very sad about that. I feel as though something must have happened in Chinese history that makes us so self-conscious. Well, I have my family here in Panama. My children bring me happiness. They are very well behaved and they do well in school."

Despite the prominence and visibility of his family name and business, Pedro almost never attends any community or social event. In contrast, Pedro's oldest brother is extremely active and visible in the

Chinese community. In fact, his brother is on the board of the Chinese Association, and he and his wife attend almost all the activities sponsored by the different Chinese organizations. To give the reader a sense of how small and interconnected this community is, Pedro's older brother is married to a distant aunt of Marco.

Pedro's narrative elaborates a range of reasons for serial migration. For his father, immigrating to Panama was a way of sustaining his family in China, and once he had achieved a level of economic success, he eventually brought his brothers to Panama. For Pedro, his multiple migrations were determined by different factors. The family's return to China from Panama, I suspect, may have been part of the mass exodus of Chinese from Panama when then-President Arnulfo Arias disenfranchised large numbers of Chinese immigrants and prohibited them from owning retail businesses. Many people I interviewed were faced with the same predicament of returning to China, immigrating to other parts of Latin America, or relocating to the Canal Zone. For the wealthier families like Pedro's, many left for China, only to remigrate back to Panama at the time of the Chinese Communist Revolution. These back-and-forth migrations, then, were consequences of hostile political situations. Finally, Pedro's migrations to the United States, Guatemala, and Nicaragua were efforts to accumulate cultural capital and to expand the family business.

Thus far the narratives have focused on Panamanian-born, middle-class men. This focus results from the question of serial migration, which specifically examines multiple border crossings over time. Up until the mid-twentieth century, migration among diasporic Chinese was primarily a male endeavor, in the sense that the majority of migrants were men, and migration was encouraged and practiced mostly by men to achieve social mobility and to fulfill certain familial duties.[23] Moreover, transnational migrations require a certain level of capital. It is not surprising, then, that the majority of such migrants came from at least middle-class backgrounds and could afford to travel. The fourth narrative offers a different perspective. As an immigrant woman who comes from a less privileged background, Victoria shows a distinctly different way of engaging serial migration.

Victoria: "I can do what a man can do"

Victoria and I met during the summer of 1994. Her close friend and colleague, Roberto Tang (who was instrumental in helping me establish my first contacts), introduced us at a dinner party. Victoria is one of those people who puts you at ease very quickly and makes you feel as though you've known her for years in just a few minutes. Within the first hour of our meeting, I had learned that she migrated from China, grew up in Colón, studied medicine in Brazil, and lived in the interior of Panama before finally moving to Panama City.

Victoria would never consider herself a "typical" Chinese Panamanian woman. She made this very clear to me from the very beginning by confiding that she is not a member of any Chinese organization, nor does she participate in the activities sponsored by the various Chinese Panamanian associations or "clubs," as she calls them. Essentially, she considers herself an outsider to these Chinese/Chinese Panamanian social networks. Since I had met most of my informants through these Chinese Panamanian organizations and social networks, I realized she could provide a distinctively different perspective on what it means to be Chinese in Panama.

Our time together is always filled with food, stories, music, more stories, and always laughter. And despite her busy schedule, she is always generous with her time and energy. She shares memories and stories with me, introduces me to her family, and takes me with her on weekend visits to her mother's house in La Chorrera.[24]

As a psychologist, Victoria makes it clear that she treats our conversations as both interview and self-therapy: "I narrate my past in order to confront my own fears and, in a sense, to heal and remake myself." Explicitly stating her own agenda in this project, Victoria makes certain that I am aware of her sense of complicity and control in the interviewing process, thereby equalizing the asymmetrical power relationship between "anthropologist" and "informant."

Victoria's parents and brother fled China and arrived in Panama at the time of the Chinese Communist Revolution in 1949. Victoria and her sister were left behind in China for a few years. During that period, the girls went into hiding, while some of their close relatives looked after them as much as they could. Reflecting two responses to trauma and memory, Victoria vividly remembers a number of incidents while her sister has no recollection of her years in China.

Victoria's family had belonged to the landed class and was therefore in danger of persecution during the Communist Revolution. She had watched her grandparents' execution at the town's center, and one of her aunts was imprisoned for almost two decades. Once released, this same aunt immigrated to Panama to reunite with her husband and family. In one of my visits to Chorrera, I met this aunt. She was quiet and removed. In her sixties, she was a small woman, no taller than about four feet. Physically, she looked frail. Her back was hunched over, and she hardly moved or made any unnecessary gestures. I never had the chance to talk with her, for fear of disturbing her or interrupting her peace. Victoria later told me that this aunt had been tortured in China and that she was imprisoned in place of her husband who had fled to Panama. Before the end of my field research in 1997, I learned that this aunt had committed suicide. The aunt's history exemplifies the extent to which the Communist Revolution affected people like Victoria and her family. Even after four decades, conversations about their lives in China brought tears to their eyes, and strong emotions of pain and rage kept resurfacing.

While most of the literature on diasporic Chinese has emphasized labor and economic reasons for migration, Victoria's story forcefully illustrates the salience of politics and political persecution in motivating emigration. Fleeing China was not a choice for Victoria's family; it was the only way they could have survived. In this sense, it is more fitting to think of Victoria and her family as political refugees than immigrants. Diasporic Chinese have been called sojourners, immigrants, and transnational migrants. Their migrations are considered to be "voluntary," yet there are many moments in history when their border-crossings are not quite "forced" but not quite "voluntary" either. Instead, they fall somewhere in between, in the ambivalent space where choice is extremely limited. Such was the case with indentured laborers who worked in the sugar plantations of Cuba and the guano fields of Peru, on the railroads in the United States and throughout Latin America.[25]

Victoria's story is another case in point. Together, these narratives point to the inadequacies of legal-political categories—such as exiles, refugees, or immigrants—to fully capture peoples' complex experiences of migration.

By the time Victoria (age 9) and her sister (age 11) reached Panama, their parents had had another son and had opened a small cafeteria in Colón City, serving breakfast to workers from the Canal Zone and the American military bases. The cafeteria opened at six in the morning and closed at noon. Victoria and her mother were the only ones in the family who woke up at two or three in the morning to start preparing the tortillas, empanadas, and plantains for breakfast. After finishing her tasks at the cafeteria, she would go to school, and by the time she returned home at four in the afternoon, the family would start preparations for the following day again. It was a difficult routine to keep up. "It was hard," Victoria remarked, "[but] I never felt sad or depressed, [I never felt] longing feelings for my grandmother and my aunt [who we left behind in China]. I guess I was just glad that at least I was here and not back in China." For immigrants who fled China in the late 1940s, most of them came without their savings. They basically had to start all over. For Victoria's family, they were fortunate to have relatives already in Panama who were able to help them set up a small business.

The first time I visited Victoria's mother in Chorrera, I was quite amused by the decor of her home. From the outside, there was nothing remarkable about her house, but as I walked through the front door, I felt as though I had magically traveled thousands of miles and suddenly stepped into a home in a Chinese village. The interior of the house was decorated in such a way that it appeared almost identical to the homes I have visited in southern China. Colors of red and gold were all around the room, and an altar of Guan Gong (the Chinese warrior saint) sat by the entrance of the living room. Victoria's mother had been in Panama for over four decades, but judging by the interior decoration of her home, it seemed as though she had never left China, or at least, had never left it behind.

Nothing in their interaction with one another suggests that Victoria and her mother have been through difficult times. However, during one of our trips, Victoria confesses that throughout high school she fought constantly with her parents, usually over issues of gender discrimination. She recognized that she and her sister were treated differently from her brothers, and she resented the fact that her parents favored the boys.

Victoria recalls, "Once [my mother] beat me with a fish in her hand, and I was very, very rebellious. I screamed at her, 'I never told you to bring me into this world.' Now, I know it was very tough for her too because she had to work, to rear children, and my father was drunk often, so she had to work alone, and she tried to get us to help her . . . The only one who helped her was me, and I couldn't understand why she never liked me. I tried to please her, but at the time, she was awful to me . . . Many times when [our fights got out of hand], my father would shut me and my sister out of the house . . . the confusion of being immigrants . . . well, right now, I can understand what happened psychologically. It was my mother projecting her devaluation onto us . . . From what she has told me about her life, I know she wasn't treated well as a child. Knowing that now helps me understand why she treated me the way she did, but at the time when I was growing up, it was hard. I didn't know why she hated me so much, even though I was the only person who helped her . . . My older brother was never around, and my father was often drunk. I remember he used to play records of Chinese operas, and he would just sit there listening, with tears flowing down his face. He was depressed a lot. I guess my mother was under a lot of pressure to keep everything together."

"During the summer of my junior year in high school," Victoria continues, "we got into a fight, and my father told us to pack our suitcases, and he took us to the school where the nuns were ...and paid for our last year of high school. I promised that I would not return anymore to my family. Instead, I studied a lot. I repressed my sadness, my fears, and my sense of powerlessness. I channeled all my energy into doing well in school, and I graduated first place in my class."

After high school graduation, she and her sister Ana lived with their non-Chinese Panamanian teachers and friends. "They are like family," Victoria explains, "the teachers have always been there for me. They have taken me in every time. They fed me, encouraged me, and gave me so much. To me, they are family." While living with their teachers, Victoria and Ana made money by crocheting and selling small items like doilies, baby socks, and clothes. With the help of her teachers, Victoria eventually won a scholarship to study at the University of Santa María Antigua (USMA), and when she decided to study medicine, she transferred to the University of Panama. "My thought was that I was going to be somebody. I was going to study . . . and this drive . . . the feeling that I knew, that I was conscious of the rage and the challenge helped push me. It was the challenge to prove to [my parents] that even though I'm a woman, I can do what a man can do. I'm proud that I achieve all my objectives."

"I started studying medicine in the University of Panama . . . but then, in 1968, the military had taken power, and it was a bad time in Panama and democracy was over, and the military government closed the University. I went to Colón and asked my father for help. You see, I had won another scholarship through the Brazilian Embassy to study medicine in Brazil. My godmother was working at the Brazilian Embassy at the time, and she told me about this opportunity. So I applied and got the scholarship. It was the only way I could pursue medicine at that time."

I interject, asking, "Was that the first time you talked to your father since before your high school graduation?"

"Yes, and he was glad [to see me] . . . It had been three years since the last time I saw him. He was very glad. When it comes to education, he has always been extremely supportive. I remember one time when he was on his knees begging my older brother to finish high school. I think he has always been proud of me in that sense. He gave me $500 [to help with my education]. In 1969, it was plenty of money."

She pauses and continues, "I think Brazil was a good period in my life. I got more autonomy, I met more people, and my professors appreciated me. I was the only Chinese in the class. Some of my patients would call me Japa, thinking I am Japanese. Well, Brazil is different from Panama in that way. There are more Japanese there than Chinese. So, instead of calling Asians China or Chino, they call us Japa." In contrast, Chino/China are the generalized terms that non-

Asian Panamanians use to refer to anyone who looks East Asian. This is the case throughout Central America. The terms "Asian" and "Asian American" as they are used in the United States to refer to the different ethnic groups in and from Asia have no cultural currency in Latin America.[26]

While studying in Brazil, Victoria met her first husband, who is also from Panama, and as soon as she graduated from medical school, she re-migrated back to Panama to join her husband in the interior. There, she did her internship and had her two children. She confides, "Those years were difficult. When my ex-husband came back to his hometown, he changed a lot. I had nobody there, and things between him and me got worse and worse and worse. So I talked to my sister, who was married by then, and she lent me the money to move back to Panama City. I left my first husband and brought my children with me. It was such a crazy period then. I was still doing my internship at the hospital, and my children were so young. My daughter was about three years old, and my son was just a toddler. Again, my teachers came through for me. They took care of my children while I worked at the hospital."

Victoria and her sister Ana have maintained a very close relationship. They've always supported one another. Ana married a Panamanian Chinese whose family has been in Panama for several generations and who has been extremely successful in his retail store and restaurant businesses. With her husband's business success and family networks, Ana's family is extremely active in the Chinese community. In fact, I see Ana and her family at Chinese community banquets and functions all the time. Victoria, on the other hand, is less inclined to participate in these activities. Part of her hesitation has to do with her sense of non-belonging in the community and her sense of non-acceptance from them. She comments, "I don't participate in these Chinese activities because, well, I didn't marry a Chinese man, and my children are racially mixed and don't speak Chinese. The old Chinese can't accept that, so I don't go to these activities very often. Once in a while, I will attend a dinner banquet sponsored by my village association. But I don't go to them regularly."

Since her relocation to Panama City almost twenty years ago,

Victoria has remarried, and she now co-owns a clinic with several other psychologists. Her children are now both in their twenties. Following in their mother's footsteps, her daughter, Alicia, is now pursuing a degree in clinical psychology, and her son, Esteban, is studying medicine in Mexico. The three of them are very close, and Victoria is extremely proud of both her children. Like their mother, Alicia and Esteban have done well in school, and like their grandfather, both are musically talented. There were evenings when the family would entertain me with hour-long performances, with Esteban playing the guitar, Victoria doing the back-up vocals, and Alicia singing the most beautiful verses. It was truly heart-warming to be in their presence.

Moving from one place to another has never been a matter of "choice" for Victoria, at least not in the sense that she had other comparable alternatives. The communist revolution had forced her to emigrate from China to Panama. The military government's shutting down of the university had compelled her to move from Panama to Brazil. And her migrations within Panama throughout her life were consequences of what she interprets to be her resistance against gender discrimination.

What I want to underscore here is her multiple migrations within Panama as well as her detours and returns within Latin America. Most of the literature on migration has focused primarily on movements from South to North, Third World to First World, developing countries to overdeveloped countries. By doing so, these studies inadvertently reinsert the North, the First World, the overdeveloped countries at the center. Furthermore, it ignores the interactions among people within the South, the Third World, and the underdeveloped world—interactions and exchanges that are crucial to the formation of these countries. Victoria's narrative and the three others above illustrate a very different migration pattern/route than what we have conventionally studied. Their field of vision is not centered on the United States, and their movements within the Americas show a different itinerary of migration altogether, one that has not been adequately explored or even acknowledged.

Conclusion: Detours and Returns

Through these narratives, I have shown how serial migration has played a critical role in shaping the lives of diasporic Chinese and their conceptions of themselves. While I have emphasized people's agency in these narratives, I have tried not to romanticize their ability to move freely across national borders. I have been mindful to present the various conditions and situations that determine their respective migrations and movements.

Several patterns emerge in these narratives. The most consistent one that links all four narratives concerns the practice of serial migration, or the practice of detours and returns. All of the interviewees and/or their family members have traveled across several national and cultural spaces. It seems that even within one generation, people have migrated at least once, sometimes more. For example, Fernando's grandparents are from Jamaica and Guyana. Marco's great-grandfather had been in the United States and Peru before he settled in Panama. Other people I have interviewed have mentioned Peru, the Dominican Republic, and Cuba in their families' migration itineraries. These narratives show how common it was for people to engage in serial migration. In many ways, they reveal the very ordinariness of serial migration in the lives of diasporic Chinese. Detailing itineraries between China and Panama, between Panama and the United States, and across different parts of Latin America and the Caribbean, they show how diasporic Chinese approach migration matter-of-factly and almost as a practice of everyday life.

By tracing migration through several generations, these narratives provide a longer historical perspective on migration and, more significantly, show how memories of migration influence the way people construct geographies of home, belonging, and community. Weaving together generations of travel and migration, Marco not only maps the various locations where family members have migrated but also connects those disparate locations with genealogies and kinship networks. Binding unfamiliar places with kinship ties, Marco incorporates them into his geography of family and community, thereby bringing those places closer to home. In contrast, Pedro's memories of his own migration only leave him feeling alienated and "not belonging" to any place.

In reference to internal migrations in Panama, the four narratives point to the steady movement toward Panama City from Colón and the interior regions. The restructuring of Panama's post–World War II economy caused a stream of migration from Colón to Panama City. The end of World War II and the removal of American army bases in Colón dramatically increased the rate of unemployment in that region. In order to offset postwar depression, the government established the Colón Free Zone in 1948. However, despite being one of the largest free zones in the world,[27] it has not improved the economic situation in the area. The Free Zone has not been able to absorb the large pool of low-skill labor left behind by the removal of American army bases. While Victoria and Fernando both grew up in Colón, they, like many of their peers, moved to Panama City, where the commercial and financial industries were expanding during the 1960s and 1970s.[28] The movement from the interior region of Panama to Panama City at around the same time can be characterized as a rural to urban migration, spurred by the deteriorating agricultural economy of the rural regions coupled with Panama City's booming service and financial sectors. Moreover, all the colleges and universities are located in Panama City. A number of interviewees have mentioned that their desire for their children to pursue higher education is what initiated their move to Panama City.

State violence and political persecution are recurrent themes in Chinese migration. Under these circumstances, migration has served as a strategy of survival. For Victoria and Pedro, political situations in both China and Panama had forced them to migrate. In China, it was the Communist Revolution and its persecution of the landed class. In Panama, it was Arnulfo Arias' exclusionist and nationalist agenda that denied the Chinese (and other immigrant groups) the rights to Panamanian citizenship and ownership of retail businesses. These incidents of disenfranchisement, persecution, and forced migration are important factors not only shaping diasporic Chinese subjectivity but also propelling serial migration.

Throughout my field research, I encountered significant numbers of diasporic Chinese who had attended college or university in the United States. For most middle-class and upper-middle-class Panamanian Chinese, studying abroad to acquire bilingual and bicultural (and in some cases triligual and tricultural) skills was both a vehicle for social mobility and an emblem of social status. For instance, having an American education enabled them to compete with their Panamanian counterparts for jobs in the American Canal Zone. It was also not uncommon for diasporic Chinese to obtain American university degrees in engineering, architecture, and finance, only to return to Panama to run family businesses. Not surprisingly, then, all four interviewees studied abroad for their university degrees, and for a variety of reasons, they all chose to return to Panama afterwards. Victoria came back from Brazil to reunite with her husband; Fernando left the United States in order to re-establish his roots in Panama; and Pedro went to Guatemala in order to help with his family's business. With regard to Fernando and Pedro, they both had the opportunity to stay in the United States after graduation but decided to return to Panama instead. As discussed above, their return migration to Panama challenges recent studies of transnational migration, which tend to emphasize unidirectional migrations from developing countries to developed nations such as the United States. The narratives in this essay address a different set of migration patterns at the same time that they challenge conventional discourses of migration, which tend to situate the "West," or the "North," as the final destination.

Indeed, the narratives convey a different itinerary of movements and provide an alternate map of detours and returns. People migrate and circulate amongst different places for a variety of reasons at different time. For some, it is to escape or to circumvent difficult and sometimes unsafe situations, for others it is a strategy of capital accumulation. Their movements sustain them, help reinvent them. By exploring migration stories, I show that serial migration—the act of moving across different places over time—is an experiential process that revises one's notions of belonging, identity, and community. Importantly, I do not want to give the impression that diasporic Chinese are nomadic or that they do not develop a sense of connection to any place. To the contrary, my interviewees' consistent returns

189

to Panama symbolically and physically mark Panama as home, and for each of them, specific places carry profound meaning. Whether it is Chicago for Fernando, Brazil for Victoria, or Taiwan for Marco, these dwelling places have informed their sense of who they are and where they belong. Serial migration, hence, not only extends the boundaries of home and community, but it also deepens their connection to particular places.

Finally, beyond simply illustrating the migrations of diasporic Chinese, this essay also provides situated life narratives that disrupt any fixed notions of what being "Chinese" means and what living in diaspora entails. Whereas Marco strives to explore all the potential facets of his identity and extensive travel actually enhances his sense of diasporic belonging, Pedro's high-profile family and his own set of migrations generate a sense of alienation. Also, whereas Fernando asserts his belonging by actively participating in community activities, Victoria retreats away from community because of her sense of non-acceptance. Each of the interviewees expresses varying degrees of belonging and alienation related to being "Chinese." By juxtaposing their migration stories against one another, I hope to work against any reductionist tropes that homogenize Chinese experience in diaspora.

In the last thirty years, trans-American migrations have increased. More and more, we see pockets of "Chinese Latinos" and "Chinese Caribbeans" emerging in cities like New York, Los Angeles, Miami, and Toronto. My conception of serial migration, hence, serves as a timely intervention. It not only provides a framework to examine these more recent trans-American migrations, but it also serves as a point of departure to explore both the linkages and the divergences among diasporic Chinese communities more generally.

NOTES AND BIBLIOGRAPHIES

Notes to the Introduction

1. While many Chinese women migrated in the nineteenth and early twentieth centuries, the vast majority of émigrés were male. I have chosen the male possessive pronoun to reflect this fact.

2. G. William Skinner, "Creolized Chinese Societies in Southeast Asia," in Anthony Reid, ed., *Sojourners and Settlers: Histories of Southeast Asia and the Chinese* (St. Leonard's, N.S.W.: Allen & Unwin, 1996), 51.

3. Lynn Pan et al., *Sons of the Yellow Emperor: A History of the Chinese Diaspora* (Boston: Little Brown & Co, 1990); Adam McKeown, *Chinese Migrant Networks and Cultural Change: Peru, Chicago, Hawaii, 1900–1936* (Chicago: University of Chicago Press, 2001); and Andrew R. Wilson, *Ambition and Identity: Chinese Merchant Elites in Colonial Manila* (Honolulu: University of Hawaii Press, 2004).

4. See Walton Look Lai, *Indentured Labor, Caribbean Sugar: Chinese and Indian Migrants to the British West Indies, 1838–1918* (Baltimore: The Johns Hopkins University Press, 1993) and *The Chinese in the West Indies, 1806–1995: A Documentary History* (Kingston: University of the West Indies Press, 2000).

5. The equivalent of the Chinese Benevolent Association existed in many overseas Chinese communities. In fact, the common Chinese term *huiquan*, which means "meeting hall" or "council," is very commonly rendered as "Benevolent Association" in English.

6. The Hakka, literally "guest people," are a socially marginalized group who migrated to the poor peripheries of South China. They are often looked down on by "native" southern Chinese (*punti*) because of their northern origins and relatively late entry into an already competitive southern economy. *Punti*/Hakka competition, compounded by social and political turmoil in south China, compelled many Hakka to migrate overseas when the opportunity arose. As a result, Hakka form a significant portion of the global Chinese diaspora and have been very successful in maintaining a distinct Hakka subgroup and encouraging those of Hakka descent to rediscover their identity.

7. See in particular Leo Douw, ed., *Unsettled Frontiers and Transnational Linkages: New Tasks for the Historian of Modern Asia* (Amsterdam: VU University Press, 1997).

8. See Linda G. Bausch, Nina Glick Schiller, and Cristina Blanc-Stanton, *Nations Unbound: Transnational Projects, Postcolonial Predicaments, and Deterritorialized Nation-states* (Langhorne, Penn.: Gordon and Breach, 1994) and Leo Douw, ed., *Unsettled Frontiers and Transnational Linkages.*

9. Adam McKeown, *Chinese Migrant Networks*, 3.

Notes to Chapter 1

1. Fujian province, the other major emigrant region, continued to send migrants during this century to the traditional destinations in Southeast Asia, but small numbers were also involved in the wider global movements of the nineteenth century.

2. The Hakkas or "Guest People" originated in North China, and relocated to the Southeast provinces as followers of the Southern Song dynasty (1127–1279). When that dynasty collapsed in 1279, several thousands remained in the region and were given the name "Guests" by locals because of their outsider origins.

3. Tait & Co; Syme, Muir & Co; Hyde, Hodge & Co.

4. See Barry Higman, "The Chinese in Trinidad 1806–1838," *Caribbean Studies* 12, no. 3 (1972): 21–44.

See also Walton Look Lai, *The Chinese In The West Indies 1806–1995: A Documentary History* (Kingston, Jamaica: UWI Press, 1998), chapter 2. Official records identified about twenty or thirty of them on the island in the 1820s, and a mere two or three by the time slavery ended in 1834.

5. There were six foreign coolie agencies at Amoy (Xiamen) in the early 1850s, five of them British: Syme, Muir and Co; Tait & Co; Hyde, Hodge & Co; Jackson, Robert & Co.; and Turner & Co. See Yen Ching-Hwang, *Coolies and Mandarins* (Singapore: Singapore University Press, 1985), p. 42, n. 43.

6. W. Look Lai, *The Chinese in the West Indies*, chapter 4.

7. Mauritius, Natal (South Africa), Queensland (Australia), Louisiana (U.S.A.), Bengal (India), Hawaii, the Philippines, Java, Fiji, Peru, Puerto Rico, as well as the older Cuba and Brazil. See Eric Williams, *From Columbus to Castro* (New York: Random House, 1970), chapter 20.

8. See David Northrup, *Indentured Labor in the Age of Imperialism 1834–1922* (Cambridge and New York: Cambridge University Press, 1995).

9. George Roberts and Jocelyn Byrne, "Summary Statistics on Indenture and Associated Migration Affecting the West Indies 1834–1918," *Population*

Studies 20, no. 1 (1966): 125–34. This does not include the inter-island movements of the West Indians themselves, which was quite substantial, especially to Trinidad and British Guiana.

10. Chinese labor in Peru was used in sugar as well as in the guano industry.

11. J. Ankum-Houwink, "Chinese Contract Migrants in Surinam between 1853 and 1870," *Boletin de Estudios Latinoamericanos y del Caribe* 17 (December 1974): 42–69.

12. Paul Leroy Beaulieu, *De la Colonisation chez les peuples modernes* (Paris: Guillaumin, 1902), vol. 1, p. 233. A 1955 study states that between 1852 and 1887, 1,300 Chinese and 500 Annamites arrived in the French West Indies. See Eugene Revert, *La France d'Amerique* (Paris: Editions maritimes et coloniales, 1955), 54.

13. Twentieth General Report of the Colonial Land and Emigration Commissioners, Appendix no. 45. *Irish University Press Series of British Parliamentary Papers. Emigration* (Shannon: Irish University Press, 1968–71), vol. 14.

14. One British pound equalled 20 shillings in British currency, $4.80 in British West Indian (BWI) currency, and $4.87 in U.S. currency. Dollars referred to in the text are BWI dollars.

15. Great Britain, Colonial Office Documents, CO 111, vol. 334, Hincks to Newcastle, 21 March 1862, enclosure.

16. The *Glentanner* to British Guiana from Fujian province in 1852/3.

17. Indeed, it was precisely the Chinese government insistence on such a provision in 1866 that led to the demise of Chinese emigration to the West Indies.

18. Many did, though.

19. See Walton Look Lai, *Indentured Labor, Caribbean Sugar* (Baltimore: Johns Hopkins University Press, 1993), 71, 75.

20. P.P., 1871, XX (C.393): Report of the Commissioners appointed to enquire into the treatment of immigrants in British Guiana.

21. See Denise Helly, ed., *The Cuba Commission Report: A Hidden History of the Chinese in Cuba: The Original English-Language Text of 1876* (Baltimore: Johns Hopkins University Press, 1993).

22. See Walton Look Lai, *Indentured Labor, Caribbean Sugar*, chapter 4, and Trevor Sue-a-Quan, *Cane Reapers* (Vancouver: Riftswoods Publishing, 1999), chapter 6, for detailed accounts.

23. Henry Kirke, *Twenty-Five Years in British Guiana, 1872–1897* (London: Sampson Low, Marston & Co., 1898), p. 216; repr. (Georgetown [British

Guiana] Daily Chronicle, 1948), p. 160.

24. Walton Look Lai, *The Chinese in the West Indies*, 205–206.

25. Trevor Sue-a Quan, Cane Reapers, chapter 6.

26. (Demerara) *Royal Gazette*, 11 March 1873.

27. See Walton Look Lai, *The Chinese in the West Indies*, chapter 9. See also *The Diaries of Abbé Armand Massé* (1878–1883), translated by M.L. De Verteuil (Port of Spain, 1988); R.P.M. Cothonay, *Trinidad, Journal d'un Missionaire Dominicain des Antilles Anglaises* (Paris, 1893); Charles Kingsley, *At Last—A Christmas in the West Indies* (London, 1871); Edward Jenkins, *The Coolie—His Rights and Wrongs* (London, 1871); Henry Kirke, *Twenty-Five Years in British Guiana 1872–1897*; Rev. H.V.P. Bronkhurst, *Wesleyan Missionary: The Colony of British Guiana and Its Labouring Population* (London, 1883).

28. See table 1.2.

29. See Walton Look Lai, *Indentured Labor, Caribbean Sugar*, Appendix 1, table 30, for Trinidad.

30. The figures in table 1.3 apply to China-born alone.

31. Many are also from Fujian province, rather than the traditional Guangdong.

Bibliography for Chapter 2

Abbreviations

CO	Colonial Office
PP	Parliamentary Papers
PRO	Public Record Office
RG	*Royal Gazette*

Manuscript Collections

Public Record Office, Colonial Office, CO 295/14

Parliamentary Papers, vol. XXXV, Correspondence Relative to Emigration of Labourers to the West Indies and the Mauritius from the West Coast of Africa, the East Indies and China, 1844 (Chadwyck-Healy 48.291–48.292)

Parliamentary Papers, vol. LXVIII, Copies or Extracts of Despatches Relating to Chinese Immigrants Recently Introduced into the Colonies of British

Guiana and Trinidad, August 1853 (Chadwyck-Healey 57.500–57.502)

Parliamentary Papers, vol. XXVII, Fourteenth General Report of the Colonial Land and Emigration Commissioners, 1854 (Chadwyck-Healey 58.239–58.241)

Parliamentary Papers, vol. XX, Report of the Commissioners to Enquire into the Treatment of the Immigrants in British Guiana, June 1871 (Chadwyck-Healey 77.174–77.178)

Newspaper Articles

Editorial, *Royal Gazette*, 12 February 1850
Editorial, *Royal Gazette*, 16 September 1869
Editorial, *Royal Gazette*, 10 November 1870
Editorial, *Royal Gazette*, 10 June 1875
Editorial, *Royal Gazette*, 15 August 1874
Editorial, *Royal Gazette*, 23 December 1875
Editorial, *Royal Gazette*, 28 December 1875
"Emigration," *Royal Gazette*, 28 January 1854
"Reports of the Stipendiary Magistrate of Districts D, E, and G in respect to the Chinese Labourers," *Royal Gazette*, 16 July 1853
"Report of Trinidad's Standing Committee on Immigration," *Royal Gazette*, 25 August 1860
"The Chinese Labourers in the West Indies," *Royal Gazette*, 16 February 1854

Books

Jenkins, Edward. 1877. *Lutchmee and Dilloo. A Study of West Indian Life in Three Volumes*. London: William Mullan & Son.
_____. 1871. *The Coolie. His Rights and Wrongs*. London: Strahan & Co. Publishers.
Laurence, K.O. 1971. *Immigration into the West Indies in the 19th Century*. Barbados: Caribbean Universities Press.
_____. 1994. *A Question of Labour: Indentured Immigration into Trinidad and British Guiana, 1875–1917*. New York: St. Martin's Press.
Look Lai, Walton. 1993. *Indentured Labor, Caribbean Sugar: Chinese and Indian Migrants to the British West Indies, 1838–1918*. Baltimore: Johns Hopkins University Press.
_____. 1998. *The Chinese in the West Indies, 1806–1995. A Documentary*

History. Barbados, Jamaica, and Trinidad and Tobago: University of the West Indies Press.

Stanley, E. 1850. *Claims and Resources of the West Indian Colonies. A Letter.* London: T & W Boone.

Williams, Eric. 1964. *History of the People of Trinidad and Tobago*. London: Andre Deutsch Limited.

Notes to Chapter 2

1. Throughout this article, the terms "Indian" and "Chinese" are used to indicate immigrants from British India and China to the West Indies. Such usage is not meant to be reductive—I am aware that the terms do not adequately describe the diverse cultural populations that composed these groups. They are used simply to facilitate reading.

2. The Emancipation Act was actually passed in 1833 but did not come into effect until 1834. At that time, although nominally free, ex-slaves were required to enter into mandatory apprenticeships on the estates. Although initially, apprenticeship was to last seven years, the practice was abolished in 1838.

3. The decline in the sugar industry in the 1800s has also been linked to soil depletion and economic downturns in the British market.

4. Extensive work on the indentured immigration of Chinese and Indian labourers to the West Indies has been completed by Walton Look Lai and K.O. Laurence. For further information, see, for example, Look Lai's *Indentured Labor, Caribbean Sugar: Chinese and Indian Migrants to the British West Indies, 1838–1918* and Laurence's *A Question of Labour: Indentured Immigration into Trinidad and British Guiana, 1875–1917*.

5. The term "coolie" or "cooly" was sometimes used in nineteenth-century British West Indian texts as a general synonym for "indentured laborer." It should be noted, however, that these documents also reveal a tendency on the part of the colonial administration to use "coolie" or "cooly" specifically in reference to migrants from India while referring to labourers from China as simply "the Chinese."

6. In his *History of the Peoples of Trinidad and Tobago*, Eric Williams claims that about 30 Chinese remained by 1814 (p. 76).

Notes to Chapter 3

I would like to thank Mr. Eastern Lee and Dr. Tanna for bringing me some materials from Jamaica.

1. Walton Look Lai, *Indentured Labor, Caribbean Sugar: Chinese and Indian Migration to the British West Indies, 1838–1918* (Baltimore: Johns Hopkins University Press, 1993); Walton Look Lai, *The Chinese in the West Indies, 1806–1995: A Documentary History* (Kingston: The University Press of the West Indies, 1998).

2. Andrew W. Lind, "Adjustment Patterns among the Jamaican Chinese," *Social and Economic Studies* (Mona, Jamaica) 7, no. 1 (1958): 144–64; Howard Johnson, "The Anti-Chinese Riots of 1918 in Jamaica," *Immigrants and Minorities* 2 (March 1983): 50–63; Jacqueline Levy, "The Economic Role of the Chinese in Jamaica: The Grocery Retail Trade," *The Jamaican Historical Review* 15 (1986): 31–49; Christine Ho, "'Hold the Chow Mein, Gimme Soca': Creolization of the Chinese in Guyana, Trinidad and Jamaica," *Amerasia* 15, no. 2 (1989): 3–25. The only exception is Lee Tom Yin's *The Chinese in Jamaica* (Kingston: Get For Company, 1957, rev. 1963). More than half of it devoted to "Who's Who" of the Chinese in Jamaica, the book was written in Chinese with few English explanations. It is essentially in the form of a guidebook, with the Chinese title *Annual of Chinese in Jamaica* on the cover and the English title *The Chinese in Jamaica* at the back. This is the first serious effort to keep the records of the Chinese in Jamaica.

3. Although Phyllis Marrow suggested that the concept of a Chinese community became "fictitious" in the early 1970s, it was still adequate to use the term in the early 1960s, as indicated in this chapter. " . . . even in Kingston, there is no longer a true 'Chinatown', and the Chinese have responded as an ethnic group only when threatened as such. For most purposes, then, the concept of a Chinese community is fictitious." Phyllis Marrow, "Chinese Adaptation in Two Jamaican Cities" (honors thesis, Harvard University, 1972), 4.

4. Eric Williams, *Capitalism and Slavery*, Andre Deutsch, 1964 [1944], 3–29. As for the study of the Caribbean slavery, the best reader is Hilary Beckles and Verene Shepherd, eds., *Caribbean Slave Society and Economy: A Student Reader* (Kingston, Jamaica: Ian Randle Publishers, 1991). Revised and expanded edition, *Caribbean Slavery in the Atlantic World* (Kingston, Jamaica: Ian Randle Publishers; Princeton: Markus Wiener Publishers, 2000).

5. Christine Ho, "'Hold the Chow Mein, Gimme Soca'," 4.

6. Chen Zexian, "The Indentured Labor System in the 19th century," *Historical Research* (Beijing), no. 1 (1963): 176–78. According to statistics, more than 780,000 Chinese indentured laborers went to the Malay Peninsula in 1881–1915; about 142,000 Chinese laborers went to Africa in 1700–1910; and Chinese indentured laborers also went to other parts of the world. See Wu Fengbing, ed., *Dongnanya Huaqiao Tongshi* (General History of Chinese Overseas in Southeast Asia) (Fuzhou: Fujian People's Publishing House, 1994), 297–98; Li Anshan, *Feizhou Huaqiao Huaren Shi* (A History of Chinese Overseas in Africa) (Beijing: Overseas Chinese Publishing House, 2000), 82–125.

7. Olive Senior, "Corollary: The Chinese Who Came from Panama," *Jamaica Journal* 13, no. 2 (1980): 79; Robert Tomes, *Panama in 1855* (New York: Harper & Brothers, 1855), 121; Chen Kwang Min, *The Chinese in the Americas* (New York: Overseas Chinese Culture Publishing Co., 1950), 696; Andrew W. Lind, "Adjustment Patterns among the Jamaican Chinese," 147.

8. "Matachin" means "butcher" in Spanish; it was assumed by others that it derives from "matar" (to kill) and "Chinos" (Chinese). Olive Senior, "Corollary: The Chinese Who Came from Panama," 79.

9. "'More than one hundred of the coolies hung from the trees, their loose pantaloons flapping in the hot wind'. Some had hung themselves with bits of rope and tough vines. Many used their own hair, looping their long pigtails round their necks and tieing the ends to a tree limb. Over 300 more were lying on the ground, their mode of suicide as varied as their ingenuity. Some tied stones to themselves and jumped into the river, others sat on the banks waiting for the waters of a freshet to come and wash them away, some bargained with their companions to kill them, some threw themselves on pointed machetes, others cut crutch-shaped sticks, sharpened the points, and thrust their necks on them." Olive Senior, "Corollary: The Chinese Who Came from Panama," 79.

10. Lucy M. Cohen, "The Chinese of the Panama Railroad: Preliminary notes on the migrants of 1854 who 'failed'," *Ethnohistory* 18, no. 4 (1971): 309–20. She used materials from contemporary newspapers to describe the miserable situation of the Chinese. See also Andrew W. Lind, "Adjustment Patterns among the Jamaican Chinese," 147–48.

11. *Daily Panama Star and Herald*, September 3, 1854, 1:107, quoted from Cohen, "The Chinese of the Panama Railroad," 312. This Chinese was most probably Wang Te-Chang, who was the interpreter on the Panama mission from Jamaica. Parliament Papers. 1854–55, XXII (1953), Fifteenth General Report of the Colonial Land and Emigration Commissioners (1855), no. 52,

Journals of the Chinese interpreter Wang Te-Chang, reporting on the state of the Chinese immigrants in Panama. Quoted from Walton Look Lai, *Indentured Labor, Caribbean Sugar*, 93.

12. Andrew W. Lind, "Adjustment Patterns among the Jamaican Chinese," 147.

13. For example, Chen Kwang Min, *The Chinese in the Americas*, 696; Lee Tom Yin, *The Chinese in Jamaica*, 30, 44; Wu Fengbin, *Qiyue Huagong Shi* (A History of Indentured Labor) (Nanchang: Jiangxi People's Publishing House, 1988), 300; Zhou Nanjing and Li Anshan, ed., *Encyclopedia of Chinese Overseas, Volume of History* (Beijing: Overseas Chinese Publishing House, 2002), 539, 541.

14. Parliament Papers. 1854–55, XXII (1953), Fifteenth General Report of the Colonial Land and Emigration Commissioners (1855), app. no. 51, White to Walcott, 7 April 1854. Quoted from Walton Look Lai, *Indentured Labor, Caribbean Sugar*, 89.

15. "Gong" is a respectful title for a man above middle age. Chen Ba returned to China and died in Hong Kong in 1902.

16. Walton Look Lai, *Indentured Labor, Caribbean Sugar*, 104; Lind, "Adjustment Patterns among the Jamaican Chinese," 149.

17. Chen Kwang Min, *The Chinese in the Americas*, 696. Walton Look Lai, *Indentured Labor, Caribbean Sugar*, 104. Another figure is 696, recorded in *Colonial Standard* (Jamaica) (July 14, 1884); see Lind, "Adjustment Patterns among the Jamaican Chinese," 149.

18. It is the name for four counties in southeastern Guangdong Province: Taishan, Xinhui, Kaiping, and Enping.

19. Ching Chieh Chang, "The Chinese in Latin America: A Preliminary Geographical Survey with Special Reference to Cuba and Jamaica" (Ph.D. diss., Department of Geography, University of Maryland, 1956), 47.

20. Lee Tom Yin, *The Chinese in Jamaica*, 118. For the dates of departure and arrival, I have used Chen Kwang Min's. See Chen Kwang Min, *The Chinese in the Americas*, 696. The ship may have arrived in Halifax first; after a change of ship, the passengers continued to Bermuda and Cuba before arriving in Kingston.

21. Lee Tom Yin, *The Chinese in Jamaica*; see also Ching Chieh Chang, "The Chinese in Latin America," 45.

22. Lee Tom Yin, *The Chinese in Jamaica*, 138. Before 1904, dead Chinese had to be buried in local cemeteries. The Chinese buried in the free cemetery were not included here.

23. The same fact was indicated the cemetery list in 1953. Among 1,289

with places of birth recorded, 1,018 were born in China, and 910 were born in Dongguan (Tung-kuan), Bao-an (Pao-an), and Huiyang (Hui-yang). In other words, nearly 90% of those born in China came from the triangular border region of the three counties in southeastern Guangdong. Moreover, among those from Dongguan, 240 were from Guanlan (Kuan-lan) and 200 from Tangli (Tang-li), two small towns. Ching Chieh Chang, "The Chinese in Latin America," 45.

24. Eastern Lee, "The Chinese in Jamaica—A Personal Account," *The Daily Observer* (Kingston), January 20, 2000, 15.

25. It is also called the Chinese Benevolence Society.

26. Besides ordinary disputes, there were special problems. For example, in order to rent a space for business, some Chinese may offer a higher payment as rent for a place that was being used by other Chinese. To prevent this, the association stipulated a specific regulation. For 1934 and 1957 constitutions of the association, see Lee Tom Yin, *The Chinese in Jamaica*, 92–102. The association also had its bad times, such as 1904–1910, when Lin Bin (James Solomon), a Chinese migrant from Costa Rica, was chairman. He caused many troubles, including employing a group of local guards to take care of his safety and using this force to bully the Chinese community.

27. On May 3, 1928, the Japanese invaded Shandong Province and killed more than ten thousand Chinese civilians. The association became very active in mobilizing the Chinese community for donations and other related activities. See Lee Tom Yin, *The Chinese in Jamaica*, 50–56. There were a lot of reports and news regarding those activities in Chinese community. See, for example, *Huaqiao Gongbao* (The Chinese Public Newspaper), August 2, 1940; February 23, March 27, and March 30, 1945.

28. Andrew W. Lind, "Adjustment Patterns among the Jamaican Chinese," 144–164; Christine Ho, "'Hold the Chow Mein, Gimme Soca'," 3–25.

29. For example, the association decided to hold a meeting of its representatives to discuss the revision of the constitution in mid-October 1961, but few people showed up and the meeting had to be changed to a group discussion. *Zhong Shan Bao* (The Chung San News, Kingston), October 17, 1961.

30. *Ru Yi Tang* was set up in 1905 in order to protest against the arbitrary character of Lin Bing, the Chairman of the Chinese Benevolent Association at that time. After Lin Bing died, *Ru Yi Tang* was gradually incorporated into the CBA and was finally closed in the mid-1940s.

31. "Chinese Public School Constitution, Issued in January 1944," Lee

Tom Yin, *The Chinese in Jamaica*, 124–26.

32. This is true in Chinese communities almost all over the world. For example, many Chinese schools appeared in Africa after the war. See Li Anshan, *A History of Chinese Overseas in Africa*, 327–42, 515–23.

33. More than six Chinese language schools were opened in Kingston, St. Andrew, etc. All the schools were of the same pattern: weekend classes were arranged with free tuition, the teaching language was Chinese, and the subjects were all China-related. The Chinese Consul Huang Zeguang even held a tea party in the Consulate at which he emphasized the importance of overseas Chinese education. As for advertisements of the Chinese schools, see for example *Huaqiao Gongbao* (Chinese Public Newspaper, Kingston), February 3, February 27, and March 2, 1945.

34. "The Chinese Consulate Bulletin 34/22," *Huaqiao Gongbao* (Chinese Public Newspaper, Kingston), March 30, 1945.

35. "Balance Report of the Chinese Public School, 1953," *Zhong Shan Bao* (The Chung San News, Kingston), May 4, 1954.

36. For example, an editorial of *Zhong Zhan Bao* once displayed strong nationalist feeling by saying, "We are Chinese and the Chinese respect and emphasize the concepts of nation and race . . . we still consider ourselves a Chinese nation, and citizens of China; we don't want to be assimilated by others, nor do our children." "How to save education for Chinese children here" (Editorial), *Zhong Shan Bao* (The Chung San News, Kingston), May 4, 1956.

37. "An Open Letter to Jamaican Chinese," *Huaqiao Gongbao* (Chinese Public Newspaper, Kingston), September 4, 1954.

38. Chen Yinghao, "Chinese Public School at Present and Suggestions for the Future," *Zhong Shan Bao* (The Chung San News, Kingston), October 28, 1955. (Chen Yinghao is the Chinese name of Rupert Chinsee.)

39. "Advertisement of Chinese Public School," *Zhong Shan Bao* (The Chung San News, Kingston), December 5, 1961.

40. "Rules of the Chinese Inpatient Department," Lee Tom Yin, *The Chinese in Jamaica*, 130.

41. The weekly donation amount was 6 shillings for a big wholesale store, 4 shillings for a middle-sized one, 2 shillings for a small one; 3 shillings for a retail store; 2 shillings for food shops; 1 shilling for restaurants; and 6 pennies for an employee. "Bulletin of the Chinese Benevolence Association (1945/3/19)," *Huaqiao Gongbao* (Chinese Public Newspaper, Kingston), March 30 1945.

42. "High Praise for Chinese Hospital," *Huaqiao Gongbao* (Chinese Public

Newspaper, Kingston), May 8, 1954.

43. Lee Tom Yin, *The Chinese in Jamaica*, 132.

44. "Bulletin of Chinese Benevolence Association (1945/3/19)," *Huaqiao Gongbao* (Chinese Public Newspaper, Kingston), March 30, 1945.

45. *Zhong Shan Bao* (The Chung San News, Kingston), October 17, October 20, November 24, and November 30, 1961.

46. "Zhanghua Yishan (Chinese Cemetery)," Lee Tom Yin, *The Chinese in Jamaica*, 134–38.

47. "Special Issue of the Donation for the Renovation of Chinese Cemetery," *Zhong Shan Bao* (The Chung San News, Kingston), July 27, 1956. The advertisement was put up by the Propaganda Department of the association.

48. This was even noticed by the local newspaper. For example, a newspaper in Jamaica published an article entitled "New Split among the Chinese" on July 24, 1954, and the Chinese Public Newspaper immediately reported this news. "Westerners Speak about the New Split among Chinese," *Huaqiao Gongbao* (Chinese Public Newspaper, Kingston), July 27, 1954.

49. Some titles may suggest this, such as Leslie R. Chin, "The Young Generation," *The Pagoda* 26, no. 5 (November 1952); B. Brown, "Sojourner, or . . . . ?" *The Pagoda* 27, no. 18 (December 1954). Unfortunately the editor was murdered by bandits in his house on October 31, 1953.

50. This is an internal name for *Zhi Gong Tang*, the secret society of the anti-Qing/restore-the-Ming movement in China. The organization was suppressed and persecuted by the Qing government (1644–1911) and many members fled abroad. As for the resistance against the plantation owners, see Chen Kwang Min, *The Chinese in the Americas*, 706; Walton Look Lai, *Indentured Labor, Caribbean Sugar*, 113; Zhou Nanjing and Li Anshan, eds., *Encyclopedia of Chinese Overseas, Volume of History*, 539.

51. The principles still reflect the character of the anti-Qing/restore-the-Ming movement that gave birth to the organization. All the newspapers run by the Chinese Freemasons in Latin American countries include the "Three Principles" in their mastheads. See, for example, *Huaqiao Gongbao* (The Chinese Public News, Kingston), *Kaiming Gongbao* (Hoi Men Kong Po, Habana), *Gong Yan Bao* (La Voz de la Colonia China, Lima), etc.

52. Their contribution was long remembered for an incident in 1922. More than three hundred Chinese arrived from Hong Kong that year but were forbidden to land in Kingston. After long negotiation, the Chinese Benevolence Association reached an agreement with the government: the Chinese immigrants could land after paying a guarantee sum of £30. The

association had just restarted and could not produce such a large sum of money, but help from other Chinese businessmen and especially the Chinese Freemasons, who together lent the association £3,000, solved the problem. Chen Kwang Min, *The Chinese in the Americas*, 698.

53. From the 1920s onward, the Chinese Benevolent Association sent several petitions to the Chinese Embassy in London and the Overseas Chinese Commission respectively, asking for help and the setup of a consulate in Jamaica. After the 1924 petition, the American consulate in Jamaica was asked to help take care of the Chinese community there, but the result was not satisfactory. Not until 1943 was Huang Zeguang was appointed as the first Chinese Consul in Jamaica. The Chinese community bought a house by donation and gave it to the Chinese Consulate as a gift. Lee Tom Yin, *The Chinese in Jamaica*, 58–70.

54. In South Africa, Mauritius and Madagascar, for example, there are quite a few Chinese organizations based on their hometowns or home villages. See Li Anshan, *A History of Chinese Overseas in Africa*, 150–62, 353–66, 459–67. For the same type of organizations in Europe, see Li Minhuang, *Ouzhou Huaqiao Huaren Shi* (A History of Chinese Immigrants in Europe) (Beijing: Overseas Chinese Publishing House, 2002), 215–34, 676–81.

55. *Huaqiao Gongbao* (The Chinese Public Newspaper), June 16, 1945.

56. *Huaqiao Gongbao* (Chinese Public Newspaper, Kingston), June 22, 1946.

57. "Constitution of the Chinese Grocery Association," Lee Tom Yin, *The Chinese in Jamaica*, 160; "Constitution of the Chinese Bakery Association," ibid., 180.

58. "Bulletin No. 4" and "Bulletin No. 7," *Huaqiao Gongbao* (The Chinese Public Newspaper), February 3 and 23, 1945; "The Choice of the Chinese Retailers," Bulletin of the Chinese Retail Association, *Zhong Shan Bao* (The Chung San News, Kingston), March 4 and November 29, 1955.

59. "Records of the Member Meeting of the Association," *Huaqiao Gongbao* (The Chinese Public Newspaper), February 6, 1945. For other issues see "Bulletin No. 12" and "Bulletin No. 42," *Huaqiao Gongbao* (The Chinese Public Newspaper), April 24 and November 23, 1945; "The Choice of the Chinese Retailers," Bulletin of the Chinese Retail Association, *Zhong Shan Bao* (The Chung San News, Kingston), March 4 and November 29, 1955.

60. *Zhong Shan Bao* (Chung San News), September 20, September 23, and October 4, 1955.

61. "Encourage the Staff of the Retail Association," Editorial, *Zhong Shan*

Bao (The Chung San News, Kingston), March 2, 1956.

62. Lee Tom Yin, *The Chinese in Jamaica*, 171.

63. *Huaqiao Gongbao* (The Chinese Public Newspaper), September 2, 1954.

64. *Spotlight* (Kingston), May 1949. Quoted from Lind, "Adjustment Patterns among the Jamaican Chinese," 162.

65. Helen Chinsee, wife of Rupert Chinsee, a member of the Legislative Council, and herself a prominent woman in the Chinese community in Jamaica, wrote an interesting article to recall her father-in-law, Pa Chinsee. It vividly described an early Chinese retailer's life in Jamaica. See Helen Chinsee, "A Chinese in Jamaica," *Jamaica Journal* (Quarterly of the Institute of Jamaica), 2, no. 1 (March 1968): 10–14.

66. See, for example, Leonard Broom, "The Social Differentiation of Jamaica," *American Sociological Review* 19, no. 2 (1954): 115–25; Lind, "Adjustment Patterns among the Jamaican Chinese," 144–64; Howard Johnson, "The Anti-Chinese Riots of 1918 in Jamaica," 50–63; Jacqueline Levy, "The Economic Role of the Chinese in Jamaica: The Grocery Retail Trade," 31–49.

67. Chang, "The Chinese in Latin America," 82.

68. One Chinese wholesaler alone handled ten percent of the food imports in 1950. Chang, "The Chinese in Latin America," 86.

69. Orlando Patterson, "Contest and Choice in Ethnic Allegiance: A Theoretical Framework and Caribbean Case Study," in Nathan Glazer and Daniel P. Moynihan, eds., *Ethnicity Theory and Practice* (Cambridge: Harvard University Press, 1975), 322–46.

70. "The Chinese grocers' main strength in attracting Creole patronage was that they endeavored to service the special needs of the laboring classes." Howard Johnson, "The Anti-Chinese Riots of 1918 in Jamaica," 56. Lind's and Levy's articles also dealt with the same issue. It is worth mentioning that in other parts of the world, the Chinese also provided the same service for the lower class. In Africa, for example, they offered a credit system, small amounts of goods, and favorable conditions for the poor. Li Anshan, *A History of Chinese Overseas in Africa*, 142–50, 162–67.

71. Russell Dwight Lee, "The Perils of Ethnic Success: The Rise and Flight of the Chinese Traders in Jamaica" (Ph.D. dissertation, Harvard University, 1979).

72. Howard Johnson, "The Anti-Chinese Riots of 1918 in Jamaica," 50–63; Christine Ho, "'Hold the Chow Mein, Gimme Soca': Creolization of the Chinese in Guyana, Trinidad, and Jamaica," 3–25.

73. The plantation owners also used other tricks to exploit the laborers. ". . . little rum bars and gambling places clustered around the estates, where the indentured labourers, after a long and hard day's work, wary and lonesome, away from home and family, went to gather a little human warmth. These were traps. For the men quickly squandered away their small wages, and what is more pawned their next week's wages, and the next and the next. . . . It was only the very determined ones among the indentured labourers who had enough will power to keep way from those shabby rum shops." Helen Chinsee, "A Chinese in Jamaica," 11.

74. "Present Challenge before our Chinese Trade Business" (Editorial), *Zhong Shan Bao* (The Chung San News, Kingston), April 1, 1955.

75. "To Encourage Ms. Hu Jingxian" (Editorial), *Zhong Shan Bao* (The Chung San News, Kingston), August 23, 1955.

76. Helen Chinsee said, "Government through J.I.D.C. is helping us organize plans for a new 7,000 sq. ft. factory on five acres of land two miles south of Falmouth. We are truly grateful for their help." See "The Unburied Talent," *Spotlight* (Monthly Newsmagazine of Jamaica and the Caribbean) 21, no. 10 (1960): 21–22. The article mistook the year of her study as 1956; it should be 1955. See "To Encourage Ms. Hu Jingxian."

77. Christine Ho, "'Hold the Chow Mein, Gimme Soca'," 3–25.

78. Lind, "Adjustment Patterns among the Jamaican Chinese," 151.

79. "An Open Letter to the Chinese in Jamaica," *Huaqiao Gongbao* (Chinese Public Newspaper, Kingston), September 4, 1954. In this letter, the author gave some examples that showed that the Chinese youngsters were changing their attitude toward China and its culture. He warned that to prevent the Chinese youngsters from being assimilated, they should receive adequate education in Chinese.

80. Clifton Neita, compiler, *Who's Who Jamaica, British West Indies, 1951* (Kingston: Who's Who [Jamaica] Ltd., 1951). Determining who in the *Who's Who* is of Chinese descent is complicated by the fact that many Chinese in Jamaica adopted English family names. Therefore, although some of those pictured in this volume appear to have Asian features, because I could not be certain that they were of Chinese descent, I have only counted those who maintained Chinese family names, such as Chen, Cheong, Chin, Chong, Chung, Lai, Wong, Woo, as Chinese.

81. "Out of many . . . . " *Spotlight* (Monthly Newsmagazine of Jamaica and the Caribbean) 24, no. 7 (1960): 16.

82. *Zhong Shan Bao* (The Chung San News, Kingston), April 9, 1954.

83. *Huaqiao Gongbao* (Chinese Public Newspaper, Kingston), August 2, 1940.

84. *Huaqiao Gongbao* (Chinese Public Newspaper, Kingston), October 2, 1954.

85. *Zhong Shan Bao* (The Chung San News, Kingston), January 7, 1955.

86. Lee Tom Yin, *The Chinese in Jamaica*, 50.

87. *Zhong Shan Bao* (The Chung San News, Kingston), November 7, November 10, December 1, and December 8, 1961.

88. *Zhong Shan Bao* (The Chung San News, Kingston), December 19, 1961.

89. *Zhong Shan Bao* (The Chung San News, Kingston), December 22, 1961.

90. David Lowenthal, *West Indian Societies* (London: Oxford University Press, 1972), 206–207.

91. "Out of many . . . ." *Spotlight* (Monthly Newsmagazine of Jamaica and the Caribbean) 24, no. 7 (1963): 15.

92. Lee Tom Yin, *The Chinese in Jamaica*, 118.

93. "Politics and Us" (Editorial), *Zhong Shan Bao* (The Chung San News, Kingston), April 15, 1954.

94. "Out of many . . . ." *Spotlight* (Monthly Newsmagazine of Jamaica and the Caribbean) 24, no. 7 (1963): 16. See also Lee Tom Yin, *The Chinese in Jamaica*, 154.

95. *Zhong Shan Bao* (The Chung San News, Kingston), September 15, 1961.

96. *Zhong Shan Bao* (The Chung San News, Kingston), September 19, 1961.

97. "The Unburied Talent," *Spotlight* (Monthly Newsmagazine of Jamaica and the Caribbean) 21, no. 10 (1960): 21; "Out of Many . . . ." *Spotlight* (Monthly Newsmagazine of Jamaica and the Caribbean) 24, no. 7 (1963): 16.

98. "Out of Many . . . ." *Spotlight* (Monthly Newsmagazine of Jamaica and the Caribbean) 24, no. 7 (1963): 15.

Bibliography for Chapter 4

Barth, Fredrik. 1969. *Ethnic Groups and Boundaries: The Social Organization of Culture Difference*. Boston: Little Brown & Company.

Black, Clinton. 1983. *History of Jamaica*. London: Collins Educational.

Bouknight, Gail. 1991. "A Study of the Chinese Retail Grocery Trade and Its Impact upon Chinese Ethnicity and Sino-Jamaican Relations." Unpublished Master's thesis, Brown University.

Broom, Leonard. 1954. "The Social Differentiation of Jamaica." *American Sociological Review* 19, no. 2 (April): 115–25.

Campbell, Persia C. 1923. *Chinese Coolie Emigration to Countries within the British Empire.* London: P. S. King & Son, Ltd.

Chai, Marie. 1983. "Chinese Social Customs and Their Retention amongst the Chinese Community in Contemporary Jamaica." Unpublished paper. Caribbean Studies in History. Dept. of History, University of West Indies, Mona, Jamaica.

Chang, Ching Chieh. 1956. *The Chinese in Latin America: A Preliminary Geographical Survey with Special Reference to Cuba and Jamaica.* Ph.D. dissertation, University of Maryland.

Clementi, Sir Cecil. 1915. *The Chinese in British Guiana.* Georgetown: Argosy.

Cohen, Abner. 1969. *Custom and Politics in Urban Africa: A Study of Hausa Migrants in Yoruba Towns.* Berkeley: University of California Press.

Cohen, Abner. 1981. "Variables in Ethnicity." In *Ethnic Change*, edited by Charles F. Keyes. Seattle: University of Washington Press.

De Vos, George, and Lola Romanucci-Ross. 1975. "Ethnicity: Vessel of Meaning and Emblem of Contrast." In *Ethnic Identity: Cultural Continuities and Change*, edited by George De Vos and Lola Romanucci-Ross. Palo Alto, Calif.: Mayfield Pub. Co.

Eisner, Gisela. 1961. *Jamaica 1830–1930.* Manchester: The University Press.

Freedman, Maurice. 1958. *Lineage Organization in South Eastern China.* London School of Economics Monographs on Social Anthropology no. 18. New York: Humanities Press, Inc.

Freedman, Maurice. 1979. *The Study of Chinese Society.* Stanford, Calif.: Stanford University Press.

Fried, Morton H. 1956. "Some Observations on the Chinese in British Guiana." *Social and Economic Studies* (Mona, Jamaica) 5, no. 1: 54–73.

Glazer, Nathan, and Daniel Patrick Moynihan. 1963. *Beyond the Melting Pot: The Negroes, Puerto Ricans, Jews, Italians, and Irish of New York City.* 1st ed. Cambridge, Mass.: MIT Press.

Gordon, Milton M. 1964. *Assimilation in American Life: The Role of Race, Religion and National Origins.* New York: Oxford University Press.

Hall, Douglas. 1959. *Free Jamaica 1838–1865: An Economic History.* New Haven: Yale University Press.

Herlinger, Elizabeth Hagens. 1972. "A Historical Cultural, and Organizational Analysis of Ozark Ethnic Identity." Ph.D. dissertation, University of Chicago.

Hicks, George L. 1977. "Introduction: Problems in the Study of Ethnicity." In *Ethnic Encounters: Identities and Contexts*, edited by George L. Hicks and Philip Leis. North Scituate, Mass.: Duxbury Press.

Hsu, Francis L. K. 1953. *Americans and Chinese: Two Ways of Life*. New York: Henry Schuman, Inc.

Johnson, Howard. 1983. "The Anti-Chinese Riots of 1918." *Immigrants and Minorities* 2, no. 1 (March): 50–63.

Latourette, Kenneth Scott. 1934. *The Chinese: Their History and Culture*. New York: The MacMillan Company.

Lawrence, Keith O. 1971. *Immigration into the West Indies in the 19th Century*. Barbados: Caribbean Universities Press.

Levy, Jacqueline. 1972. "Chinese Indentured Immigration to Jamaica during the Latter Part of the 19th Century." Unpublished paper, Department of History, University of the West Indies, Mona, Jamaica.

Levy, Jacqueline. 1967. "The Economic Role of Chinese in Jamaica: The Grocery Retail Trade." Unpublished paper, Dept. of History Post Graduate Seminars, University of the West Indies, Mona, Jamaica.

Lind, Andrew W. 1958. "Adjustment Patterns among the Jamaican Chinese." *Social and Economic Studies* (Mona, Jamaica) 7, no. 2.

Look Lai, Walton. 1993. *Indentured Labor, Caribbean Sugar*. Baltimore: Johns Hopkins University Press.

Lyn-Shue, Maureen. 1979. "The Chinese In Jamaica." Ph.D. dissertation, Dept. of History, University of the West Indies, Mona, Jamaica.

McLean, Esther. 1979. "Language and the Chinese Minority in Jamaica." Unpublished paper. Caribbean Studies in History. Dept. of History, University of the West Indies, Mona, Jamaica.

Morrow, Phyllis. 1972. "Chinese Adaptation in Two Jamaican Cities." Unpublished honors thesis, Dept. of Anthropology, Harvard University.

Nettleford, Rex. 1978. *Caribbean Cultural Identity. The Case of Jamaica*. Kingston: Institute of Jamaica.

Patterson, Orlando. 1983. "Context and Choice in Ethnic Allegiance: A Theoretical Framework and Caribbean Case Study." In *Ethnicity: Theory and Experience*, edited by Nathan Glazer and Daniel P. Moynihan. Cambridge, Mass.: Harvard University Press.

Patterson, Orlando. 1978. "Migration in Caribbean Societies: Socio-economic and Symbolic Resource." In *Human Migration, Patterns and Policies*, edited by William H. McNeill and Ruth S. Adams. Bloomington and London: Indiana University Press.

Rex, John. 1983. "Review of 'The Ethnic Phenomenon'." *Ethnic and Racial*

Studies 6:368–71.

Richardson, Mary. 1983. "Out of Many, One People—Aspiration or Reality: An Examination of the Attitudes to the Various Racial and Ethnic Groups within Jamaican Society." *Social and Economic Studies* (Mona, Jamaica) 32, no. 2.

Roberts, George W. 1957. *The Population of Jamaica*. London and New York: The University Press.

Roberts, George W. 1974. *Recent Population Movement in Jamaica*. C.I.C.R.E.D. Series. Paris: C.I.C.R.E.D.

Shibutani, Tamotsu, and Kian M. Kwan. 1965. *Ethnic Stratification: A Comparative Approach*. New York: MacMillan.

Silin, R. A. 1962. "Survey of Selected Aspects of the Chinese in Jamaica." Unpublished honors thesis, Dept. of Anthropology, Harvard University.

Straw, Carol. 1986. "Anti-Chinese Prejudice in Jamaica, 1918–1938." Unpublished paper. Caribbean Studies in History. Dept. of History, University of the West Indies, Mona, Jamaica.

Takaki, Ronald T. 1989. *Strangers from a Different Shore: A History of Asian Americans*. Boston: Little, Brown.

van den Berghe, Pierre L. 1981. *The Ethnic Phenomenon*. New York: Elsevier North Holland Inc.

van den Berghe, Pierre L. 1977. *Inequality in the Peruvian Andes: Class and Ethnicity in Cuzco*. Columbia: University of Missouri Press.

Williams, Lea E. 1966. *The Future of the Overseas Chinese in Southeast Asia*. New York: McGraw-Hill Book Company.

Williams, Lea E. 1960. *Overseas Chinese Nationalism: The Genesis of the Pan Chinese Movement in Indonesia, 1900–1916*. Glencoe, Ill.: The Free Press.

Williams, Lea E. 1976. *Southeast Asia: A History*. New York: Oxford University Press.

Yin, Lee Tom, ed. 1963. *The Chinese in Jamaica*. Kingston: Chung Sun News, Ltd.

Notes to Chapter 4

1. Jimmy Lee (pseudonym), interviewed by author, Kingston, Jamaica, July 11, 1990.

2. Beverly Chin, interviewed by author, Kingston, Jamaica, June 20, 1990; Jimmy Lee, interviewed by author, Kingston, Jamaica, July 11, 1990; Faye Soltau, interviewed by author, Kingston, Jamaica, August 9, 1990.

3. Jimmy Lee, interviewed by author, Kingston, Jamaica, July 11th, 1990; Yuet Chang, interviewed by author, Kingston, Jamaica, June 29, 1990; Sammy Chin, interviewed by author, Kingston, Jamaica, June 7, 1990.

4. Yuet Chang, interviewed by author, Kingston, Jamaica, June 29, 1990.

5. The *Daily Gleaner*, May 23, 1913.

6. The Chinese population in Jamaica increased dramatically in the first half of the twentieth century. By 1943, Chinese in Jamaica outnumbered those in Trinidad and Guyana (Look Lai 1993:202).

7. Earl Loshusan, interviewed by author, Kingston, Jamaica, July 12, 1990; Yuet Chang, interviewed by author, Kingston, Jamaica, June 29, 1990.

8. Little Greene and Elva James, interviewed by author, Kingston, Jamaica, June 26, 1990; Yuet Chang, interviewed by author, Kingston, Jamaica, June 29, 1990; Sammy Chin, interviewed by author, Kingston, Jamaica, June 7, 1990; Faye Soltau, interviewed by author, Kingston, Jamaica, August 9, 1990.

9. Beverly Chin, interviewed by author, Kingston, Jamaica, June 20, 1990.

10. Beverly Chin, interviewed by author, Kingston, Jamaica, June 20, 1990.

11. Philip Lee, interviewed by author, Kingston, Jamaica, July 11, 1990; Yuet Chang, interviewed by author, Kingston, Jamaica, June 29, 1990.

12. Philip Lee, interviewed by author, Kingston, Jamaica, July 11, 1990.

13. Earl Loshusan, interviewed by author, Kingston, Jamaica, July 12, 1990.

14. Yuet Chang, interviewed by author, Kingston, Jamaica, June 29, 1990; Sammy Chin, interviewed by author, Kingston, Jamaica, June 7, 1990; Earl Loshusan, interviewed by author, Kingston, Jamaica, July 12, 1990.

15. Records of ownership were sometimes difficult to assess because documentation for registered business ownership did not always coincide with the buying or selling of these markets. A business owner may register before the business has been physically established, and an establishment may go out of business or change hands before it is officially documented with the Registrar.

16. Earl Loshusan, interviewed by author, Kingston, Jamaica, July 12, 1990.

17. In 1954, of the 187 large and small bakeries, 141 were owned and operated by the Chinese (Chang 1956:86).

18. Beverly Chin, interviewed by author, Kingston, Jamaica, June 20, 1990; Sammy Chin, interviewed by author, Kingston, Jamaica, June 7, 1990.

19. Sammy Chin, interviewed by author, Kingston, Jamaica, June 7, 1990.

20. Annual General Report, Protector of Immigrants, 1910–1911, Departmental Reports, p. 162.

21. Lawson Davis, interviewed by author, Kingston, Jamaica, June 12, 1990; Neville Smith, interviewed by author, Kingston, Jamaica, June 7, 1990, Sammy Chin, interviewed by author, Kingston, Jamaica, June 7, 1990; Yuet Chang, interviewed by author, Kingston, Jamaica, June 29, 1990.

22. Owners identified as East Indian owned 7.1 percent of the grocery retail shops and others identified as Syrian owned 1.4 percent of the grocery retail shops (Bouknight, 1991).

23. Earl Loshusan, interviewed by author, Kingston, Jamaica, July 12, 1990.

24. "Occidental Chinese Wall," *Spotlight* (October, 1952): 4, 7.

25. Letter to the Editor, The *Star*, Friday, August 9, 1963, p. 13.

26. "Occidental Chinese Wall," *Spotlight* (October, 1952): 4, 7.

27. The two oldest organizations are Chee Kung Tong, formed in 1887, and Chinese Benevolent Society, formed in 1891. Newer organizations include the Chinese Cultural Development Center (CCDC) and the Chinese Society of Jamaica, which merged in 1990 to form the Chinese Cultural Centre. The former two represent members of the local-born population, while the latter reflects foreign-born members.

28. Jimmy Lee, interviewed by author, Kingston, Jamaica, July 11th, 1990.

29. The local-born Chinese population is descended from the first, second and third large-scale migration waves, whereas others are foreign-born but have spent a great deal of their lives, beginning in childhood, as Jamaicans. Many of the first immigrants were from southeastern China. Later immigrants come from Hong Kong. Differences between local-born and foreign-born are reflected in the spoken dialects as well. Local-born Chinese may still speak the Hakka dialect because their forebears migrated from southeastern China. Post–nineteenth century migrants from China tend to be Mandarin speakers. Recent Hong Kong migrants are predominantly Cantonese speaking.

30. The term "dark person" is used most often when referring to an Afro-Jamaican in a mixed union. (Tina Chin, interview by author, June 10, 1990; Faye Soltau, interviewed by author, Kingston, Jamaica, August 9, 1990.)

31. Sammy Chin, interviewed by author, Kingston, Jamaica, June 7, 1990.

32. Johnson 1983, 3.

33. Johnson 1983.

34. *New World Fortnightly*, no. 24, 1965.

35. Beverly Chin, interviewed by author, Kingston, Jamaica, June 20, 1990; Little Greene and Elva James, interviewed by author, Kingston, Jamaica, June 26, 1990.

36. The *Daily Gleaner*, Wednesday, September 7, 1932.

37. Beverly Chin, interviewed by author, Kingston, Jamaica, June 20, 1990.

38. Neville Smith, interviewed by author, Kingston, Jamaica, June 7, 1990; Lawson Davis, interviewed by author, Kingston, Jamaica, June 12, 1990.

39. Some claim that ethnic groups may be established and maintained by boundary maintenance (van den Berghe 1981, Barth 1969, De Vos 1975, Herlinger 1972). However, the definitions of what constitutes the boundary vary: it may be a form of social organization (Barth 1969), a cultural symbol system (Herlinger 1972), a social and physical creation by territoriality (van den Berghe 1977), or psychological in nature (De Vos 1975). While boundaries may be constructed culturally, psychologically, socially and physically, what is significant is that they are constructed with interaction. Therefore, the focus should be on the conditions under which a category becomes a group.

40. Patterson suggests that economic interests based on context and choice are primary factors for ethnic identity. (Patterson 1988:337). However, social, cultural and historical factors within the economic context of the grocery retail industry as mentioned above— role of the family, kin affiliation, and social organizations—also influenced the construction of both ethnic identity and interethnic relations.

Notes to Chapter 5

1. *El Comercio* (Cienfuegos), 23 March 1923, 1.

2. From 1847 to 1874 about 100,000 Chinese also signed contracts to work in Peru. For the commission's report, see China, Zongli geguo shiwu yamen [Office for the General Management of Foreign Affairs], *Chinese Emigration: Report of the Commission sent by China to Ascertain the Condition of Chinese Coolies in Cuba, 1874* (English ed., Shanghai: Imperial Maritime Customs Press, 1876; reprint ed., Taipei: Ch'eng Wen Publishing Company, 1970). See also the paperback reissue of this document, *The Cuba Commission Report: A Hidden History of the Chinese in Cuba*, introduction by Denise Helly (Baltimore: The Johns Hopkins University Press, 1993). Between 1865 and 1874, only 2,000 Chinese returned to China. Helly, introduction to *The Cuba Commission Report*, 25. For works on the coolie trade to Cuba, see Duvon C. Corbitt, *A Study of the Chinese in Cuba, 1847–1947* (Wilmore, Kentucky:

Asbury College, 1971); Denise Helly, *Idéologie et ethnicité: Les Chinois Macao à Cuba: 1847–1886* (Montreal: Les Presses de lUniversité de Montréal, 1979); Juan Jiménez Pastrana, *Los Chinos en la historia de Cuba: 1847-1930* (Havana: Editorial de Ciencias Sociales, 1983); Evelyn Hu-DeHart, "Chinese Coolie Labour in Cuba in the Nineteenth Century: Free Labour or Neo-slavery?" *Slavery and Abolition* 14, no. 1 (1993): 67–86; and Juan Pérez de la Riva, *Los culíes chinos en Cuba (1847–1880): Contribución al estudio de la inmigración contratada en el Caribe* (Havana: Editorial de Ciencias Sociales, 2000 [1967]).

3. Pérez de la Riva, *Los culíes chinos en Cuba*, 178–83. According to Pérez de la Riva, precise numerical data is not available for the Chinese who migrated to Cuba from California in the second half of the nineteenth century, as customs registered them according to the last port of exit (Mexico and New Orleans). His demographic analysis reveals that the "Californians" were particularly numerous between 1865 and 1875 and continued to arrive afterward.

4. U.S. War Department, *Report on the Census of Cuba 1899* (Washington: Government Printing Office, 1900), 69–71, 472–75; Corbitt, *A Study of the Chinese in Cuba*, 89.

5. *The Havana Daily Post*, 14 October 1913, 5.

6. Despite a U.S.-imposed immigration restriction of 1902 (Order No. 155) banning Chinese laborers from entering Cuba, they continued to arrive with false papers under the categories of merchant, student, diplomat, and tourist. Official census records underreport the numbers of Chinese entering after the establishment of the Cuban Republic in 1902. For example, the Cuban census of 1919 reported no entries of Chinese between 1908 and 1917, seven in 1918, and 1,100 in 1919. In contrast, the Chinese Consulate in Havana recorded 6,258 Chinese immigrants between 1903 and 1916, along with data such as name, date of entry, name of ship, and category of immigrant. Cuba, Oficina Nacional del Censo, *Censo de la República de Cuba 1919*, 175; Corbitt, *A Study of the Chinese in Cuba*, 95–96.

7. Corbitt, *A Study of the Chinese in Cuba*, 89. Spanish-speaking Chinese in Chinatowns of New York and San Francisco were most likely migrants from Cuba or elsewhere in Latin America and the Spanish-speaking Caribbean.

8. Chen Mengyu, "Guba huaqiao shenghuo gaikuang" [General Situation of the Lives of Overseas Chinese in Cuba] Part 2, in *Huaqiao banyuekan* 31 (16 September 1933): 14–18.

9. Antonio Chuffat, "Los Chinos y la diversidad de dialectos, carácter de cada provincia y regiones, los imperialistas y los republicanos," in *El Comercio*

(Cienfuegos), 11 September 1926, 4.

10. Corbitt, *A Study of the Chinese in Cuba*, 115; José Baltar Rodríguez, *Los Chinos de Cuba: Apuntes etnográficos* (Havana: Fundación Fernando Ortiz, 1997), 91–92.

11. Chuffat, "Los Chinos y la diversidad de dialectos." For a perceptive analysis of Antonio Chuffat's role in the Chinese Cuban community, see Lisa Li-ShenYun, "An Afro-Chinese Caribbean: Cultural Cartographies of Contrariness in the Work of Antonio Chuffat Latour, Margaret Cezair-Thompson, and Patricia Powell," in *Caribbean Quarterly* 50, no. 2 (June 2004).

12. Violeta Luis and Mitzi Espinosa Luis, interviews by author, March 1999, June 2000, and March 2002, Cienfuegos, Cuba. The foundations for Lü Fan's operation had already been laid in the Cienfuegos region by former indentured laborers who filled an economic niche cultivating vegetables for local consumption. Typically, Chinese truck farmers leased land and carted their produce to local markets. Duvon Corbitt states, "The production and sale of vegetables passed almost completely into their hands, where it long remained." Corbitt, *A Study of the Chinese in Cuba*, 89. Cuba, Oficina del Censo, *Censo de la República de Cuba bajo la administración provisional de los Estados Unidos 1907* (Washington: Oficina del Censo de los Estados Unidos, 1908), 31.

13. *La Correspondencia* (Cienfuegos), 21 April 1934, 1.

14. These networks extended to other Chinese communities throughout the diaspora. In his study of Chinese in Chicago, Peru, and Hawaii, Adam McKeown demonstrates that Chinese migrants in their local contexts can best be understood through a transnational perspective that examines the networks linking them to each other and to Chinese villages. Adam McKeown, *Chinese Migrants and Cultural Change: Peru, Chicago, Hawaii, 1900–1936* (Chicago: The University of Chicago Press, 2001).

15. Interview by author, Meige, Xinhui County, China, November 2001.

16. Lin Datian, interview by author, Dulian, Xinhui County, China, August 2001. Lin Datian is the current editor of "Dulian News" (a *qiaokan* or magazine geared toward Chinese overseas) and the son of a Chinese migrant to Cuba, Lin Gengsheng.

17. Chen Mengyu, "Guba huaqiao shenghuo gaikuang" [General Situation of the Lives of Overseas Chinese in Cuba], Part 1, *Huaqiao banyuekan* 29 (15 August 1933): 7–11.

18. Guangdong Provincial Archive, Guangdong sheng youzheng guanli ju [Guangdong Province Postal Service Management Office], 29 quanzong

[archive], 2 mulu [catalogue], 372 juan [volume], "Guowai qiaobao ji guonei qiaojuan dizhi diaocha biao, jinchukou qiao you tongji biao, 1948" [Address chart of foreign overseas Chinese and their domestic dependents, chart of incoming and outgoing overseas Chinese mail, 1948].

19. For the role of *jinshanzhuang* or "Gold Mountain firms" in providing Chinese overseas remittance services, see Madeline Y. Hsu, *Dreaming of Gold, Dreaming of Home: Transnationalism and Migration Between the United States and South China, 1882–1943* (Stanford, Calif.: Stanford University Press, 2000), 31–40.

20. Interview by author, Meige, Xinhui County, China, November 2001. Hsu, *Dreaming of Gold*, 40–54.

21. Lin Datian, interview by author, Dulian, Xinhui County, China, August 2001.

22. Interview by author, Meige, Xinhui County, China, November 2001.

23. Corbitt, *A Study of the Chinese in Cuba*, 90. Scholars have attributed the gender imbalance in Chinese migration to the Americas to patriarchal standards in China that confined women to the home, high costs of transport, the preference of labor recruiters for males, and bureaucratic hurdles and legal restrictions to entry. See Sucheng Chan, *Asian Americans: An Interpretive History* (New York: Twayne Publishers, 1991), 103–107.

24. Liu Chongmin, *Taishan xian huaqiao zhi* [Taishan Overseas Chinese Gazette] (Taishan: Taishan County Overseas Chinese Affairs Office, 1992), 164. For the impact of male migration on families in China, see Evelyn Nakano Glenn, "Split Household, Small Producer, and Dual Wage Earner: An Analysis of Chinese-American Family Strategies," *Journal of Marriage and the Family* 45, no. 1 (February 1983): 35–48; Hsu, *Dreaming of Gold*, 90–123.

25. Liu Chongmin, interview by author, Guanghai, Taishan County, China, August 2001; Han Mei [Liu Chongmin], "Yi ge guba huagong shi" [History of a Chinese Laborer in Cuba] *Wuyi qiaoshi* 7 (1989): 32–33.

26. Hsu, *Dreaming of Gold*, 91.

27. Lü family, interview by author, Xinhui County, China, August 2001.

28. Although she has never met them, Baoqin's eldest daughter refers to Lourdes and Violeta as "Third Auntie" (*san yi*) and "Fourth Auntie" (*si yi*). Growing up, she had a total of "four aunties": her mother (Baoqin), her mother's sister (Mali), and her mother's two Cuban half-sisters.

29. Lü family, interview by author, Xinhui County, China, August 2001. In the summer of 2001, with information provided by the Cuban daughters and the assistance of the local overseas Chinese affairs office, my research assistant and I were able to locate and meet the elderly Chinese daughters.

They still live in Lü Village and maintain the house that their father built upon his first return trip from Cuba in the early twentieth century. Since then, communication with their Cuban relatives has resumed. I extend my deepest appreciation to Chen Liyuan and to the Daze Overseas Chinese Affairs Office for their role in reuniting the two sides of the Lü family.

30. Zhou Nanjing, ed., *Huaqiao huaren baike quanshu* [Encyclopedia of Chinese Overseas], *Shetuan zhengdang juan* [Volume of Organizations and Parties] (Beijing: Zhongguo Huaqiao Chubanshe, 1998), 151–52; Chen Kwong Min, *Meizhou huaqiao tongjian* (The Chinese in the Americas) (New York: Overseas Chinese Culture Publishing Co., 1950), 641–42. By 1882 the Zhonghua zonghuiguan (Chinese Consolidated Benevolent Association or Chinese Six Companies) was established in San Francisco from the various district associations to represent the Chinese community. It became the most influential of the Chinese organizations in the Americas. See L. Eve Armentrout Ma, *Revolutionaries, Monarchists, and Chinatowns: Chinese Politics in the Americas and the 1911 Revolution* (Honolulu: University of Hawaii Press, 1990), 14–21.

31. By 1950 it housed 170 Chinese residents. Chen, *Meizhou huaqiao tongjian*, 641–42. It was common practice for Chinese associations throughout Cuba to stipulate that in the event of dissolution, remaining funds would go to the Asilo de Anciano Chinos de Jacomino.

32. Chen, *Meizhou huaqiao tongjian*, 641–42; Zhou, *Huaqiao huaren baike quanshu*, 151.

33. See Chan, *Asian Americans*, 64. Today, for example, the remaining Chinese from Xinhui County have joined the Zhongshan regional society in Havana.

34. By 1950 there were 2,500 members, and plans were underway for another 100 beds to be added to the existing 140. Chen, *Meizhou huaqiao tongjian*, 644–45.

35. Chen, *Meizhou huaqiao tongjian*, 641–42; Napoleón Seuc, *La Colonia China de Cuba (1930–1960): Antecedentes, memorias y vivencias* (Miami: Ahora Printing, 1998), 82.

36. Archivo Provincial de Cienfuegos (hereafter APC), Cementerio de Reina, Libro de Exhumaciones, 1899–1936, Folio 23; APC, Registro de Asociaciones, Legajo 28, Expediente 422, "Lung Kuan (Gran China)." Cemetery records in Cuba indicate the name of the deceased, date of interment, location of tomb, and, if an autopsy was performed, cause of death.

37. Chen, *Meizhou huaqiao tongjian*, 641–42. Bones were sent to China through Donghua Hospital in Hong Kong.

38. Zhou, *Huaqiao huaren baike quanshu*, 152.

39. APC, Registro de Asociaciones, Legajo 27, Expediente 581, "Asociación Cienfueguera de Agricultores Chinos," Folios 85–86.

40. Ma, *Revolutionaries, Monarchists, and Chinatowns*, 21–29. The Triads have variously been called Sanhehui, Sandianhui, Yixinghui, and Hongmen.

41. In 1946 its name changed again to the Hongmen Minzhidang. Zhou, *Huaqiao huaren baike quanshu*, 150.

42. It became a political party named Zhigongdang in 1925, with Chen Jiongming (Governor of Guangdong province from 1920 to 1923) elected titular head. Him Mark Lai, "The Kuomintang in Chinese American Communities before World War II," in Sucheng Chan, ed., *Entry Denied: Exclusion and the Chinese Community in America, 1882–1943* (Philadelphia: Temple University Press, 1991), 170–212 (179, 203–204 n. 38). As in China, over time, Triads overseas became less political and revolutionary and more involved in mutual aid and smuggling of opium and illegal immigrants.

43. APC, Registro de Asociaciones, Legajo 28, Expediente 420, "Centro Republicano Asiático," Folios 155–56.

44. *La Correspondencia* (Cienfuegos), 17 July 1928, 12.

45. In 1905 Sun Yat-sen elucidated three major principles of nationalism (*minzu*), democracy (*minquan*), and people's livelihood (*minsheng*), which were later developed into the Three Principles of the People (*sanminzhuyi*).

46. Chen, *Meizhou huaqiao tongjian*, 672–73; Huang Dingzhi, "Guba de sanminyue shubaoshe" [The *Sanmin* Study Society of Cuba], in *Huaqiao yu xinhai geming* [Overseas Chinese and the 1911 Revolution] (Beijing: Zhongguo shehui kexue chubanshe, 1981), 312–30.

47. Chen, *Meizhou huaqiao tongjian*, 672–73.

48. Huang, "Guba de sanminyue shubaoshe"; Ma, *Revolutionaries, Monarchists, and Chinatowns*, 150. See subsequent articles in *The Havana Daily Post*, 10 April 1913, 10 January 1914.

49. Lai, "The Kuomintang in Chinese American Communities," 182.

50. Pablo L. Rousseau and Pablo Díaz de Villegas, *Memoria descriptiva, histórica y biográfica de Cienfuegos y las fiestas del primer centenario de la fundación de esta ciudad* (Havana, 1920), 339.

51. Lai, "The Kuomintang in Chinese American Communities," 180–88.

52. Ibid., 190–91.

53. Baltar, *Los Chinos de Cuba*, 70–71; Jiménez Pastrana, *Los Chinos en la historia de Cuba*, 144; Zhou, *Huaqiao huaren baike quanshu*, 151. In 1929 they established the clandestine monthly publication *Gongnong husheng* ("Grito Obrero-Campesino" or "Call of the Worker and Peasant"). For parallels with

the purge of leftist Guomindang elements and the beginning of organized Marxists among Chinese in the United States, see Lai, "The Kuomintang in Chinese American Communities," 190–91.

54. For a detailed description of the contents and significance of hometown publications, see Cen Huang and Michael R. Godley, "Appendix Chapter: A Note on the Study of *Qiaoxiang* Ties," in Leo Douw, Cen Huang, and Michael R. Godley, eds., *Qiaoxiang Ties: Interdisciplinary Approaches to 'Cultural Capitalism' in South China* (London: Kegan Paul International, 1999), 306–342; Hsu, *Dreaming of Gold*, 124–55.

55. Select copies of the first three newspapers from the 1930s to 1970s made their way to the foreign newspaper collection of the National Library of China in Beijing (Guojia Tushuguan). The library also holds copies of the Communist *Guanghuabao* after 1959.

56. Seuc, *La Colonia China de Cuba*, 37.

57. See, for example, *Minsheng ribao* (Havana), 27 March 1942, 4.

58. Chen, *Meizhou huaqiao tongjian*, 649–51. My translation.

59. For Nationalist Party activities in the United States during World War II, see Lai, "The Kuomintang in Chinese American Communities," 194–97.

60. Liu, *Taishan xian huaqiao zhi*, 165–70.

61. Liu Kongye was Liu Chongmin's uncle. Liu Chongmin, interview by author, Guanghai, Taishan County, China, August 2001.

62. Lü family, interview by author, Xinhui County, China, August 2001.

63. Yen Ching-Hwang, *Studies in Modern Overseas Chinese History* (Singapore: Times Academic Pres, 1995), 144.

64. Chen, *Meizhou huaqiao tongjian*, 647–48; Zhou, *Huaqiao huaren baike quanshu*, 244–45.

65. See Yong Chen's discussion of Chinese overseas participation in the resistance to Japanese aggression. Yong Chen, *Chinese San Francisco, 1850–1943: A Trans-pacific Community* (Stanford: Stanford University Press, 2000), 233–37.

66. Gonzalo de Quesada, *Los Chinos y la revolución cubana* (Havana: Úcar, García y Cía., 1946). In March 1931 the ceremony for the laying of the foundation was attended by overseas Chinese leaders, Cuban government officials, and Chinese diplomatic representatives. With the interruption of the Japanese invasion of China, it was not until April 1946 that the official unveiling ceremony was held, presided over by Chinese Minister Li Dijun and Cuban President Ramón Grau San Martín. Chen, *Meizhou huaqiao tongjian*, 634–35. The monument is inscribed in Spanish ("No hubo un chino cubano desertor; no hubo un chino cubano traidor") and Chinese ("Guba

zhongguo ren wu you daoge zhe, guba zhongguo ren wu you tiaowang zhe").

67. Archivo Nacional de Cuba (hereafter ANC), Secretaría de la Presidencia, Legajo 25, Expediente 42, "Reporte del periódico 'El País' de 7 de mayo de 1926, relativo a los problemas creados en el Casino 'Chung Wag'" [no folio numbers]. For an analysis of the struggles for control of Havana's Chinatown, see Reinaldo Ramos Hernández, Arturo A. Pedroso Alés, and Flor Inés Cassola Triana, "Luchas por el control del Barrio Chino de la Habana (1926)," *Catauro* 2, no. 2 (2000), 34–49.

68. ANC, Secretaría de la Presidencia, Legajo 25, Expediente 52, "Expediente mecanografiado y manuscrito que contiene cartas, acuses de recibo, informes policiacos, decreto, reportes de periódicos, actas, etc.; en relación con la causa 1091 de 1926 seguida por el juzgado especial, por el asesinato del asiático Andres Chiu Lión y la complicidad de la sociedad China 'Chi Kong Tong' en el mismo" [no folio numbers].

69. *El Comercio* (Cienfuegos), 2 September 1926, 4.

70. ANC, Secretaría de la Presidencia, Legajo 25, Expediente 52, "Expediente mecanografiado y manuscrito . . . en relación con la causa 1091 de 1926 . . ." [no folio numbers].

71. For example, the Cienfuegos branch of the Zhigongtang, known as the "Centro Repúblicano Asiático," was investigated on December 22, 1926. APC, Registro de Asociaciones, Legajo 28, Expediente 420. The file contains copies of official correspondence from Havana detailing previous investigations of the Zhigongtang and the assassination.

72. Ma, *Revolutionaries, Monarchists, and Chinatowns*, 21–29.

73. ANC, Secretaría de la Presidencia, Legajo 25, Expediente 52, "Expediente mecanografiado y manuscrito . . . en relación con la causa 1091 de 1926 . . ." [no folio numbers].

74. ANC, Secretaría de la Presidencia, Legajo 25, Expediente 51, "Cuadro comprensivo de la arteria principal del barrio chino, donde viven los asiáticos en completo hacinamiento y faltos de toda higien; y relacíon de las casas de comercio de tercer orden que radican en dicho barrio; enviados al parecer al Secretario de Sanidad por el Secretario de Gobernación," 28 August 1926.

75. *El Comercio* (Cienfuegos), 11 September 1926, 4.

76. For the impact of competition from foreign labor on the Cuban working class, see Louis A. Pérez, Jr., *Cuba: Between Reform and Revolution* (New York and Oxford: Oxford University Press, 1995), 201–205. In 1882 the United States Congress had passed the Chinese Exclusion Act, banning the future immigration of Chinese laborers. When the U.S. occupied Cuba from 1899 to 1902 and again from 1906 to 1909, restrictive anti–Chinese immi-

gration laws were enforced by American military authorities.

77. *La Correspondencia* (Cienfuegos), 21 August 1922, 1.

78. *The Havana Daily Post*, 2 October 1913, 4.

79. ANC, Secretaría de la Presidencia, Legajo 25, Expediente 52, "Expediente mecanografiado y manuscrito . . . en relación con la causa 1091 de 1926 . . ." [no folio numbers]. My translation.

80. *El Republicano*, 14 September 1915.

81. Chen, *Meizhou huaqiao tongjian*, 645.

82. *El Comercio* (Cienfuegos), 25 June 1926.

83. Chuffat, "Los Chinos y la diversidad de dialectos."

84. Seuc, *La Colonia China de Cuba*, 96.

85. Chen, *Meizhou huaqiao tongjian*, 645–46; Corbitt, *A Study of the Chinese in Cuba*, 114; Seuc, *La Colonia China de Cuba*, 92–96.

86. Alejandro de la Fuente, *A Nation for All: Race, Inequality, and Politics in Twentieth-Century Cuba* (Chapel Hill and London: University of North Carolina Press, 2001), 104–105; Chen, *Meizhou huaqiao tongjian*, 645–46; Corbitt, *A Study of the Chinese in Cuba*, 114. For the impact of the Nationalization of Labor decree on Jews, see Robert Levine, *Tropical Diaspora: The Jewish Experience in Cuba* (Gainesville: University Press of Florida, 1993), 52–59.

87. Seuc, *La Colonia China de Cuba*, 85–87.

88. Chen, *Meizhou huaqiao tongjian*, 643–44.

89. Chen, *Meizhou huaqiao tongjian*, 643–44; Corbitt, *A Study of the Chinese in Cuba*, 111–12. Corbitt gives the year of the investigation as 1932.

90. Chen, *Meizhou huaqiao tongjian*, 645–46.

91. Ibid.

92. *La Correspondencia* (Cienfuegos), 16 April 1934, 2.

93. Independence leader José Martí (1853–95) summoned the participation of all races and classes in the formation of the new nation. Jose Marti, "Mi raza" (*Patria*, 16 April 1893), in *Obras completas*, 28 vols. (Havana: Editorial Nacional de Cuba, 1963–73), vol. 2, 299; Fernando Ortiz, *Cuban Counterpoint: Tobacco and Sugar* (Durham: Duke University Press, 1995). For race in Cuba and contending notions of *cubanidad*, see de la Fuente, *A Nation for All*, 23–53.

94. APC, Juzgado de Primera Instancia, Expediente 6652, "Rollo de apelación en expediente sobre subsanación de error en la inscripción de nacimiento de José Wong Alonso" (1945).

95. According to Alejandro de la Fuente, the term was used by late-nineteenth-century scientists "to denote the extensiveness of miscegenation in

the island, but it was opposed on the ground that it designated so many racial mixtures as to become scientifically meaningless. . . . It was precisely the ambiguity of the term, however, that made it attractive. In opposition to other racial labels such as *negro* or *mulato*, deemed to be more precise in Cuban racial imagery, the denomination *mestizo* had the virtue of detaching a significant portion of the Cuban population from blackness." De la Fuente, *A Nation for All*, 31–32.

96. V.P. Oswald Horton, ed., *Chinese in the Caribbean, 1911–1941* (Kingston, Jamaica: Gleaner Co., 1942), 146–47; Chen, *Meizhou huaqiao tongjian*, 549–50, 643–44; Guillermo Tejeiro, *Historia ilustrada de la Colonia China en Cuba* (Havana, 1947).

97. This phenomenon had parallels with the Qing society pattern of one son training for the imperial civil service exams and one son learning the family business.

98. President of the Overseas Chinese Student Association Kong Lu Cheung, "Why Should We Come Back to China to Study," *Nanda yu huaqiao* 1, no. 1 (1923): 1–12. Original in English.

99. Ibid.

100. *Nanda yu huaqiao* 1, no. 3 (1923).

101. Seuc, *La Colonia China de Cuba*, 46–52.

102. Baltar, *Los Chinos de Cuba*, 159, based on interview with ex-actress Yolanda Eng, who in her childhood and adolescence worked in two companies. For Chinese Cuban opera troupes, see Chen, *Meizhou huaqiao tongjian*, 649–50; Baltar, *Los Chinos de Cuba*, 156–66; Baldomero Álvarez Ríos, *La inmigración china en la Cuba colonial: El Barrio Chino de la Habana* (Havana: Publicigraf, 1995), 74–76.

103. It was called the Three Principles of the People Society (Asociación Juventud China de "San Min Chu I" or Sanminzhuyi Qingniantuan). Tejeiro, *Historia ilustrada de la Colonia China*.

104. For the equivalent youth organization in the United States in 1941, see Lai, "The Kuomintang in Chinese American Communities," 195.

105. Baltar, *Los Chinos de Cuba*, 157–58.

106. ANC, Registro de Asociaciones, Fondo 54, Legajo 334, Expediente 9910, "Asociación Nacional Chino-Cubana."

107. Baltar, *Los Chinos de Cuba*, 105–107, 174; Pablo Rodríguez Ruiz, "Relaciones inter-étnicas e interraciales en el Barrio Chino de La Habana (Un estudio desde los chinos y sus descendientes)," *Catauro* 2, no. 2 (2000): 103–126 (115). Yet Rodríguez cites the case of the son of a Chinese father and white, Catholic mother who speaks, reads, and writes Chinese, took first

communion, and professes the "cult of the ancestors" (126).

108. Karen Isaksen Leonard, *Making Ethnic Choices: California's Punjabi Mexican Americans* (Philadelphia: Temple University Press, 1992), 7–8.

109. Seuc, *La Colonia China de Cuba*, 1–3. My translation. His mother, along with his younger brother and two sisters, became "refugees of war" in their Cantonese town during the Japanese occupation.

110. Napoleón Seuc, interview by author, Miami, September 2000.

111. Parroquia "La Purisima Concepción" S.I. Catedral de Cienfuegos, Libro de Bautismos, Tomo 15, Folio 242, Número 698.

112. Chen Lanbin visited Cienfuegos on April 24, 1874, to investigate the treatment of Chinese workers on two nearby estates. In Cienfuegos he stayed at the Hotel Unión, which has been recently restored. Rousseau and Díaz, *Memoria descriptiva, histórica y biográfica de Cienfuegos*, 184.

113. Enrique Edo y Llop, *Memoria histórica de Cienfuegos y su jurisdicción*, 3rd ed. (Havana: Úcar, García y Cía, 1943), 626–27.

114. Blas and Santiago Pelayo Díaz, interviews by author, Cienfuegos and Havana, Cuba, March 1999 and December 1999.

115. Leonard, *Making Ethnic Choices*, 214–15.

116. Matthew Frye Jacobson, *Special Sorrows: The Diasporic Imagination of Irish, Polish, and Jewish Immigrants in the United States* (Cambridge, Mass.: Harvard University Press, 1995), 5.

117. Blas Pelayo, "Short Chronicle of the Visit of the President of the People's Republic of China, Jiang Zemin, to Havana, from November 21, 1993 to November 22, 1993." My translation.

118. Interview by author, Dulian, Xinhui County, China, November 2001.

119. According to Casino Chung Wah President Alfonso Chao, in 1998 there were about 430 remaining ethnic Chinese, with an average age of about 80, and about 3,200 descendants of Chinese. There are also a handful of ethnic Chinese who were born in Cuba. Angus MacSwan, "Cuban Chinatown enjoys revival but lacks Chinese," Reuters, 9 December 1998.

120. Map and pamphlet "Presencia China en Cuba" (Havana: Fundación Fernando Ortiz, Grupo Promotor del Barrio Chino, Ediciones GEO, 1999); Álvarez, *La inmigración china en la Cuba colonial*, 49–54; Isabelle Lausent-Herrera, "El renacimiento de la comunidad china en Cuba," *Oriental* (December 1998). The inaugural issue of *Fraternidad 2* was published in May, 2002. The magazine *Fraternidad* was originally founded in 1934 as the official organ of the Union of Commercial Retailers of the Chinese Colony in Cuba (Unión de Detallistas del Comercio de la Colonia China en Cuba).

121. For five days every spring, the Festival de Chinos de Ultramar

(Festival of Chinese Overseas) commemorates the arrival of the first ship of Chinese coolies to Havana on June 3, 1847, with the participation of Cuban and international scholars, businessmen, and community members. The theme of the Fifth Festival of Chinese Overseas held in Havana in May of 2002 was "Chinatowns of the World as Zones of Tourist Attraction."

122. A similar phenomenon exists among Jewish Cubans. See Ruth Behar's documentary on the search for identity and memory among Sephardic Jews with Cuban roots, *Adio Kerida*, VHS, 82 min. (New York: Women Make Movies, 2002).

123. Felipe Luis died on September 7, 2003, at the age of 99.

Notes to Chapter 6

1. The construction of the Capitol began in May of 1926, and it was inaugurated in May of 1929.

2. The queue was a Manchu men's hairstyle consisting of a high shaved forehead and a long braid down the back. The Manchu Qing dynasty that ruled from 1644 to 1911 decreed that all Chinese men adopt the hairstyle or risk execution.

3. Martha Sawyers, *Extremo Oriente: Enciclopedia en colores* (Barcelona: Tumun Mas., 1964).

4. Ibid.

5. Yamilet García Zamora, *Los contextos en* Paradiso (Havana: Editorial Letras Cubanas, 1997), 27–28.

6. He is most likely referring to the canal (called the *Zanja Real* or Royal Canal) that brought water to the formerly walled city of Havana. Chinatown initally grew along this canal, and Zanja Street retraces much of its original course.

7. Ana Cairo, "Apuntes sobre los chinos en la literatura cubana," *Catauro* 2:2 (2000): 167–74 (171–72). Quoting from *La nueva lira criolla* (Havana: Imprenta La Moderna Poesía, 1907).

8. Guan Yu was a general of the Three Kingdoms who was posthumously called "Venerated Ancestor Guan" and eventually became the patron of Chinese immigrants to Cuba.

9. This legend has been immortalized in Luo Guanzhong's *Romance of the Three Kingdoms*.

10. José Baltar Rodríguez, *Los Chinos de Cuba: Apuntes etnográficos* (Havana: Fundación Fernando Ortiz, 1997), 154.

11. "Jakuey" is the pronunciation of a Cantonese pejorative term for blacks.

Notes to Chapter 7

1. For the facts of "la trata amarilla" see Evelyn Hu-Dehart, "Chinese Coolie Labour in Cuba in the Nineteenth Century: Free Labour or Neo-slavery?" *Slavery and Abolition* 14, no. 1 (April 1993): 67–86.

2. This is not meant as an acquittal of the Castro regime for its treatment of Cuban Chinese citizens. The ultimate or underlying motivations for the policies that alienated the Cuban Chinese is a highly complex issue. Whether or not these policies arose from official racism, no-one could blame the Cuban Chinese for feeling collectively oppressed.

3. As an example of this pattern, my grandparents arrived in the U.S. at the turn of the twentieth century and opened a grocery and a milliner's store in the 1930s. The greater lag time between their arrival and entry into small business reflects their immigrating as children and the impact of the Great Depression.

4. This is again comparable to the experience of my own family—my parents and their siblings entered into accounting and teaching.

5. Andrew Wilson, *Ambition and Identity: Chinese Merchant Elites in Colonial Manila, 1880–1916* (Honolulu: University of Hawaii Press, 2004).

6. Seinfeld Episode 16, "The Chinese Restaurant." Original air date: May 23, 1991.

7. Cristina García, *Monkey Hunting* (New York: Alfred A. Knopf, 2003), 45–47.

8. Carsey Yee, "Ming Loyalist Poetry in Eighteenth-Century Vietnam," paper delivered at the AAS Annual Meeting, Washington, D.C., April 6, 2002.

Notes to Chapter 8

Acknowledgement

I thank Andrew Wilson for his comments and suggestions on earlier drafts of this article.

1. The term Greater China signifies a social formation and geographical area that includes China, Taiwan, Hong Kong, and Macao.

2. The key places my interviewees indicated include Jamaica, British Guiana, Nicaragua, Peru, and the United States.

3. For instance, see Madeline Hsu, *Dreaming of Gold, Dreaming of Home: Transnationalism and Migration between the United States and South China, 1882–1943* (Stanford: Stanford University Press, 2000), Sucheng Chan, *Asian Americans: An Interpretive History* (Boston: Twayne, 1991), Andrea Louie, *Chineseness Across Borders* (Durham: Duke University Press, 2004).

4. James Clifford, *Routes: Travel and Translation in the Late Twentieth Century* (Cambridge: Harvard University Press, 1997).

5. Inherent in the concept of step migration is the teleology of movement from less developed countries to more developed ones. Serial migration refuses this kind of teleology.

6. For instance, see Wang Gungwu, "Upgrading the Migrant: Neither Huaquiao nor Huaren" in Elizabeth Sinn, ed., *The Last Half Century of Chinese Overseas* (Hong Kong: Hong Kong University Press, 1998), 15–34, and Kyeyoung Park, "'1,000 Señora Lees': The Changing Gender Ideology of Korean-Latina-American Women in the Diaspora," *Amerasia Journal* 28, no. 2 (2002): 161–80.

7. Linda Basch, Nina Glick Schiller, and Cristina Szanton Blanc, *Nations Unbound: Transnational Projects, Postcolonial Predicaments, and Deterritorialized Nation-States* (Amsterdam: Gordon and Breach Press, 1994).

8. Roger Rouse, "Mexican Migrants and the Social Space of Postmodernism," *Diaspora* 1 (Spring 1991): 18–23.

9. For more details, see Karen Leonard, *Making Ethnic Choices: California's Punjabi Mexican Americans* (Philadelphia: Temple University Press, 1992) and Andrea Louie, *Chineseness Across Borders.*

10. For more details, see Jeffrey Lesser, ed., *Searching for Home Abroad: Japanese Brazilians and Transnationalism* (Durham: Duke University Press, 2003), Takeyuki Tsuda, *Strangers in the Ethnic Homeland: Japanese Brazilian Return Migration in Transnational Perspective* (New York: Columbia University Press, 2003), Joshua Roth, *Brokered Homeland: Japanese Brazilian Migrants in Japan* (Ithaca: Cornell University Press, 2002), and Daniel Linger, *No One Home: Brazilian Selves Remade in Japan* (Stanford: Stanford University Press, 2001).

11. The word "diaspora" is derived from the Greek verb *speiro*, meaning "to sow," and the preposition *dia*, meaning "over." It describes the process of dispersal or migration from one place to multiple locations.

12. Paul Gilroy, *The Black Atlantic: Modernity and Double Consciousness* (Cambridge: Harvard University Press, 1993).

13. Ibid., *'There Ain't No Black in the Union Jack': The Cultural Politics of Race and Nation* (Chicago: University of Chicago Press, 1991).

14. The scholarship on overseas Chinese in Southeast Asia offers many examples. See, for instance, William G. Skinner, *Chinese Society in Thailand: An Analytical History* (Ithaca: Cornell University Press 1957) and *Leadership and Power in the Chinese Community of Thailand* (Ithaca: Cornell University Press 1958); Maurice Freedman, *Chinese Family and Marriage in Singapore* (London: Her Majesty's Stationery Office, 1957) and *Chinese Lineage and Society: Fukien and Kwangtung* (London: Athlone Press, 1966).

15. For instance, see Aihwa Ong and Donald Nonini, eds., *Ungrounded Empires: The Cultural Politics of Modern Chinese Transnationalism* (New York: Routledge Press, 1997), and Madeline Hsu, *Dreaming of Gold, Dreaming of Home*.

16. See, for instance, Gillian Hart, *Disabling Globalization: Places of Power in Post-Apartheid South Africa* (Berkeley: University of California Press, 2002), Lane Hirabayashi, Akemi Kikumura-Yano, and James Hirabayashi, eds., *New Worlds, New Lives: Globalization and People of Japanese Descent in the Americas and from Latin America in Japan* (Stanford: Stanford University Press, 2002), Adam McKeown, *Chinese Migrant Networks and Cultural Change: Peru, Chicago, Hawaii, 1900–1936* (Chicago: University of Chicago Press, 2001), and Lok Siu, "Diasporic Citizenship: the Politics of Belonging for Chinese in Central America and Panama," *Social Text* 69 (Winter 2001).

17. "Paper sons" came to the United States bearing papers documenting them as sons of Chinese who had returned to China to marry and produce children. The Great Earthquake of 1906 in San Francisco had destroyed immigration records, along with other official records of the U.S. government. In the process of redocumentation, Chinese immigrants falsely reported the number of children they had in China in order to get papers for others to immigrate.

18. For a more detailed discussion, refer to Edward Said, *The World, the Text, and the Critic* (Cambridge; Harvard University Press, 1983) and Caren Kaplan, *Questions of Travel: Postmodern Discourses of Displacement* (Durham: Duke University Press, 1996).

19. Stuart Hall, "Cultural Identity and Diaspora," in Jonathan Rutherford, ed., *Identity: Community, Culture, Difference* (London: Lawrence & Wishart, 1990), 222–37.

20. For a more detailed discussion of the United Fruit Company in Central America, please refer to Philippe Bourgois, *Ethnicity at Work: Divided Labor on a Central American Banana Plantation* (Baltimore: Johns Hopkins University Press, 1989).

21. *Sal Si Puedes* literally means "leave if you can." There are different versions of why Chinatown became known as Sal Si Puedes. One is that the area
is so crowded with merchants and their outdoor stands that visitors can barely find their way out once they enter. Another refers more explicitly to the
danger of wandering into the Chinese neighborhood, where one may not survive the tricks and booby traps of the sly Chinese merchants. This second
version reflects the orientalist portrayal of the Chinese as mysterious and
dangerous, as a people who cannot be trusted and should be feared.

22. Pedro is referring to the first Chinese school that was established in the
1930s and which has since been destroyed. It was a primary school that
taught Cantonese in addition to the regular Panamanian curriculum. It was
attended mostly by children of Chinese descent living in the Chinatown
area.

23. This is not to say that women were not migrating. They did, though
not in the same proportions. Moreover, their migrations did not have the
same connotation of being masculinist adventures to seek family fortunes.
Migration, for women, simply did not have the same glory attached.

24. La Chorrera is a suburb west of Panama City, across the Bridge of the
Americas. Since the 1980s, La Chorrera has become the city with the largest
percentage of Chinese immigrants in Panama. Most of the Chinese there are
Hakka speakers from the Guangdong Province of China and had immigrated
to Panama during the Manuel Noriega military regime. The Chinese living
in La Chorrera are primarily involved in distribution, small retail businesses,
and restaurants. As the next largest city west of Panama City, it serves as a
major transit point between the urban capital and the smaller towns in the
interior of Panama (the provinces of Coclé, Herrera, Los Santos, and
Veraguas). Because of its central location, La Chorrera has become a central
distribution center for produce and commercial products to both Panama
City and the interior.

25. This "in-between" category applies not only to the Chinese, but also
to South Asian indentured laborers, native Americans, as well as West Indian
laborers (to name a few) who worked under the contracted labor system
throughout the 1800s and early 1900s. For a more detailed discussion, refer to
Denise Helly, introduction to *The Cuba Commission Report: A Hidden History
of the Chinese in Cuba: The Original English-Language Text of 1876* (Baltimore:
Johns Hopkins University Press, 1993), and Watt Stewart, *Chinese Bondage in
Peru* (Durham: Duke University Press, 1951).

26. The term "Asian American" emerged during the 1960s in order to
mobilize a political coalition of the different ethnic Asian groups in the

United States. By putting forth a collective identity, it helped articulate shared experiences of racial oppression. Since such a movement did not take place in Panama, a collective "Asian Panamanian" consciousness was never achieved. Indeed, ethnicity and nationality remain the central frameworks by which Panamanians categorize difference.

27. Tom Barry, *Panama: A Country Guide* (Albuquerque: the Inter-Hemispheric Education Resource Center, 1990), 49.

28. With Panama's currency being the U.S. dollar, and with the passage of the 1959 bank secrecy law, followed by the 1970 banking law that made all bank deposits tax-free, Panama City (the capital of Panama) quickly became a center of international finance.

ABOUT THE EDITOR AND CONTRIBUTORS

ANDREW R. WILSON is an associate professor in the Department of Strategy and Policy, U.S. Naval War College. He is the author of *Ambition and Identity: Chinese Merchant Elites in Colonial Manila, 1880–1916.*

WALTON LOOK LAI is a lecturer in the History Department at the University of the West Indies in Trinidad & Tobago. He is the author of *Indentured Labor, Caribbean Sugar: Chinese and Indian Migrants to the British West Indies 1838–1918* (1993), and *The Chinese in the West Indies 1806–1995: A Documentary History* (1998).

ANNE-MARIE LEE-LOY is an assistant professor in the Department of English at Toronto's Ryerson University. She is currently revising her doctoral dissertation, on the representation of the Chinese in Jamaica, Trinidad, and Guyana, for publication.

LI ANSHAN is a professor at the Institute of Afro-Asian Studies, School of International Studies, and Peking University where he teaches courses on African history and culture and on Sino-African relations. He is also vice-director of the Center for African Studies, Peking University, and vice president of the Chinese Society of African Historical Studies. A leading expert on Chinese in Africa, Professor Li is the author of several books and dozens of articles, including *A History of Chinese Overseas in Africa.* His interest covers African history, Chinese international migration, and comparative nationalism.

GAIL BOUKNIGHT-DAVIS, director of the Multicultural Center at Williams College, is a former faculty member and Director of Multicultural Affairs at Landmark College in Putney, Vermont. She holds a Ph.D. from Brown University in anthropology, specifically ethnic studies, and her research is focused on ethnic minorities and economic development in the Caribbean.

About the Editor and Contributors

KATHLEEN LÓPEZ holds an M.A. in Asian Studies from Cornell University and is currently a doctoral candidate in history at the University of Michigan. Her dissertation research is on Chinese migration to Cuba in the late nineteenth and early twentieth centuries. She was a 2002–2003 visiting researcher at the Center for the Study of Ethnicity and Race at Columbia University.

MITZI ESPINOSA LUIS was an archivist and librarian in the Provincial Archive of Cienfuegos in Cuba (Archivo Histórico "Rita Suárez del Villar") from 1996 to 2004. She is a member of the Chinese association Sue Yuen Tong, and she continues her involvement with the Grupo Promotor del Barrio Chino and her work in recovering documentation on the Chinese in Cuba.

ANDREW MEYER is an assistant professor of history at Brooklyn College. An intrepid explorer of New York's culinary landscape, Dr. Meyer is also an expert in Chinese philosophy and the history of Classical China.

LOK SIU is an assistant professor of anthropology and Asia/Pacific/American Studies at New York University, where she teaches courses on Central America and the Asian-American experience. The author of several articles on the Chinese in Panama, she is in the process of finishing a book-length study entitled *Memories of a Future Home: Geopolitics and Diasporic Chinese in Panama*.